DOWN BUT
NOT OUT

DOWN BUT NOT OUT

THE INCREDIBLE STORY OF SECOND WORLD WAR AIRMAN MAURICE 'MOGGY' MAYNE

MAURICE MAYNE WITH MARK RYAN

First published 2014

The History Press
The Mill, Brimscombe Port
Stroud, Gloucestershire, GL5 2QG
www.thehistorypress.co.uk

British Library Cataloguing in Publication Data.
A catalogue record for this book is available from the British Library.

ISBN 978 0 7509 5206 4

Typesetting and origination by The History Press
Printed in Great Britain

CONTENTS

INTRODUCTION: NOSE-DIVE

1 APRIL 1942

So this was it. The steep dive told me that the pilot, Wing Commander Paddy Boal, had finally selected his target and we were going in for the kill. Pretty soon we'd level out just above the waves, drop our torpedo at the German ship, and turn for home.

These were the seconds that mattered. As a gunner in the turret of a Bristol Beaufort, you had long periods of inactivity. Then suddenly all your senses were heightened, your finger was on the trigger of your Browning, and you were ready to do your bit.

We were just off the Norwegian coast, we'd found the convoy after coming down through the clouds and now there was no time to waste.

Even so, this felt like the steepest dive I'd ever been in. Crazy bugger, Paddy Boal. We all knew he'd had too much to drink in the officers' mess the night before. The word had gone round like wildfire; he'd danced a jig and played the fool in front of his men. He was the boss; he could do what he liked.

Trouble was, our lives now depended on the speed of his reactions, on his ability to have recovered from the booze. How much was still in his system? He seemed to have lost all fear and the extreme angle of the dive was putting a hell of a strain on the aircraft. I'd just heard some of the furniture cracking up front towards the cockpit. Maybe it was a foldaway table snapping or something; but I was more worried about finding something to shoot at.

I loved to open fire, I don't mind admitting it. I couldn't wait, but as I looked out of my turret all I could see was thin air. At the back of the plane, coming down at this steep angle, I couldn't find a target. It was frustrating; but when we levelled out, I'd be ready to hit those Germans with everything I'd got.

What I didn't know was that we weren't going to level out. Those sounds like cracking furniture had been shells coming in from that German ship. Paddy Boal hadn't taken us into a steep dive because Paddy Boal was dead – hit by a shell, straight up through his seat. The plane was out of control, we were about to slap into the freezing sea.

If I'd known, I might have had time to wonder why the hell I'd stayed as a gunner, when I'd finally been given the chance to train as a pilot. There might have been a few seconds to wonder why the friendships I'd made among my fellow gunners and wireless operators had meant more to me than the chance to control my own destiny. There might have been a moment to say goodbye in my head to Sylvia West, my girlfriend down in Devon, and to my family back in London.

Maybe it was better I didn't know. There were four of us in our crew. One was already dead, another had only seconds to live … and he was one of my best pals.

1

FLASH OF BLADE AND THUD OF GLOVE

I was lucky to be born at all. My dad, George, was a private in the Royal Fusiliers during the First World War. Somehow he managed to survive being sent over the top in the first wave on the very first day of the Battle of the Somme, when about 60,000 men were killed or wounded.

He charged through the shells and bullets and reached the German trenches alone. Later he recalled:

> Out of breath and to gather my wits and strength, I dropped into a shell hole just in front of the German wire. I peeped over the edge, fired a shot at a round hat on a German head that suddenly appeared, rushed the last few yards and jumped into the German trench. I saw nobody there, friend or foe. It was very eerie but I recall facing our old front lines and being appalled at the poor positioning of them. They were absolutely clearly overlooked by the enemy for all those terrible months preceding the battle. Sitting ducks we must have been, I thought.
>
> I then went on to the second-line trench and jumped in, to see a German soldier lying on the parapet. With fixed bayonet I approached, then I saw his putty-coloured face which convinced me he was mortally wounded. The German brought up an arm and actually saluted me. I understood no German language but the poor chap kept muttering two words: '*Wasser, wasser*' and '*Mutter, mutter*.' It took me a minute or so to realise he wanted a drink of water. The second word I could not cotton on to. I am glad to this day that I gave him a drink from my precious water.

The other word my dad's German acquaintance had repeated was 'Mother, mother.' My father felt sorry for him and was never ashamed for having shown some compassion. More than a million men became casualties on the Somme eventually. It was a miracle my dad came home in one piece because most didn't.

Did he receive a hero's welcome? Hardly. He couldn't find any work at all in London for the first few months. Eventually a friend managed to get him a job at the Victualling Yard in Deptford. That was where they used to keep all the supplies for the navy, including the rum. My father found himself working in the department where they used to mix rum with lime. Each day all the workers got a ration of rum, same as the navy boys got, but some blokes didn't want their ration, so they gave it to my father, because they knew he liked it. My mother said he came home one day in a wheelbarrow.

I was born in Deptford and spent my first few years in that part of East London. But as a youngster I used to go up to White Hart Lane with my dad, to watch Tottenham Hotspur play. We'd walk all the way through the city to North London to get to the matches. And if we were running late, he would literally drag me along through the crowds, to make sure we arrived on time. I remember having the skin scraped off my knees in the desperate rush to the Lane. It didn't put me off, though; the atmosphere was amazing. Those were the days when we all stood, and they passed youngsters over the heads of the grown men and put them down at the front, where they could have a better view of the match. I loved it.

When I was eight years old I asked my father whether he knew how to attack with a fixed bayonet. He said he did and showed me how to put the bayonet on his rifle, which he still had.

'See? Like this.' He demonstrated, sliding the thing down once it was on. But he didn't stop there. 'First foot forward … plunge! Twist! That's very important. Pull it out again.'

Some people think you twisted a bayonet to do maximum damage to your enemy's vital organs, and that could have been a consequence, but the main reason was that if you didn't twist a bayonet, you didn't leave enough air around the metal to pull it out again. The 'meat' closed in around the blade and then you were stuck. You'd end up tugging for ages and ages, pulling the body along.

'Thrust! Twist! Come out again!' He showed me one last time for good measure. 'In! Twist! Out!' He didn't mind teaching me, even though I was so young. Perhaps he thought I might have to fight one day. In a way he was right.

When I was ten or eleven we moved across to West London – Paddington, to be precise – so that my dad could run his brother's textile shop. I went to the Polytechnic Secondary School there. By then I wasn't known as 'Maurice Mayne' to my friends. For some reason they called me 'Moggy' – and the nickname stuck.

Everyone studied a foreign language at the polytechnic, which was a grammar school. You could choose between French, Spanish or German. I chose German. I don't know why because it wasn't as if I thought they'd try to invade us or take over the world. I just remember finding it easier than French. German would prove very useful later on – in captivity and then when I was on the run among the Nazis, having escaped on my own.

I also learned to box at an early age, because the school was big on it. Even though I was only small, I discovered that my fists packed a punch and I was nifty on my feet. Quite a few opponents were surprised to find themselves sitting on their backsides before they could land much glove on me.

They had boxing competitions every year at the polytechnic, and the parents were all invited along to watch. I won the first fight I had in a ring because I went in with my fists flying and overwhelmed my opponent. But the second fight I had at school was very different. I went straight in again, as though I was going to murder the other chap, but I left myself exposed and he got me. I took quite a pasting.

I remember going back to the classroom in a state. Mr Chipperfield, the head of the scholarship class, took a good look at my face. It was still smudged with blood and he said to me, 'Don't go in for boxing. It's not nice.'

It may not be nice but it's a great skill to have and it came in handy during the times of trouble in wartime. When you're trying to fight for what's right in a prisoner-of-war camp and some trouble-maker challenges you, what are you going to do if you can't back up your words with your knuckles? If you're on a death march in the snow and you have to rip a man's coat off his back because you think he has stolen it off your mate, you have to be able to give the culprit a look that tells him he'll get a fearful beating if he tries to fight for that stolen coat. How are you going to do that if you don't know how to look after yourself? Boxing's not nice, Mr Chipperfield said. So what? Life's not nice sometimes.

After I took that schoolboy beating in the ring, you could say I was down but not out. I carried on fighting, partly because the Boy Scouts were big on it too. I was a Scout in Paddington – 43rd Troop, West London. They held boxing bouts every month and I had the opportunity to box against boys in other Scout troops. I don't think I ever lost a fight in the Scouts. I was learning more about the noble art every time I fought. I understood where to put my hands by then, to keep them up to protect myself from counter-punches.

As well as boxing and football, I loved cricket too. I was good at it and played for an adult team called the Old Vauxonians. In 1934, at the age of fourteen, cricket gave me a special experience, because I met Jack Hobbs! Imagine the current cricket England captain and attach to him the celebrity of David Beckham. Now you're getting an idea of Jack Hobbs' status in British sport at the time. He scored 199 first-class centuries and over 61,000 runs, despite his career being interrupted for five years by the First World War, during which he flew for the Royal Flying Corps. How many runs would he have scored if that First World War hadn't broken out?

He'd already become a journalist by the time I met him, which hadn't stopped him from scoring 221 against the touring West Indians in 1933 – in his fiftieth year! All the best journalists worked in London's Fleet Street in those days, so that's where I went to find him. I was going to pick up an award for the highest-scoring batsman on the London schools circuit that summer.

I climbed some stairs to his office and before I knew it Jack Hobbs, living legend, was greeting me.

'Congratulations!' he said warmly. 'Keep it up! And remember to keep a straight bat!'

Not only did he give me advice, he gave me a junior cricket bat. It was slightly smaller than the average cricket bat, just right for my age and size. And the best thing was, he autographed it for me too. He wrote his initials on it, which for me in 1934 was the cricket equivalent of being blessed by the Pope.

I didn't have the heart to tell him I'd only come to collect the prize for a mate called Bert Page. But Bert let me use his Jack Hobbs cricket bat whenever I wanted, and I scored quite a few runs with it too! The Old Vauxonians record for 1936 was played 20, won 11, drawn 7 and lost 2 – so I didn't do them any harm that year.

I won certificates in other sports too. It sounds like boasting but I'm only telling you all this because it helps to explain why I survived while others died as a prisoner of war. I was naturally athletic, you see – even though I was still short and never did grow much beyond 5 feet 7 inches tall. I'd had plenty of practice at racing around. We lived on quite a busy road and there had been a lot of accidents involving bicycles, so my dad told me I wasn't having one. I'd started to run everywhere instead, especially from the age of fourteen, when I'd begun to get really fit. That's how I became such a good all-round athlete. It stood me in good stead for the death marches at the end of the Second World War, when only the fittest were going to survive. It also helped me live into my nineties.

Competition is good for you, it's lovely. Sport at school really is important. People talk about competition not being important when you're growing up. The same kind of people say boxing is bad for you. What a load of rubbish! When you grow up what chance are you going to have when it's dog-eat-dog, if you were never encouraged to be competitive at school?

My father knew all this after what he'd been through in the First World War. Now he was doing everything he could to make his family comfortable and was moving up in the world. But he didn't want us to be soft. He left his brother's business in Paddington and opened a textile shop of his own in Bermondsey. It sold all kinds of clothing materials and started to do so well that he opened another one in Peckham. That shop began to do even better.

Leaving school at sixteen, I was still a world away from any life-or-death situations – at least to start with. What was soon in danger was my chosen career. The irony was that I played it very safe and joined an accountancy firm. This went well for a couple of years, until I broke the company's most prized possession – their calculator. I was swinging it over my shoulder when I dropped it. The boss

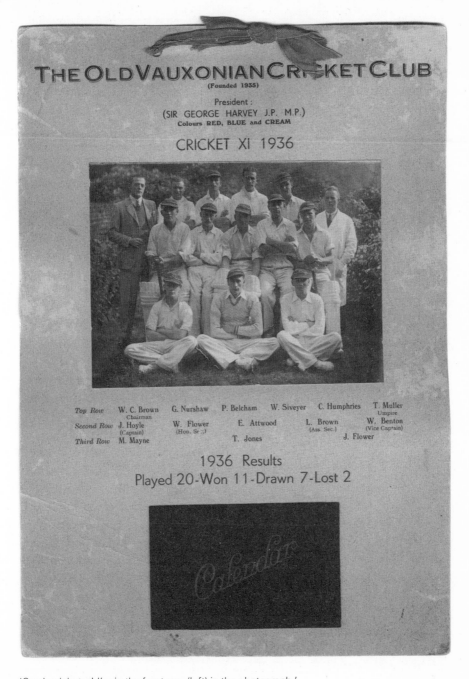

'Crack cricketer! I'm in the front row (left) in the photograph.'

wanted me to pay for it, which would have taken me at least a year on my wages. So I went to work for my father at his textile shop in Peckham instead.

My family was very friendly with a lot of Jewish people in the East End of London, because a lot of Jews were textile wholesalers. But not everyone was so friendly towards the Jews. Don't think for a moment that it was only in Nazi Germany where they had anti-Semitism in the 1930s. There was plenty of anti-Semitism in London too, and there were all sorts of derogatory names for Jews flying around – too terrible to mention here. A lot of people down the East End of London, where they settled, didn't like them at all. If you've lived in a place for a long time and it suddenly changes, you take a dislike to the change, I suppose.

But the Jews were trying to integrate and took up a lot of things that the East Enders thought were their prerogative – such as boxing. They found some excellent boxers among their number. The locals were quite surprised by that. And the Jews had musicians – marvellous musicians – people who really understood music.

I had no problem with the Jews; I liked them. I'm not going to lie, though; you had to be pretty sharp when you dealt with some of them, because when it came to business, well … let's just say they really were business people! You had to fight hard to hold your own and survive alongside them in business. But overall we got on well, the Jews and I. Business was brisk, life was good.

Then the war started and people started joining up. There was a bloke living round the back of my father's shop and his name was Ken Reeves. When he was on leave, Ken used to walk past the shop in his RAF uniform, all blue and smart. I saw him a few times and thought, 'Look at that uniform! I want to look that good.' I was struck by the sheer elegance of his appearance and the way he carried himself. I watched him go past several times and each time I wanted that uniform a little bit more.

'That's it,' I said to myself. 'I'm going to be a pilot!'

But I didn't do anything about it until, one Thursday afternoon in the early summer of 1940, I went out for my lunch break and saw a bunch of blokes on a big area of greenery called Peckham Rye. It was a lovely sunny day and I was there to enjoy the fine weather; but these lads were there for a purpose – they were new recruits under instruction. They wore army uniform and they were learning how to fire a rifle while lain down on the ground. I was stretched out on the grass too; but I wasn't doing anything useful like they were. Suddenly I got this peculiar urge telling me I'd got to join up. But I didn't want to join the army like them; none of those blokes looked as smart as Ken Reeves.

I went straight over to Eltham, where they were recruiting in a public house called Yorkshire Grey. I told them, 'I want to join the RAF.' I could have added, 'I want to look like the bloke who keeps walking past my dad's shop in Peckham,' but they wouldn't have cared about that. They were more interested in giving me a quick medical – there and then.

A Scot in a long white coat said, 'Let's have a sample of yer watter!'

I worked out what he meant and did this little drop in a jar for him. He looked at it and said, 'I want a bit more than that, laddie!' So I filled the jar up. I took it over to him and he looked annoyed. 'I said "a bit more"; I didn't say have a damn great piss!' I was staggered at that sort of language from a doctor.

Despite having had the cheek to empty my bladder, they accepted me – or so I thought. My 'Notice Paper' to join the Royal Air Force Volunteer Reserve was dated 29 May 1940. I've still got it. Maurice George Mayne of 175 Peckham Rye, Peckham, London SE15, 'buyer/salesman in outfitters' became 'number 1253284'.

Within a couple of weeks they'd sent me for a full air crew medical over at Uxbridge in West London. When I got there though, I quickly realised it wasn't just a medical, it was a full-scale interview. They put me in front of a panel of high-ranking RAF officers, who asked me various questions.

'What do you want to be?'

'I want to be a pilot.'

There was a collective sigh. Then one officer said, 'Do you realise that every man who comes in here says he wants to be a pilot?'

I nearly said, 'Of course they bloody do – you're the RAF!' Instead I remained silent.

'There simply aren't enough places on the courses,' said another member of the panel. 'It would be six months before we could even think about sending you on the training course to become a pilot – and the nearest would be Babbacombe in Devon.'

Six months seemed like a long time. Then one of the officers asked me another question. 'Did you do any sport at school?'

'Yes, I love sport,' I said.

'Did you do any boxing?'

'Yes,' I confirmed. 'I did a lot of boxing and I was good at it.'

'That's settled then,' said another officer, the debate apparently over before it had started. 'Air gunner.'

Just because I'd done a lot of boxing, they made me an air gunner. No choice! I suppose they thought a gunner had to be a tough, aggressive type. Anyway, the dream of becoming a pilot was over – for now. 'At least I'm going to be flying,' I told myself. I was going to see more than my share of danger, too.

Aged nineteen, I took the oath in Uxbridge on 18 June 1940. It went like this:

I, Maurice George Mayne, swear by Almighty God that I will be faithful and bear true allegiance to His Majesty King George the Sixth, His Heirs and

2

ROYAL AIR FORCE VOLUNTEER RESERVE.

Certified Copy of Attestation.

No. _1253284_ .... Name _MAYNE, MAURICE George_ ....

Questions to be put to the Recruit before Enlistment.

You are hereby warned that if, after enlistment, it is found that you have wilfully or knowingly made a false answer to any of the following questions, you will be liable under the Air Force Act to a maximum punishment of two years' imprisonment, with hard labour.

1. What is your name ?

1. (Christian Names) _MAURICE GEORGE_
   (Surname) _MAYNE_

2. Where were you born ?

2. In the Parish of _NEW C ROSS_
   in, or near, the Town of _LONDON_
   in the County of _LONDON_

3. What was the date of your Birth ?

3. _20th DECEMBER 1920_

4. What is your full permanent postal address (including the County, or in London, the Metropolitan Borough) ?

4. { _175 PECKHAM RYE_
   PECKHAM
   LONDON S.E. 15 }

5. Are you of pure European descent ?

5. _YES_

6. Are you a British subject by birth ?

6. _YES_

7. Are your parents both British subjects by birth? If not, state separately their nationality at birth : (a) Father. (b) Mother.

7. { _YES_
   (a) .... (b) .... }

8. Are you, or is either of your parents, a naturalised British subject ?

8. _No_

9. If so, state the date(s) of the naturalisation certificate(s).

9. ....

10. What is your Trade or Calling ?

10. _BUYER SALESMAN in OUTFITTERS_

11. What is your Religious Denomination ?

11. _CHURCH OF ENGLAND_

12. Are you married ?

12. _No_

13. Have you ever been convicted by the Civil Power ? If so, give particulars and dates of all convictions.

13. _No_

*14. Do you now belong to, or have you ever served in the Royal Navy, the Army, the Royal Air Force, the Royal Marines, the Militia, the Special Reserve, the Supplementary Reserve, the Territorial Force (or Army), the Imperial Yeomanry, the Volunteers, the Auxiliary Air Force, the Army Reserve, the Air Force Reserve, the Militia Reserve, or any Naval Reserve Force, or any O.T.C. or Cadet Unit, or the armed forces of Eire or of any other Dominion or in a Reserve of any such force ? If so, state particulars of all engagements.

14. { _No_ }

* If so, the Recruit is to be asked to produce, if possible, his Certificate of Discharge and Certificate of Character, which should be returned to him, on re-enlistment, conspicuously endorsed in red ink, as follows :

(Name) .... Re-enlisted in the Royal Air Force on the (Date) .... 19 ...

If Certificate of Discharge and Certificate of Character is not produced, state briefly the circumstances ....

'I'm still only 19 when I join up.'

3

15. Have you truly stated the whole of your previous service, if any ?   15. .... YES ....

16. Did you receive a notice, and do you understand what it means ? Who gave it to you ?   16. { ....
Name..........................

17. Do you understand that every person in the Royal Air Force Volunteer Reserve will be liable, if medically fit, to carry out duty in the air in any type of aircraft and may be ordered to serve in any part of the world, ashore or afloat ?   17. .... YES ....

18. Are you willing to serve upon the following conditions provided His Majesty should so long require your services ?—

For the duration of the present Emergency, which means that you will be required to serve for so long as His Majesty should require your services in connection with the Emergency for which you are now enlisting, and that if you are still serving at the termination of the Emergency you will be discharged as soon as your services can be dispensed with thereafter.   18. .... YES ....

19. Are you in receipt of a disability pension ?   19. .... No ....

I, _Maurice George Mayne_ do solemnly declare that the foregoing answers made by me to the foregoing questions are true, and that I am willing to fulfil the engagements made.

SIGNATURE OF RECRUIT _Maurice G. Mayne._

NAME OF WITNESS _A. H. Greenzil_

125328Y ACH¹/ₜ WOₜ/AG

VolunteeR

FORM 2168

ROYAL AIR FORCE VOLUNTEER RESERVE.

NOTICE PAPER.

DURATION OF THE PRESENT EMERGENCY.

Signature of Man receiving the Notice Paper.......*Maurice G Mayne.*..........

NOTICE to be given to a Man at the time of his offering to join The Royal Air Force Volunteer Reserve.

Date....*29ᵗʰ May*....19..*40*....

The General Conditions of the Contract of Enlistment that you are about to enter into with the Crown are as follows :—

1. You will engage to serve His Majesty as an airman for the duration of the present Emergency, provided His Majesty should so long require your services.

2. On enlistment into the Royal Air Force Volunteer Reserve, you will be liable, if medically fit, to carry out duty in the air in any type of aircraft and may be ordered to serve in any part of the world, ashore or afloat.

3. Your term of Service shall begin to reckon from the date of Attestation.

4. The age given by you on enlistment will be accepted as your true age, and you will be liable to be held to serve on the engagement for which you attest notwithstanding that at some future date you may prove that your age given on enlistment is incorrect.   You will not, however, be eligible for family allowance until you attain the true age at which family allowance will be issuable.

5. Men in receipt of a disability pension are not eligible for enlistment.

6. You will be attested by the Attesting Officer.   On completion of your attestation you will be subject to all the provisions of the Air Force Act for the time being in force.

7. You will be required by the Attesting Officer to answer the questions printed on pages 2 and 3, to take the oath shown on page 4, and you are warned that if at the time of your attestation you wilfully or knowingly make any false answer to him you will thereby render yourself liable under the Air Force Act, to a maximum punishment of two years' imprisonment with hard labour.

8. If after arrival at the R.A.F. Receiving Centre, you refuse to enlist for personal reasons, you must be prepared to make your own arrangements for your return journey home.   No undertaking can be given that a free warrant would be issued to you.

Signature and Rank of the Officer or Non-Commissioned } ....
Officer serving the Notice

'"Present Emergency" … That's the Second World War!'

4

OATH TO BE TAKEN BY RECRUIT ON ATTESTATION.

I, *Maurice George Maygel* swear by Almighty God that I will be faithful and bear true allegiance to His Majesty King George the Sixth, His Heirs and Successors, and that I will, as in duty bound, honestly and faithfully defend His Majesty, His Heirs and Successors, in Person, Crown and Dignity against all enemies, and will observe and obey all orders of His Majesty, His Heirs and Successors, and of the Air Officers and Officers set over me. So help me God.

CERTIFICATE OF ATTESTING OFFICER.

The Recruit above named was cautioned by me that if he wilfully or knowingly made any false answer to any of the foregoing questions, he would be liable to be punished as provided by the Air Force Act.

The foregoing questions were then read to the Recruit in my presence.

I have taken care that he understands each question, and that his answer to each question has been duly entered as replied to. He has been inspected by me, I consider him fit for service in the Royal Air Force and due care has been exercised in his enlistment. The said Recruit has made and signed the Declaration and taken the Oath before me at *UXBRIDGE* on this *18th* day of *June* 19 *40*

Name of Attesting Officer..

I certify that the foregoing is a true copy of the Attestation of the above-named Recruit.

....Approving Officer.

C35724) 50,000 9/39

'Allegiance to the King.'

Successors, and that I will, as in duty bound, honestly and faithfully defend His Majesty, His Heirs and Successors, in Person, Crown and Dignity against all enemies, and will observe and obey all orders of His Majesty, His Heirs and Successors, and of the Air Officers and Officers set over me. So help me God.

I wasn't likely to receive any direct orders from King George VI, was I? It was more about getting me to obey the orders of the officers. Disobey your superior officer and it was like disobeying the king. That was the gist of it. I didn't intend to disobey, I wanted to do my bit 'For King and Country' and I was excited about it, proud to take that oath. It was the beginning of quite an adventure, I can tell you.

2

THE FACE IN THE WINDOW

Britain faced invasion and the Battle of Britain loomed. Despite this critical situation, no one seemed in too much of a hurry to get me into the air, or even into the war for that matter. I was sent home and told to wait for a letter. Eventually, after about ten weeks, that letter arrived and I was told to report to St Pancras station on 4 September and catch a train to Blackpool.

My mother and father and younger brother came to the station with me. There were crowds of people waiting on the platform, photographers too. As a young man you feel such a fool when your parents are there and your mother is making a tearful fuss of you. It's nice to be loved but it was also a relief to get on the train and sit down, four lads to each group of seats.

I was happy and excited when we set off. I was also in the money because I'd withdrawn £40 from my account to make sure I had a bit of spending power for my first few weeks in the armed forces. We knew it was going to be a long journey and we needed something to pass the time so one of the lads said, 'Fancy a game of cards?' Well, you can probably guess the rest before I tell you. By the time we reached Blackpool, I'd lost my £40.

The very first night we were in Blackpool, twenty-six of us were put into a boarding house. The blokes were all getting friendly with one another by then. They weren't just going to go quietly to bed; this was a seaside town and a potential adventure awaited. Everyone decided to go out into town and they chose the 'Manchester Bar' as the place to meet up but I couldn't go because I didn't have any money. Another Londoner was in the same situation. It was just the two of us, left in the boarding house while all the others went out. We felt sad, forlorn and foolish – we didn't know what to do. We were just twiddling our thumbs, thinking of all the others having a great time out on the town when suddenly we saw a solution.

In the corner of the front room we spotted what looked like a Christmas stocking, with some coins in it. I know, you normally find chocolate coins in a Christmas stocking; but these coins weren't made of chocolate. I'm ashamed to say it, but it didn't take long to empty the coins out of the stocking and join the others in the Manchester Bar. I promised myself I'd make sure that money found its way back into the stocking as soon as I got luckier playing cards! I'm not sure it ever did, though.

By day, at least, military life in Blackpool involved a strict routine: square-bashing or gym work in the mornings, Morse code in the afternoons. The next day they'd do it the other way round to give us some variation. Lessons in Morse were held in the sheds where Blackpool's famous trams were housed overnight. I enjoyed Morse code more than drill. It was like a refresher course for me because I'd already learned Morse in the Boy Scouts, along with semaphore. You might wonder why I wasn't firing any machine guns yet; but officially I was training as a 'WOP/AG' – a Wireless Operator and Air Gunner. Blokes were supposed to be interchangeable in those two roles. If you were going to be an air gunner, you had to be trained to work the radio too.

In October we had a photograph taken of our group – Class 1, Squadron B, Wing 5. In that photo I'm sitting down at the very front of the group and I look about as proud and relaxed as it's possible to look in a military snap. I was a serviceman, I liked this new life, and it showed on my face.

Our time in Blackpool drew to a close before Christmas because you never stay in any one place for too long when you're training. Suddenly we were sent right down to the other end of the country. That didn't mean the routine changed, though. At Yatesbury in Wiltshire there was more radio in the morning, drill in the afternoon and vice-versa. We might just as well have stayed in Blackpool, except that it was midwinter by now.

When was I going to be allowed to start firing a machine gun from the turret of an airborne plane? When could I learn the trade for which I'd been earmarked in the first place? We were just getting settled in Yatesbury when it was time to move back up north again. At the end of February 1941, at Catterick in Yorkshire, my new radio skills were at least put to the test in more of a wartime environment. Except that I didn't have to be very skilful. I had a job based in a caravan just off the base, surrounded by sheep and newborn lambs. There was a fighter squadron at Catterick and they were practising their landings. Where did I come in useful? I'd be in this caravan which had an aerial on top. Camp headquarters would phone through to tell me where to point the aerial. This gave the fighter pilots a fix on where they were supposed to be coming in. But they were training too and there was always the potential for disaster.

One night I heard and felt a terrible twang and realised one of the fighter aircraft had hit the aerial on the caravan. I was just below the collision, right there inside the caravan! It could so easily have been the end of my war, not to mention the flying days of that dodgy pilot. But luckily the aerial didn't bring the plane down, so we both lived to fight another day. I was happy to hear that my next destination was to be Stormy Down in Porthcawl, Wales. It wasn't that I had any special connection with Wales; I was just pleased to be leaving Catterick at the end of April before a pilot could land on me.

Stormy Down was where I was going to do my gunnery course. I'll never forget arriving at the air base. Just inside the gate we saw a Fairey Battle, a monoplane, which had crashed and was still up on its nose. That was the angle it had gone in at by the look of it, so the wreckage looked a bit horrific. I wondered whether they had left the aircraft there as a warning to us, or if the crash had just happened.

The bloke who was driving us into the base in a lorry, a very nice chap, saw us eyeing the crash scene and said casually, 'That prang happened the other day. Two men killed, including the pilot.' We went right past the plane, almost as though we were being given a stern lesson in the cost of being careless in the air. Terrible, that was.

My mood didn't improve when we were told there was so little accommodation that we'd have to sleep on the beach. Were they trying to toughen us up or were they just incompetent logistically? The result was the same. We weren't billeted anywhere, there were no huts or anything, so we were left to our own devices

'Young and proud! I'm in the front row, second left.'

at night. There were some fairground merry-go-rounds on the sea-front and I slept under one of those every night. A lot of the lads did the same. We'd go into town and have a pint if we could, then down to the beach for the night. It was early spring but the weather was still terrible, so it was miserable being out on the beach. I paddled in the sea once or twice to try to cheer myself up but I never dared take a proper swim there – the water was too cold.

Not having a roof over our heads at all seems a bit of an RAF oversight, looking back. We were issued with ground sheets and a couple of blankets; but basically we were sleeping rough. It was chilly and I got terrible back-ache down there. Still, we were young, we thought we were tough enough to cope with it, and we just got on with it. Luckily Stormy Down offered more exciting things than back-ache too. The first time I laid my hands on the Vickers Gas Operated machine gun (VGO) was on the ground there. I had a bit of instruction on how the weapon worked from a member of the ground staff. Then I went up with a pilot in a Fairey Battle and fired the VGO from the air. I was sitting just behind the pilot and he would point to the aircraft ahead, which was towing a tubular drogue behind it. We got a diagonal angle on it, so that I wouldn't be shooting my own pilot or firing into the plane dragging the drogue. Then I was given the signal to open fire. The murderous clatter of the VGO was music to my ears. I suppose if a new gunner like me had got over-excited, he could easily have fired into the other plane and brought it down. Fortunately I didn't do that and I never heard of anyone who did. You had to stay cool and concentrate on what you were doing.

There were a hundred rounds in each pan and so it only lasted about five seconds. Then you had to slap a new pan on top of the breech. So there was a lot to be said for making sure you were economical and accurate with your fire. It was a thrill to fire the machine gun and I was good at it too. You left marks on the drogue if you'd hit it and every tracer had a different colour, so you knew whether you were hitting the target or not by the trajectory of the tracer and the holes you created. I was accurate alright; my pay-book carries a note from my instructor saying 'very efficient at air-gunnery'.

Inevitably it was soon time to move on to a fresh training centre, one I hoped might even have a bed waiting for me under a roof. My back-ache had become so bad that I needed a couple of the blokes to carry one of my kit-bags out of Stormy Down. I had two huge bags, absolutely full of kit, and I couldn't carry them both any more. Sleeping rough had taken its toll.

Elated at my success with the machine gun and buoyed by the news that my back wasn't going to have to get any worse, I moved on to Chivenor, a nice little base in North Devon at the start of June 1941. When we got there, I was the one given the official papers, which meant I was more or less in charge of sixteen other blokes. Trouble was, I soon lost them all. A big group just left the base and went down the pub in Braunton, a few miles away. I booked them all in at Chivenor and then decided to go and look for the ones who had gone down the pub. Just to make sure I hadn't forgotten anyone, you understand me, because then I'd have been in trouble. It was nothing to do with wanting a beer myself!

I'd walked a fair way on a warm day and I was feeling tired by the time I reached Braunton, so the sight of a park there was very welcome. It gave me the chance to sit down and have a little rest in the sunshine. I didn't take my shirt off, I had to keep my uniform on, but at least I could relax a bit. There were some houses bordering the park, just across the road from where I was. I looked over and that's when I spotted her. A face in the window of a house, quite some distance away, looking out towards me. I couldn't make out her features too clearly at first, but it was a female face, I could tell that much; and that was enough to attract my interest. She looked at me and I looked at her. She looked quite pretty as far as I could tell, but we were so far away from each other, I wasn't even sure if she was smiling. Still, we both knew our gaze had met, because she moved away from the window when I looked at her. After a short time she came back to the window again, to see if I was still there, I thought. When I looked over again, she moved away once more. This went on for quite a while, like a game of cat and mouse. She'd sneak back, I'd catch her looking over, she'd move back from the window again. It was quite fun, but an older man, who was probably her father, suddenly appeared at another window and that broke the spell a bit. Eventually I had to move on to find that pub and check the blokes were there. It had been thirsty work, that long walk, so I enjoyed a pint with the rest of the lads once I'd found them. For a day or two I thought no more of the girl in the window, because I had plenty to think about at Chivenor.

We discovered we were going to be flying in Bristol Beauforts, quite chunky planes which could carry bombs or even torpedoes in theory. There was nothing very beautiful about a Beaufort, but she had a reputation for being quite a sturdy aircraft. She had two windowed areas jutting out at the front. The main, Perspex nose housed the navigator, who was closest to any land or sea target which might loom below us. But above and slightly behind the navigator was the pilot's cockpit, which was also surrounded by Perspex windows. Naturally the cockpit contained all the most important controls, and the pilot's steering column featured a button. Press that and he could drop bombs or a single torpedo if ever we were to be given one.

Behind the pilot, just the other side of a thin steel screen, you had the wireless operator and his radio. He could walk round the screen if he wanted to get to the pilot or down to the navigator for any reason; he wasn't closed off in his own little room. But generally it was easier to communicate with each other over the intercom. That was especially true for me as gunner, because I was nowhere near the rest of the lads, really. Way back from the other three, much nearer the tail than the nose; that was my domain, in a little machine-gun turret at the rear. It didn't have its own door from the outside and I had to climb in through a hatch nearer the front with the radio man and the navigator (the pilot had his own hatch and dropped straight down into his seat in the cockpit). Then I'd step through a bulkhead, walk to the back and squeeze into the turret. The two machine guns were on a platform which you could move from left to right or vice-versa using pedals, to give yourself the maximum angle of fire. I realised it was going to take some pretty nifty footwork if I was going to give myself a chance of hitting an enemy plane flying straight across my field of vision. But I relished the prospect of making a difference in my new role. If I could find something worth firing at, I'd be able to blast away from my turret and make the target sorry it had ever aroused my interest. The first priority of course was to miss our own tail, which stretched out below me. As long as the target wasn't crafty enough to place itself in a position where my own tail was blocking my line of fire, he was going to be in trouble.

Beauforts weren't very glamorous and apparently they weren't that easy to fly either. We all tried to make ourselves as comfortable and efficient as we could be in our respective compartments. We'd need a lot more training to make sure our roles and different compartments became one in action – a true team capable of destroying our enemy. But the first thing to do at Chivenor was to sort ourselves into these four-man crews, so that we could begin to gel.

Chivenor was being run by a larger-than-life, twenty-six-year-old Northern Irishman called Wing Commander Samuel McCaughey 'Paddy' Boal, DFC. He had flown Beauforts, seen plenty of action, and won a DFC before completing his tour. Paddy Boal was happy to let us 'crew up' of our own accord, because that was the typical RAF way. It was as easy as adding two plus two. Crewing up meant I needed to team up with another WOP/AG (wireless operator/air gunner) – and then find a pilot-and-navigator partnership to make up a four-man crew. We were just told to find ourselves other people – and when we got over the shock at being handed this sudden power, we found it was a marvellous process, very informal. What we didn't realise during this strange ritual was that it could be such a lottery. Indeed this game of chance and how it unfolded might well decide whether you lived or died later.

You only had so much influence over your own fate at this key moment. Instinct and gut feeling could play a part in 'crewing up'. But basically you just mooched around until it happened naturally. And when it was over that was probably your fate sealed, one way or another. Of course this mingling didn't feel like a life-or-death moment at the time; it felt like fun. I'd seen one lad's face before, on the gunnery course at Stormy Down. We actually looked a bit like each other, blond lads with ready smiles, though his face was a bit wider than mine. We had a chat and he was a straight-talking bloke from Sheffield in Yorkshire. His name was Stan Clarke and we sensed instantly that we'd get on. We decided to crew up together and we became friends straight away.

Now we had to find another two. The pilot you ended up with was the one who'd have your life in his hands eventually. Stan and I mingled with the others in a crowded room until we met a mild-mannered pilot called Tommy Lee. He was a typically-English type, taller than me with light brown hair; but what set him apart was his big, broad smile. Tommy was already with a navigator named Jonny Foster, an outrageous Canadian, it turned out; a man who claimed to have been a conman before he had joined up! Despite being obvious opposites, Tommy and Jonny had paired up. Suddenly that was it – we had all found one another, we were a four-man crew, and we would face the mighty guns of the German navy together before long. Without having a clue what Tommy and Jonny were like, or how they would perform when it mattered, I had placed myself at their mercy. You could have a certain amount of influence with the machine guns; but no real control over what was happening most of the time. That was down to the pilot – and I hadn't been selected to train as one of those. Apparently, due to the fact that I'd boxed at school, my life now depended on Tommy Lee.

Such things don't bother you when you're young and carefree. We were all just glad to be in a four-man crew with other young men who seemed like decent blokes. The training would start soon enough; and in the meantime there was another welcome opportunity to head towards Braunton and the pub.

It was two or three days after that little rest in the park. I was walking down the street in Braunton with a friend called Tommy Keegan, from another crew. It was about 9 p.m. and that's when I saw her again – the girl from the window, coming out of the cinema. She looked a bit younger close up but she was even prettier than I'd thought. She had lovely brown hair and high cheek bones; I couldn't wait to see her smile. I started walking straight towards her.

'I've got to go Tommy, there's that girl!' I told him.

'Oh God, he's off baby-snatching!' I heard Tommy say as he headed to the pub to meet the other lads. I didn't care; I wanted to talk to 'the girl from the window'. When she looked up, she recognised me and realised I was heading straight for her.

She was with a friend and started tugging on her arm. I could see her saying, 'It's that bloke from the park Eileen, don't go, don't leave me with him!'

That didn't put me off because I went straight up and said hello – I didn't have any chat-up lines.

'I saw you at the window,' I smiled. She didn't deny it. 'What's your name?'

'Sylvia. And this is my friend Eileen.' Then this radiant smile just lit up Sylvia's whole face.

Sylvia remembers how difficult I was to get rid of: 'He just tagged along with us, because it wasn't far from the cinema back to where I lived. So we walked along the road, the three of us.'

At some point along the way, Sylvia's friend Eileen dropped away tactfully and gave us some space. Maybe she could already sense this was going to be serious!

Once I was left alone with this lovely girl, I said, 'Are you doing anything tomorrow?'

'Nothing special,' she replied.

'Would you like to come out with me, then?' I'd been bursting to ask her.

And I must have put Sylvia at ease somehow; because she said, 'Yes, alright.'

We arranged to meet at the cinema the very next night. (It was too early in the relationship for me to be calling in at her house and meeting her parents.)

Before I left the barracks to meet her, I had to make my excuses to the lads. I told Tommy Keegan, 'I shan't be going down the pub tonight, mate. I'm going out with that girl I met yesterday.'

'Don't tell me. Off baby-snatching again!' he said with a smile, remembering how young she looked. He was a bit older than us, so Sylvia had probably looked even younger to him.

Sure enough my 'baby' turned up for the date and we introduced ourselves properly. Sylvia West – that was her full name. She was only seventeen and I was 20. But it didn't bother me that Sylvia was a bit younger. We went out as planned and had a great time. We just sort of fitted as a pair, relaxed in each other's company. It all felt right. I thought she was the most beautiful girl I'd ever seen – and I'd seen a few before!

Sylvia remembers how it felt right from the start. She said:

We got on well; we both had the same sense of humour. It all just fell into place. We went out every night from then on. I had a passion for dancing, I really loved it. There was a dance on at the Parish Hall every other night in those days. We did the foxtrot and the tango – and the Canadian servicemen had brought the 'jive' with them. I'd already left school of course, so dancing was what we girls did in the evenings.

At the time I was helping out with housework at a big house owned by a couple who had two children. They'd wanted Eileen, but she had started working full-time somewhere else, so I offered my services, just for the mornings. There was an old Scotch nanny and they had a cook too, a local woman. It was quite a posh place but it needed a lot of cleaning. When the couple had to go away for any reason, I used to go up there at night to sleep with the nanny, just to keep her company and help look after the children.

I started walking her up to the big house where she worked, and we always had fun. We'd stroll up the lane hand in hand and sing one of the popular songs of the day. Our favourite was called 'Amapola'. The Jimmy Dorsey Orchestra had brought out a version of the song that spring with Helen O'Connell and Bob Eberly singing. It was still massively popular and went like this:

> Amapola, my pretty little poppy,
> You're like the lovely flower so sweet and heavenly.
> Since I found you, my heart is wrapped around you,
> And, seeing you, it seems to beat a rhapsody.

I'd wrap my arms around Sylvia when we were singing it. The next verse went:

> Amapola, the pretty little poppy
> Must copy its endearing charms from you,
> Amapola, Amapola,
> How I long to hear you say 'I love you'.

We sang each other the song, but we didn't say we loved each other, not properly. Everything was so perfect that we didn't need to weigh ourselves down with loaded words.

Sylvia explained later, 'I was a bit too young and embarrassed to use the word "love" or anything like that.' She was living for the moment, but we'd become an item before we knew it. From the very beginning I thought to myself, 'This is a girl I could settle down with one day.'

The lads in the RAF couldn't understand it. What had happened to me? Why was I always with this girl, when the boys were having so much fun on their own nights out? But I loved Sylvia's company most of all, and I didn't really care what the lads thought about it.

I didn't always have to choose. There were times when everyone could be together at dances in the Parish Hall, so some of the boys met Sylvia. For example I introduced her to Stan Clarke, because he wasn't the sort of bloke who was going to embarrass me in front of her. Also I thought it would be nice for her to know a friend who was in the same plane as me. Sylvia and Stan got along fine; but they didn't have the chance to become good friends because she and I just wanted to be alone together most nights.

Even my parents saw less of me than they would otherwise have done. I'd been all ready to visit my parents on a spot of leave just before I met Sylvia. They were staying with my uncle in Lydney, much nearer Chivenor than London. I still didn't go, because I just wanted to stay with Sylvia instead.

I couldn't do enough for her. I even used to keep small pieces of chocolate for her. Chocolate was in very short supply during the war but I'd get a piece from the RAF canteen at Chivenor and keep it for her until it had almost melted. I'd give it to Sylvia when I saw her in the evening … until I realised she wasn't keen. Sylvia admitted later, 'I wasn't a chocolate-lover at all.' It emerged that she was giving those pieces of chocolate to her dad when she got home.

That didn't do me any harm, though. Before I knew it, she had invited me round to meet her parents. Her father took me for a walk and he was giving me a lecture about something or other; but he had such a thick Devon accent that I couldn't make out what he was saying. Was he trying to make sure my intentions were honourable? Every time there was a pause and I could tell he wanted a reply, I had to say, 'I beg your pardon?' He would say a bit more to me; and I'd have to say it again, 'I beg your pardon?' Suddenly he stopped, turned round, looked me in the eye and said, 'What's a matter with'ee? Dafe?'

He thought I must be hard of hearing, because how else could I have failed to understand him so many times? He seemed to like me, though. At least he didn't mind me by then, having enjoyed the chocolate I'd unintentionally given him.

Sylvia's parents would sometimes take us out for a drive; we did some lovely day trips, just exploring. She and I would sit in the back of her dad's car, grinning like school kids … and we'd snatch the odd kiss too. Cars didn't have mirrors in those days, or at least his didn't. We took advantage of that!

These were happy times in the glorious Devon summer of 1941. If I wasn't with Sylvia – and I almost always was – I sat with the lads getting drunk in

a pub somewhere. I was supposed to be at Chivenor to prepare to fight a war. Instead it felt like I was falling in love. The boys probably thought I'd chosen the wrong moment so when I was out with them I tried to make sure we had as much fun as possible – not that this set of characters needed any encouragement to be outrageous or cause a bit of chaos.

'Looking smart. I scrub up quite well in RAF uniform.'

3

THE BOYS

The boys in our group were mostly going to be shot down and killed. But long before people started to realise that was quite likely, most of us already liked a drink. Tommy Keegan and our navigator Jonny Foster led the way to the pubs, along with a gunner called Bill Carroll – who was also from the Peckham area. Tommy Keegan was a little bit older than us but he was a great guy, always laughing and joking. The other WOP/AG from his plane, Jock Miller, was fun too.

Keegan and Jock were part of a crew with Pilot Officers Seddon and McGregor, who spent their time in the officers' mess, so they weren't part of our gang. The RAF separated officers and NCOs (non-commissioned officers) into different messes; and that social divide remained for most other activities too. But on our plane Tommy Lee, the pilot, was only a sergeant and Jonny Foster wasn't an officer either so we were all one team in the plane and in theory we could still have been a team when we climbed out of it. I don't remember Tommy Lee coming out with us very much, though. I don't think he really drank.

When I was out with Bill Carroll you never knew what would happen. One night we saw this glass sign on top of a petrol pump at a filling station in Barnstaple. The name on the sign was 'Ethyl Pratt'. We thought this was so funny that we had to have the sign, so one of us lifted up the other and went to work. We unscrewed the glass sign, took it off the pump, and took it back to Chivenor air base as one of our souvenirs.

No one was more outrageous than Jonny Foster, though. He kidded us that he was preparing to break into the WAAF's quarters at night. Then he actually did it. I don't think any of the WAAFs were willing to risk their careers by welcoming him there for the night – he didn't get very far with them. But he was still quite proud of having got into their sleeping quarters – and we were impressed too.

Jack Featherstone, a lad I'd first known at Yatesbury, was out with us a lot. He was another WOP/AG, a really nice, decent chap and we stayed friends right through the training process. Jack was on the same crew as Bill Carroll but couldn't take his drink as well as Bill could. Somehow he ended up climbing onto a train after some boozy night out in Barnstaple and falling sleep. Poor Jack woke up in Bristol. We all thought it was hilarious when he called Bill at the base the next morning, wondering how to get back without getting into trouble.

Nights out like that helped us to knit together as a group. I may have been besotted with Sylvia, but I spent enough nights with the gang here and there to remain very much one of the lads. Everything was treated as a bit of a laugh in those days; we were enjoying ourselves while we could.

There was no moment when training in Beauforts made me think, 'I'm probably going to be joining a really dangerous squadron from here.' Besides, what did the prospect of danger matter, when what I'd really wanted to do was become a Spitfire pilot? That would have put me in more danger than almost anything else, because at the height of the Battle of Britain, Spitfire pilots had lasted about two weeks on average. I wanted excitement. I wanted to defend my country. And the idea of being in the turret was exciting, because you never knew when you might have to open fire.

In theory it could have been Stan Clarke on the guns and me on the radio, but I didn't like that idea. You didn't see much of the action when you were operating the wireless. Luckily Stan didn't want to be on the guns any more than I wanted to be on the radio. 'Being on the guns gives me a funny feeling,' he said one day.

'What do you mean?' I asked him.

'Well, it's being in the turret. Makes me feel like I'm going to fall into the sea. I don't like it.'

I could see why he felt like that, because we were barely skimming over the waves half the time. Flying at 50 feet, with not much more than Perspex to protect you, wasn't for everyone. So the radio space in the middle of the plane suited Stan better. If he wanted to, he could almost shut out what was going on outside his 'office'.

I said, 'Alright, I'll do the guns all the time and you do the radio all the time.'

'Thanks Moggy, you're on!' he said. And that was that.

There wasn't much room in the turret but I didn't mind. I was quite a small bloke really, I wasn't a big eater and I could move around alright.

When Tommy took off and flew us out beyond the North Devon coastline, there was nothing but a vast expanse of sea to look at most of the time. I used to imagine there were spots in the sky that I could shoot at. Once we were out over the sea, I could ask the pilot's permission to test the guns, to make sure they were working. I was always quite anxious to let a burst go down into the water, if I'm honest. We were still using the Vickers Gas Operated (VGO) machine guns in those days, with just those hundred rounds in each pan, so it was all over very quickly.

We didn't stay airborne for very long at first anyway, because the pilots had to get as much practice as they could at taking off and landing. 'Circuits and bumps,' we called it. Take off, come round, land again. Didn't seem too hard – but then again I wasn't the one doing it.

At around this time a letter arrived for me – an official one from the RAF/Air Ministry. It explained that a place had been found for me on a pilot's course, if I was still interested. I thought about it but felt the moment had passed. I had all my mates among the crews, we were already a close-knit group, and that was very important. We trainee crews were nearly ready for the real thing. We knew we still had another course to do, but we also knew it couldn't be long now before we went operational. To go off on a pilot's course would have sent me back to square one. And there was something else I took into account – or rather someone else – Sylvia. I was enjoying our summer together so much that I wanted it to last as long as possible before we went into action.

I wrote back saying 'thanks but no thanks' to the offer of becoming a pilot. And in that moment I denied myself the chance to have some real control over my own destiny, or at least what control you can have in a totally unpredictable war. In that moment I gave myself up to the pilots who would fly me and I placed my trust in them. My life would depend on their skill, their nerve, their mood, even their drinking habits. Of course, when you're young, you don't think about it all too deeply. My decision at the time could be summed up far more simply. 'I'm not leaving my mates. And I'm not leaving my girlfriend until I have to leave her to go to war.'

So I continued my training at Chivenor. All the crews were taking it in turns to do circuits and bumps one day when something went wrong. I'd heard there was a design fault on the Beaufort; if you didn't handle her just right when you reached the top of a climb, she could come right back down again with a thump. I don't know if it was true, but what happened next didn't give me any reason to disbelieve the rumour.

One crew took off in their Beaufort and went into low cloud at the corner of the airfield. The pilot's name was Pilot Officer S.H. Last. On the crew with him was a Canadian called Pilot Officer V.J. Hall and two sergeants named Wesley and Fell. Last must have turned over in the cloud, because by the time they came down from that cloud there was an awful screaming of the engines and that Beaufort seemed to be heading straight for the river. We were all watching and it was a question of whether or not the pilot could find a solution and pull out in time. He couldn't. They all died when the Beaufort slapped into the river. I remember the silence after the impact and then the terrible sound of bubbles as the aircraft quickly sunk below the water.

The official squadron records described how Last's '… Beaufort got out of control in a cloud and dived vertically from 500 feet into the River Taw half a mile south of Chivenor Aerodrome at 10.15hrs.'

They had no chance of surviving and the rest of us felt quite unnerved. The sound of bubbles turned to silence. The lives of these poor men were over forever. It could have happened to anyone.

That's when we heard the order: 'All go up! Five minutes!'

I thought, 'That's just cruel, after what we've just witnessed.'

We'd never seen an accident happen before our eyes like that. We didn't want to take off at such a terrible time. But that was exactly why Paddy Boal had issued the order. He realised that if we didn't get back in the air straight away, some of us would lose our nerve completely and never have what it took to become airmen. So each crew took it in turns to go up and do circuits and bumps again, until we had our nerve back. As for that poor crew which had crashed, they were fished out of the river, what was left of them, and buried at the local churchyard on the hill.

We did a slow funeral march all the way up there for a church parade and service. The band was playing mournful music. It was the first time I'd marched like that for any genuine reason and it was quite moving. But as soon as the service was over and it was time to march down again, the band started to play this really happy, up-beat music. How strange that was! It was amazing how quickly the blokes wore a different look on their faces and almost felt like dancing. It is part of military custom. Go to a funeral? You're sad. Come back? You're happy. I suppose it isn't that different to civvy street, where you have the funeral, often followed by some kind of wake. It's just that in the military the shift in mood is more sudden and pronounced.

Sylvia and I walked up to the graveyard privately soon afterwards, to pay our own respects. We'd had so many happy days that summer, she and I, but that definitely wasn't one of them, and the crash served as a warning to all of us who were still training at Chivenor.

There was no getting away from it; the war was going to be tough when we went operational. We knew by now the Beauforts were designed for attacking German ships in ports or even ships out on open water. One heroic Scot called Kenneth Campbell had already flown his Beaufort right into Brest harbour in north-west France on 6 April, and dropped a torpedo before being shot to pieces. The torpedo had blown a hole in a mighty German battle-cruiser called the *Gneisenau*, which had been put out of action for months as it was repaired. Campbell, who doubtless saved more slaughter on our merchant vessels out in the Atlantic thanks to his suicidal determination, was awarded a posthumous Victoria Cross.

Kenneth Campbell set the standard for other Beauforts in the Second World War. There could be little doubt that we'd have to sacrifice ourselves too, if a given situation demanded it. Our lives would be risked to ensure the success of any mission deemed sufficiently vital. Ultimately, we'd be seen as expendable. And although we had no confirmation at this stage, it didn't take much imagination to guess where our efforts might eventually be concentrated.

The German ships either sailing the seas around Britain in that summer of 1941 or preparing to do so again were truly formidable. Fortunately the most fearsome of all – the mighty *Bismarck* – had already come a cropper, though not before sinking the Royal Navy's finest, the SS *Hood*. The *Bismarck* had used eight, 15-inch guns, housed in four twin-gun turrets to sink the *Hood*. No less than fifty-six further guns were available around the *Bismarck*'s deck to help finish the job. All but three of the *Hood*'s 1,419 crew were lost when she slipped beneath the waves on 24 May 1941. In Britain it was considered a national tragedy.

But a Royal Navy ship called the *Prince of Wales* softened up the *Bismarck* by scoring three hits, even as the *Hood* was fatally wounded. The *Prinz Eugen*, herself a mighty battle-cruiser escorting the *Bismarck*, noted an oil slick behind the biggest German ship. The *Bismarck* had suffered damage to an oil-tank and they rushed towards the safety of the French ports. But fifteen Fairey Swordfish planes left the *Ark Royal* on 26 May and managed to achieve a minor miracle. They did irreparable damage to the *Bismarck*'s rudder assembly with one of their torpedoes. Left to swim in a fatal circle, the pride of the German navy was soon sunk by the British Navy. Of the 2,200 who had sailed on the *Bismarck*, only 114 survived. No one on either side delighted in the huge loss of life when giant ships went down; but there was much relief that Winston Churchill's vital trans-Atlantic supply lines had some breathing space again.

We all knew it wasn't over, though. The Kriegsmarine, Hitler's navy, had plenty more firepower. The *Tirpitz*, sister ship to the *Bismarck*, could still tip the balance of the war in Hitler's favour if left to wreak havoc unchecked. Sooner or later she would have to be destroyed, and we were the kind of people who might have to do it. Meanwhile the *Prinz Eugen* had made it back to the safety of Western France, where two more giant ships, the *Scharnhorst* and the *Gneisenau*, were being refitted and repaired. Campbell had bought precious time for the Allies when he sacrificed his life for the cause but the threat hadn't been removed permanently, and the *Scharnhorst* and *Gneisenau* had already shown how destructive they could be. Back in June 1940, they had combined to sink the British aircraft-carrier, HMS *Glorious* and two accompanying destroyers, HMS *Ardent* and HMS *Acasta*. The *Scharnhorst* had been damaged and had undergone repairs, just as the *Gneisenau* was doing while we trained. It was only a matter of time before they'd be brought back to full capability. When German repairs were done and our training was over, our little Beauforts and those massive battleships would be on collision course. Whether we quite grasped the uneven nature of that looming fight was another matter entirely.

★   ★   ★

It was mid–August 1941, when I had to leave Chivenor and felt Sylvia's warm embrace for the last time that year. We both put on a brave face. We'd had such fun and we didn't want it to end in a miserable scene.

'I'll write to you,' I promised. 'I'll call you when I can, too.'

Sylvia smiled encouragingly. She recalls:

> It was sad but I wasn't in tears. For all I knew, Maurice would only be going a little distance away. A place called Abbotsinch was where Maurice was going to be posted next, but I didn't know where that was. Maurice would still be in Britain, he said; that was the main thing. I was confident we'd see each other again before too long.

Seeing her again in the near future was going to prove difficult, because we were posted up to Scotland. We were going on a torpedo-training course in Abbotsinch, which later became better known as Glasgow airport. Some ships in the German navy could be dispatched with bombs but others would need torpedoes. It was at Abbotsinch that we would learn how to drop torpedoes.

I remember arriving at Abbotsinch and all the blokes were packed into a tiny new barracks, everyone making a terrific din. They were all in high spirits but I felt more sombre. They didn't bother with me, I wasn't important; the gang just wanted to go out on the town and see what Paisley or Glasgow was like. I'd been the only chap serious with a girl at Chivenor, so the rest of them were looking forward to 'fresh fields'. All I wanted to do was sit on my bed and write Sylvia a letter. I was quite upset about leaving her.

The flying up in Scotland helped me stay cheerful. Though I didn't have that much to do when we were airborne, it felt exhilarating all the same. If you're thinking it was my responsibility, as gunner, to make sure the torpedo was dispatched at the right moment, you couldn't be more wrong. That was the job of the pilot. He pressed his button on his steering column and away the 'torp' went.

I didn't see a lot of what the pilot and navigator were doing at any point, but I could try to keep an eye out for the wake and course of the torpedo from the turret, to see if it hit the target as we turned away. Torpedo training also helped me to get used to low-level flying. We had to fly just a few feet above the mountains on the initial approach to the target. We'd go through the gaps between mountains as we lined up our dummy attack, almost skim the waves at 50 feet, then rear up slightly to drop the dummy torpedo from between 60 and 80 feet. We did a lot of this kind of flying while we were up there; it was a pretty intensive course, especially for the pilots. It was all down to skill, timing and the success of the pilot in getting down low enough to carry out the strike.

Some pilots got it wrong and paid with their lives and those of their crew. This was a dangerous business, flying down through valleys between mountains and out over open water almost at wave level. But Tommy Lee was a steady bloke with a cool nerve and he negotiated the challenges with a calm focus that reassured us all. As for me, I couldn't do much up there. The air gunners weren't given a target to fire at. Once Tommy had veered away and was taking the plane out of the killing zone, they might have told us to aim at something. They didn't. So when the time came for a real mission, we gunners would have to rely upon the sort of accuracy we'd achieved at places like Stormy Down, if we were going to make our little difference to the war.

You may wonder how it was possible to drop a torpedo from a plane and make it swim through water in the direction you wanted it to go. Well, first of all, the torpedo had a tail to make it aerodynamic, because it was a bit of a monster and you didn't want it to drop like a stone. It weighed about 1,500 pounds, was 15 feet long and about 18 inches in diameter. The torpedo was attached to two cables which ran to a drum in the bomb bay. The line of cable connected to the torpedo's tail stayed attached to the drum for a split-second longer than the line of cable connected to the torpedo's main section. This sent the torpedo off at a downward angle of 17 degrees – just right to fly through the air for 250 yards and enter the water while maintaining its course. A rod on the torpedo took away the tail on impact with the sea, leaving four fins on the main section to stabilise it in the water.

As I said, we were using dummy torpedoes at Abbotsinch, so they didn't have explosive warheads ready to do serious damage on impact with their target. But Tommy and the other pilots still had to get the distances right in preparation for the real thing. With a real warhead, propellers within the torpedo's internal engine had to power it through the sea for 350 yards at 40 knots, before the warhead was finally activated and the whole thing was ready to blow up on impact with an enemy ship's hull. So Tommy Lee knew he needed to drop the dummy torpedo while there was still at least 600 yards between the plane and the ship: 250 yards of air flight and then the 350-yard swim. It was safer to leave a bit more distance, but you had to make sure you weren't too far away as well. If you released the torpedo from more than a thousand yards away, you couldn't rely on its accuracy and it might lose momentum. So about 800 yards was just the right distance for Tommy to press the button and tell us 'torpedo gone'.

Even dummy torpedoes were valuable commodities, so when they lost their momentum on the torpedo range, they were caught in nets. Scuba divers would go down quickly to retrieve or at least get a precise fix on them, before these dummies were lost to us forever.

The whole Abbotsinch experience was a good bonding exercise and probably sharpened our collective senses for real action. Meanwhile when we weren't in the air, we found that Glasgow could be fun and rough in equal amounts.

My father had a shop assistant called Rose Gonnella at one stage, and her brother was a well-known band leader called Nat Gonnella. When we heard he was playing in Glasgow, we couldn't resist it. Bill Carroll and I went along with two commissioned officers – I think one of them was Tommy Carson, a pilot who'd been to Cambridge and still liked a good time.

When we arrived at the club, Nat Gonnella and his jazz band were already playing, and Bill shouted over to the compere, 'He knows Nat's sister back in Peckham!'

'Hiya Nat!' I shouted, as though we were the best of mates.

Nat heard this and listened to what the compere was telling him. Then he came over to the side of the stage, where we were standing.

'Is it true?' he asked as his band played on.

'Yeah, your sister Rose used to work for my dad!' I said.

Nat was very good about it. He even interrupted the show so that a table and chairs could be brought in at the side of the stage. He sent for some beer and we watched the rest of the show from that privileged position. It felt brilliant to get the special treatment and of course the rest of the boys were impressed.

Another night, I was drinking with Bill Carroll and a couple of others in a bar in Paisley when a man came over and said he was on the board at Glasgow Rangers Football Club. 'Would you like to come and see a match?' he asked us. 'Rangers are playing one of your English teams – Preston North End. It's a pre-season friendly.'

We all liked football so we weren't going to turn that down. He promised to fix us up with some tickets.

'Just one thing,' he said. 'They're a good lot, the Rangers fans, but they're rough too. I wouldn't let them hear your English accents – and make sure you cheer for the right team.'

He came up with the tickets and we went along to Ibrox Park. We couldn't believe the atmosphere. This was anything but a friendly, if the mood of the crowd was anything to go by.

The English goalkeeper accidentally punched the Scottish striker as they went up for a high ball together. That caused uproar. The Rangers fans around us started throwing bottles. They wanted to invade the pitch to get at the English players. But it was the kids who ended up invading the pitch – to pick up the bottles. They were prepared for a mini-riot like this, because they had sacks all ready for the job. They'd fill them up and disappear again, ready to head for the shops and win a little fee for giving the bottles back.

Luckily the police came out on horseback and eventually quelled the crowd. But when everything had cleared, there were blokes lying on the terraces unconscious. Someone had taken the opportunity to hit them on the head with a bottle. Some servicemen had been targeted and were out cold. If I'd been down there instead of up near the directors, I might have been knocked out too. The Preston players got out alive, partly because they lost 3–1.

It had all been in aid of the war effort – for the Lord Provost's Central Fund. We hadn't expected the Glaswegians to start a war of their own.

We were back in that bar in Paisley a couple of nights later and the same man came in. 'Did you enjoy the match?' he asked?

'Yes thanks,' we assured him. We didn't want to offend him by mentioning the crowd trouble.

'Good,' he said. 'Because next week we're playing Celtic. That one won't be so friendly – it's a big affair up here. But if you want to go I'll get you tickets for that too.'

He was good for the tickets again, a real gentleman. And he gave us an even more serious warning. 'It's very important tonight that you support Rangers. If they score, you've got to cheer as loud as the rest of them. They'll punch you otherwise.'

We had a great view from near the directors' box, but even up there the atmosphere seemed full of hate. We didn't need to be reminded how to react. We supported Rangers as though our lives depended on it – which they probably did. They were 2-0 up when their goalkeeper Jerry Dawson gave away a penalty. He saved it, too, which was too much for the Celtic fans. Fighting broke out; scores of bottles were thrown onto the pitch. Those enterprising young kids went out with their sacks again and collected loads of them, ready to get rich on the return fee. What a week those lads had, with two riots in the space of a few days! The police were too busy with the Celtic crowd to pay much attention to the youngsters. They waded in, truncheons drawn, and eventually restored order. Rangers won 3-0.

You'd never have thought there was a war on – except between Celtic and Rangers! In fact there was some talk after that of stopping the Old Firm matches until the end of the real war! We went back to have a drink with our benefactor and everyone was behaving as though the match had been nothing out of the ordinary.

That was life in Glasgow and beyond. Danger in the air, flying close to mountains and sea. Danger on the ground … or rather in Rangers' ground!

But the funny thing was, I couldn't get that girl Sylvia out of my mind, my sweet seventeen-year-old from Devon. I was missing her so much that I realised I really had fallen in love with her. I wrote to her from Scotland and told her so. She wrote back and expressed similar feelings. But this was all strange new emotional territory, and we didn't know what to do about it. I wrote again and told her I'd call her house at a certain time one evening.

'I was sitting beside the phone, waiting,' Sylvia remembers fondly.

But when she picked up the phone, I was tongue-tied.

'Everything alright down there, Sylvia?' That was about the best I could manage.

'I'm fine thanks,' she said.

'Will you keep writing?'

'Yes, Maurice, write to me again and I'll write to you again.'

Then there was a silence, which I broke clumsily.

'What did you do tonight?'

She told me as best she could.

'What are you going to do tomorrow night?'

Was I starting to sound jealous and possessive?

Sylvia still remembered the awkwardness as we sat together more than seventy-two years later! 'The first time you called me, we didn't know quite what to say, did we? It was very difficult. I was happy that you'd rung, but it was just awkward. It was just you asking questions and me answering questions. I don't remember getting to ask a question.'

I didn't mean for it to go like that, but I was very curious about what she was doing when I wasn't there. At the same time I was just trying to make conversation – it didn't go very well.

We didn't know how to handle the physical separation and we didn't want to get miserable about it either. We had our own worlds, and I suppose we were most comfortable just living as we would if we hadn't met each other. So we went out with other people if the occasion arose, without telling each other.

Sylvia can explain the reasons. 'You go to a dance and you can't just dance by yourself, can you? I was seventeen years old. You can't expect a girl to stay indoors. You have to enjoy yourself. Maurice and I had been together for less than three months the previous summer. But I still had feelings for Maurice. Always.'

The calls and letters continued. We got used to speaking on the phone as well as writing, and we knew we had the makings of something special. But we weren't going to let it rule our lives, either. How could I let Sylvia dominate my thoughts when I had Adolf Hitler to fight?

Our crew left Abbotsinch in one piece. Tommy Lee seemed to know what he was doing with a torpedo by then. He was hitting those static targets like nobody's business. The fact that the German ships would be moving when the time came to use a real torpedo – and they'd be firing at us furiously too – didn't seem to enter the equation. We had done what we were there to do and now, finally, it was time to join the war.

4

ON OPS

I didn't like the sound of what I was hearing. We were going to join 217 Squadron in St Eval, Cornwall. That was part of Coastal Command, we were told.

'Coastal Command? That's not the war. That sounds like digging sandcastles!' I said to the rest of the crew. 'At best we'll be patrolling, and I haven't joined up for that.'

Then I found out that quite a few of the other crews were going to 217 Squadron as well, Bill Carroll included, so that wasn't so bad.

We flew down to St Eval, a nice little place and one of the most western bases in Britain. That's when I saw something which made me question my own eyes. It couldn't be … but it was. One of the first people I saw at St Eval was the smart RAF man whose uniform I'd liked so much when I saw him walking past my dad's shop in Peckham. How was that possible? I went over and introduced myself and he told me his name was Ken Reeves. He was quite well established on 217 Squadron.

I told him, 'You were the reason I joined up!' He looked confused. 'Peckham! Because you looked so stylish in that uniform!' He smiled at that.

Neither of us could quite believe the coincidence – it was a long way from Peckham to Cornwall. But Cornwall wasn't very far away from Sylvia in Devon, which should have helped my love life. Trouble was, we were kept so busy that I couldn't get away so Sylvia and I still had to make do with phone calls and letters.

Before we knew it, Tommy, Stan, Jonny and I were flying real operations. We were in the war. The torpedo training wasn't going to be very useful yet because we had bombs in the bomb-bay for now. The first trip was gentle enough – although still a bit nasty. I remember we were going out towards the Atlantic and our Beaufort was invaded by a terrible smell – really terrible. I was on the radio that day for some reason – very unusual. I soon wished I hadn't been.

Tommy said, 'Who's done something?'

I said, 'Not me, skip. Honestly. Not me!'

But down the side near my position there was a toilet and just beyond that there was a hatch. I opened up the toilet and immediately I realised from the stench that it hadn't been emptied since the last flight by the previous crew. Reluctantly, I realised the only thing to do was to pull the bucket out and empty it right there, in mid-air. No one was below because we were over the sea at the time. Down the hatch! You probably think I'm going to tell you that all this horrible stuff blew right back in my face – but it didn't. Instead the slip-stream was so great that I watched it disappear behind us in a tiny black spot. It narrowly missed the tail-plane. Trouble was, as I followed its progress, I noticed that the back-drop of blue sea wasn't there any more. Instead this black spot of filth was zooming down towards land – and maybe even people. Taking Jonny Foster's advice, Tommy Lee had decided to take a short cut towards the Atlantic. He'd gone over southern Ireland.

When I told my mate Bill Carroll later, he said, 'Moggy! Congratulations! You're the first man to bomb Dublin!'

But I'm pretty sure we hadn't been going over a city … at least I don't think we were.

On another occasion Ireland was more deliberately part of the plan. We were off up the south-west coast of Ireland, on the look-out for Tunney-fishing boats. The brief was to make a note of what they were up to. A Tunney-boat is like an ordinary rowing boat but it's about five times the size. If we saw one, we were under strict orders not to open fire – just to note their position. The whole thing was a mystery to me.

By pure luck, we'd just touched the west coast of Ireland and pulled out a bit to fly over the sea when we spotted something. I could see a vessel from my turret because I was on the guns that day. Pretty soon the Tunney fishing boat was directly below us and it was packed on both sides with Irishmen. They were heading out westwards, these men packed in like sardines. Even if they'd wanted to do any fishing, they couldn't have – there was no room for them to move. We were so low I could see right into the boat, I could look into the faces of these Irishmen, some with their flat caps on, packed tight all around this big boat.

I didn't like the look of them. I knew something wasn't right and my instinct told me to machine-gun the whole lot of them. I had the urge, I wanted to do it. But I had no orders like that to act upon, only my own suspicions – and they weren't enough to justify me letting rip with the VGO. I didn't dare do what I wanted to do. I kept my discipline and I didn't open fire. I found that frustrating, though.

When we got back, I asked the others on our crew for their opinion of what we had seen. They didn't seem that bothered. They certainly weren't alarmed. But I was alarmed and I was very concerned about what I'd seen. In fact I insisted that Tommy and Jonny report everything to the bosses in detail. Somehow that still didn't seem to be enough to appease me, though. So I went to speak to the intelligence officer to seek an explanation.

He said, 'We've been receiving information that Irishmen in these boats have been giving information to German submarines. But also, we've heard there are Irishmen who want to join up with the German Army.'

The German Army was made up of lots of different nationalities, battalions of foreign troops from countries they'd invaded – and some they hadn't. The Irishmen I'd seen in that Tunney-boat must have been heading out to one of the German submarines in the area, so they could be taken to Germany. They probably reached that submarine and went on to fight for the Nazis, all because I hadn't stopped them.

I never saw a single thing about that in the British press, I've always wondered why. Maybe they thought it would be bad for morale to know that some people so close to Britain wanted to help the Nazis. I know these Irishmen had their own reasons and motivations, historical hatred for the British, linked to the Irish potato famine and much more. But this was war against the Nazis and they wanted to destroy us. In fact they wanted to destroy everybody's freedom. And some Irishmen still wanted to help them. Their hatred for the British was so great that they didn't want to see beyond it.

Do I wish I'd opened up on that boat and killed the lot of them? Yes I do. In that moment they were the enemy. They should have been eliminated right there – just as sure as if they had been Nazis.

I remember going out with Bill Carroll and some of the boys not long afterwards and I said, 'Pity I didn't shoot the bastards!'

'Too late now,' he said.

A spot of 'gardening' helped to take my mind off it. I'm not talking about planting a few cabbages in an allotment at St Eval. Gardening was the term given to mine-laying outside the French ports. The Kriegsmarine had some of their most powerful battleships hidden away in places like Brest or La Pallice, where German submarines also went. You planted the mine and hoped it would bear fruit by colliding with and blowing up some German vessel.

We'd fly low all the way to the mouth of an estuary outside one of these Nazi-occupied ports. Then we'd drop the mine just where we thought a German ship might have to sail, if it came out of one of these ports. Job done, you turned round and came home. No one fired on us so it felt easy.

'Gardening at Brest.'

'Gardening at La Pallice.'

That's how the pilots recorded these trips in their log-books. There wasn't much in it for an air gunner like me. I had to be ready, focused, searching the skies. But apart from testing my weapon I didn't have to use it in anger.

The next mission I remember was even stranger – but this·time it was over enemy-occupied territory. We were told we were going to drop pamphlets over a city called Nantes, a port on the west coast of France. Hitler was planning to execute fifty civilians because one of the top German officers in France had been assassinated.

Even Franklyn Roosevelt was getting involved. We knew that because we got a chance to look at the leaflets we were dropping. Roosevelt and Churchill were warning Hitler of dire consequences if the executions were carried out. They would hold him personally responsible for these atrocities, which would outrage the free world and create a terrible retribution.

There was also a message of hope to the French population – 'Keep undermining the Nazis and one day we'll help you to be free again,' that sort of thing. But for the French who had taken the easy option and collaborated there was a stark warning: the day of reckoning would come.

It was interesting stuff, because the Americans weren't even in the war in that autumn of 1941. This was one of the first examples of the Allies openly ganging up against Hitler – leaving him in no doubt about how it would turn out if he carried on.

We bombed the port of Nantes a bit first. Tommy Lee swooped in low over the docks and released the bombs; then we came back over the city at a higher altitude – about 5,000 feet. It was up to me to send the pamphlets down the flare chute. I opened the chute when the signal was given, but I cut the string on the first batch of pamphlets too soon. That meant a lot of them just whooshed straight back up the chute and into the plane. They blew all over the place and one even stuck to the back of Tommy Lee's head at the front of the plane.

I soon realised what I'd done wrong. The other batches were released from their string ties a little later on their way out. That meant they flew down the chute and fluttered over the skies of Nantes before landing for the local population and occupying Nazis to read. It felt satisfying to have given some hope to the locals and warned the Nazis what would be coming to them.

From what I heard though, the local Nazis went ahead and executed those poor civilians anyway, because Hitler insisted on it. But there was a local Nazi commander who had started to doubt the wisdom of these executions. He pressed hard not to repeat them in the future. When he didn't get the response he'd hoped for from Berlin, I think he became deeply troubled by the whole thing. He even killed himself in the end.

It wasn't the Nantes executions that brought the USA into the war, though. Pearl Harbor in Hawaii was bombed by the Japanese in December and that did it. It was a momentous development.

I had a bit of leave in December and I remember going back to see my mother in East Dulwich, where the family was living at the time.

I told her about the momentous development in my own life. 'Mum, I've met a girl.'

I'd met dozens of girls, but Mum had never heard me say it like this before.

She looked at me and said, 'Oh Maurice. Oh dear.'

But there was more, of course. I said, 'Mum. She's only seventeen.'

Mum didn't say anything about that.

You might wonder why I didn't go straight down to Devon to see Sylvia. But I hadn't seen my parents for ages, partly because I'd been with Sylvia all summer. So it was their turn and I knew it was right to go and see them.

Jonny had a bit of leave like the rest of us. He went to Peckham with my mate Bill Carroll, because his own family was over in Canada. Jonny charmed Bill's mum into cooking a lovely steak for him, with whatever food rations he had left. But once Jonny ate that steak, he left Bill and his family quite abruptly after that and ended up going gambling on his own in London. That started a fatal chain of events which led to the end of Jonny's life.

Meanwhile, Bill came looking for me, short of some company all of a sudden. We had a great time at some pub in Peckham, went dancing and got roaring drunk. Typical clowning about by young men who didn't know what was coming next.

Jonny got back to the barracks early, because he'd lost all his money and that was his last chance to have some fun. We'd switched bases from St Eval to Thorney Island in Hampshire by then.

Anyway, Jonny went from one pilot called Lee to another pilot called Lee. Tommy Lee had been his first pilot; Mark Lee was to be his last. It just happened by chance; the whole thing was a lottery, as I said before. The rest of us were on leave but Mark Lee wasn't. He'd had some issues with a navigator who seemed almost middle-aged to young men like us. Mark had a spare spot in his plane and although he was known for some bumpy landings, Jonny didn't mind.

'Want to come on a trip with us for a change?' Mark Lee asked.

'Sure, why not?' said Foster, probably anxious to put his recent setback behind him.

It was always considered bad luck to switch crews. But there was a job to do – a job against the Nazis – and Jonny was determined to do it. If he was the only spare navigator and Mark Lee needed a navigator, then that was that. The superstitions about new crew members would have to be put out of their minds.

Off they went on this mission on 11 December – Mark Lee, Jonny Foster, Harry Carter and John Chadaway. They didn't come back. The other two aircraft on the trip made it home, so we heard what had happened. They attacked a ship called the SS *Madrid* off the Hook of Holland. A South African Flight Lieutenant called Ginger Finch led the attack. His bombs hit home and he got away, despite almost being caught in his own blast. Mark Lee went in next but the *Madrid* was fighting back by then. Lee took a shell in his portside engine and went down in flames before he reached the ship. He took Jonny Foster, Carter and Chadaway with him.

A pilot called Arthur Aldridge, who had joined up from Oxford University and was a good friend of Mark Lee's, saw what happened but still had to attack last. His bombs finished off the *Madrid* but he lost a wing-tip on the ship's bracing wire. Somehow he stayed in the air and managed to get home OK. The two surviving pilots were awarded the Distinguished Flying Cross. But we had all lost friends.

The operational record book concluded, 'F/Lt Finch and Pilot Officer Aldridge were awarded the DFC. Congratulations!'

Finch and Aldridge were brave men and deserved their medals. Mark Lee, Jonny and the others had been no less brave, but they were dead.

We were still on leave, Bill Carroll and I. Jonny Foster would have been too, if he hadn't lost all his money on that card game. We didn't even know what had happened to him at that stage. When we got back to Thorney Island, they told us and we felt desolate. That Canadian had been a big favourite among the lads. We'd lost our navigator so there would have to be changes. That might bring more bad luck.

No more Jonny, the life and soul of our nights out on the beer. What a character he had been, what fun, so full of good humour. Now that he was gone, it was just me and Stan Clarke from our crew out on the booze, because Tommy Lee was a self-contained type. Gradually Stan and I teamed up more with Bill Carroll, from Tommy Carson's crew, and a few others.

Bill came back home to Peckham with me on our second spell of December leave and we carried on living life the way Jonny Foster would have wanted us to. Bill helped me celebrate my twenty-first birthday, which was on Boxing Day, 1941. Stan was there too and we had a great old time.

My father had arranged a party for me and I had to look after the drinks. One of my dad's First World War muckers was there – a really tough naval bloke who loved a drink.

My father told me that night, 'Don't forget to keep your uncle Alf supplied with drink all evening.'

He wasn't my uncle but I spent much of the evening looking after him and making sure I kept his glass topped up. I plied him with Scotch very conscientiously, until eventually he was flat out on the floor.

There were girls around that night, including an old girlfriend of mine. I knew Sylvia was the one for me; but in wartime you live for now and I'm not going to say I rejected the attentions of my old flame because I didn't. It was all just a bit of fun and I remember locking Bill and my Peckham girlfriend's sister in a toilet under the stairs, just for a laugh. It was some time before anyone noticed they were missing and managed to get them out.

Back at the new barracks in Thorney Island, things were a bit quieter. Another Londoner, Sid Knight, was in the bed next to mine. Sid was a great bloke and we stayed friends long after the war. He lived so close to me in London that he reckoned he already knew my parents. Sid was a card player. I didn't play cards much but I used to watch Sid play pontoon with the others in the barracks and quite a lot of money used to change hands. Some lads lost £10 or more – a tidy sum in those days if you were on airmen's pay. But the losers just had to take it on the chin and the games didn't harm the growing sense of camaraderie between us. It wasn't quite the same without Jonny Foster, though. By the time the New Year came around, it would have been easy enough to conclude that many more of us were going to go the same way. But I refused to think like that; I was positive and confident and I never thought I'd be shot down.

I told myself I'd get the chance to see Sylvia before long too. We were still writing to each other and I was calling her, but we hadn't seen each other for months. Life on 217 Squadron was hectic. That summer of sheer bliss down in Chivenor seemed a lifetime ago. One day soon, I promised myself, Sylvia and I would be together again, though.

★　★　★

In early 1942 it became clear that the Germans were ready to do something big – something that had been on the cards for some time. The *Scharnhorst*, *Gneisenau* and *Prinz Eugen* were all in Brest harbour. If they broke out, these huge cruiser-class battleships could still be a massive threat to our shipping in the Atlantic. The *Scharnhorst*, having been repaired earlier, had waited for her sister ship, the *Gneisenau* to have the hole in her hull mended, the one that Campbell VC had put in her. Once the *Prinz Eugen* had joined them, they became an even more formidable force. Any convoy unlucky enough to meet these ships on the open seas had probably had it.

We didn't know where this trio wanted to go or what they wanted to do but by early February, rumours were flying around our base at Thorney Island that they were preparing to sail.

We knew what was coming and there were undercurrents of anxiety among the boys. Things were said to us to make it clear that 217 Squadron in particular were going to be on the trail of the German Fleet.

'We're going to chase them …'

'… It's going to be your job …'

'… they want us to do this one …'

Phrases like that practically guaranteed us some serious action before long. There was anxiety but there was even more excitement. We were young men getting ready for something big – and we knew it.

We were under new leadership. Squadron Leader Larkin, a New Zealander, had taken over from our outgoing C/O, Wing Commander Bower, in January. But on 8 February, on his very first operational trip, Larkin failed to return. He had crash-landed on the sea and been taken prisoner by the Germans. Some mischievous rumours circulated, speculating that Larkin had worked out just how bad our situation was, and had virtually surrendered to the enemy. I'm sure those rumours were unfair and Larkin would have made a good leader, had he had more of a chance to show what he was made of. But the size of the challenge the rest of us faced could hardly be exaggerated.

The German ships were giants, and we would be little more than flies trying to irritate them, unless we got very lucky with our torpedoes. We also knew it would be the most dangerous thing we had ever done, by some distance. The firepower these ships had was frightening. Against that storm, each of our planes had just one torpedo. And we had never even been fired upon before, in all our operations as a crew.

Were we up to the task? Our new C/O, Squadron Leader Taylor, DFC, AFC, was confident that we were and we'd find out soon enough. If I got the chance, I was going to let rip with my machine guns and make some of those German sailors wish they had never dared to come so near the British Isles. If I could kill the enemy from my turret I wouldn't hesitate to do so, but I knew I couldn't sink a battleship with bullets. That would be down to Tommy Lee and his torpedo. Could he do it? Such things were known to be possible, whatever the odds.

We knew you could do damage to even the biggest German ship if you got lucky – that Fairey Swordfish attack on the *Bismarck* the previous year had proved it. When their torpedo had jammed the *Bismarck*'s rudder, leaving it doing circles, that squadron could take most of the credit for the sinking of the biggest ship in the German fleet. It had only been a matter of time before some of our own ships closed in for the kill and finished her. Campbell had shown that Beauforts could do some serious damage too, if they adopted the correct angle of attack and took the right opportunity. Whether you came home or not was another matter, but Churchill had already explained that the naval battle was the most important of all, and great sacrifices might have to be made to win it. If our supply ships didn't get through from America, Britain could be forced out of the war due to a lack of fuel, raw materials and food. The situation was about as serious as it could get, though we'd been holding our own in a sense, by containing the giants in the German Fleet where they couldn't do any harm.

Tommy Lee, Stan Clarke and I had been joined by a new navigator called John Sinclair. He was a twenty-year-old English ex-public schoolboy, an unremarkable sort of character. He had originally tried to train as a pilot, but had been switched to navigating for some reason. He played squash with Stan Clarke quite often, but they weren't socially close like Stan and I were. John wasn't particularly jolly and didn't come out for a drink with us; he seemed a bit intense, a little cold and remote but he hadn't let us down so far and we accepted that it took all sorts to make up a plane crew.

Tommy Lee wasn't exactly one of the lads either, because he didn't come out for a drink with us much. But he sort of made up for it with the natural warmth he exuded when we were around him. Above all, Tommy was steady and calm, and that's just what we wanted from a pilot. We didn't need him to be a wild character or a big drinker. In fact, we would have been worried if he had been like that. What we required from Tommy was stability and dependability – and we'd got that from him every time we flew. I always thought he was a first class pilot. We'd seen even less of him in the sergeants' mess than usual in January and the first week of February. Bill Carroll always said that Tommy had fallen in love with a WAAF he knew and it had changed his outlook completely. Perhaps they'd had a Christmas romance, perhaps it was more serious. We didn't know her, we didn't care. We certainly had no reason to think it would have any impact on us. I was still in love with Sylvia but I don't think it changed me as a person. Everyone was focused, waiting for something big. Our personal lives had to take a back seat. The rumours of an imminent break-out intensified. All leave for 217 Squadron was cancelled on 9 February. The French Resistance must have got wind of final preparations in Brest. Now it was only a question of which day the Germans would choose to make their move.

Back at Thorney Island we felt we had one last chance to enjoy ourselves. The WAAF medical department had organised a dance and we were determined to go. Bill Carroll wanted to come to the party but he was part of Tommy Carson's duty crew that night. He was supposed to remain on standby, ready to react to any threat or urgent mission he was called upon to perform.

Bill being Bill, he decided he had his own urgent mission to perform – and that was to get to the WAAF party as soon as possible and enjoy himself as much as possible before he was ordered back. By the time I got there – a bit late for some reason or other – Bill was already there and the dancing was in full swing.

That didn't cause me any problem and I certainly didn't miss the boat as far as the WAAFs were concerned. A certain WAAF must have had her eye on me from before, because as soon as I walked through the door, something strange happened. She was dancing with this other bloke but when she saw me, she stopped dancing with him and came straight over to dance with me. I didn't mind at all. Given the situation we were in, we all took the chance to have what fun we could have, while we could have it. She stayed dancing with me for the rest of the evening and she was very welcome!

The party didn't last so long for poor Bill Carroll, though. The first announcement ordered the duty crew back across to where they should have been, closer to their aircraft. When that didn't work and Bill carried on partying, a fresh announcement ordered the duty crew to man their Beaufort immediately. That did the trick, and apparently Bill's anxious pilot Tommy Carson, who understood the situation immediately, told Bill to get in his turret and say nothing. That way no one would find out whether he had been drinking or not! As it turned out, there was no mission for them to fly, which might have been just as well in Bill's case. But his superiors had managed to get him out of the party – which could very well have been his last.

5

THE CHANNEL DASH

On 12 February it happened. Not that we knew much about it first thing that morning.

The Kriegsmarine had chosen their moment well. Cloud cover helped their escape, then gaps between RAF patrols meant we didn't spot what was going on as early as we should have done. The weather worsened, the confusion increased. We didn't even know for sure if it was the *Scharnhorst*, *Gneisenau* and *Prinz Eugen* on the move, because no one told us. We didn't know which way they were heading either.

In reality, the German ships and their accompanying fleet weren't trying to break out into the Atlantic. So our long-suffering supply ships weren't the target this time. Instead the German fleet was heading right up the English Channel, perhaps on their way back to bases in Germany, perhaps destined for somewhere else. If we could have hit them early enough, there would have been time for more attacks and our chances of knocking out their most dangerous ships would have increased. But we were being told it wasn't the *Gneisenau* or the *Scharnhorst* or the *Prinz Eugen*. The official word was that we were facing a German fleet of a few merchant ships, nothing more. If that was the case, what was all the commotion about? Thorney Island was alive with talk and excitement. At one stage it looked as though we were about to be given the order to take off and hit the enemy, because we were told to go to the planes. But then we were brought back again for an early lunch.

It was late afternoon before we finally took off. And even then we weren't told to fly at the Germans. We were ordered to fly from Thorney Island to Manston, an air base in Kent. We were meant to remain airborne and pick up an escort of Spitfires there. After becoming separated from most of our squadron, Tommy Lee entered an orbit above Manston and waited for the Spitfires … and waited … and waited some more. By now there was only Tommy and one other pilot, Arthur Aldridge, left from our squadron. Finally we decided to land and find out what was going on.

We didn't find out the true extent of the communication failings until later. Our radios were of a different type and were on a different frequency to the Spitfire radios. The commanders were trying to contact us on the Spitfire frequency. How was Stan Clarke supposed to know that? All we knew was that there were no Spitfires left to escort us. They had already gone into battle. So had the rest of our squadron, it seemed. So now we were going on the biggest trip of our lives without a fighter escort, with only one other plane for company, in murky weather.

At least after all the chaos we knew by now that we were targeting the three big ships from Brest – the *Scharnhorst*, *Prinz Eugen* and *Gneisenau*. But where were they? We didn't have much of a clue and neither did our superiors with any amount of precision.

As we prepared to take off again, a pilot officer stood on the runway just pointing.

'That way!' he yelled. 'That way.' He pointed some more. 'Fly in that direction, more or less!'

'Oh right,' I thought. 'Thanks for that. Can't miss 'em now!'

Was it nerve-wracking as we took off into mist and clouds? Absolutely! The weather was getting even worse and we didn't know what was going on. But there was never any doubt that we were going to go and do what we had to do. We flew up into the murk and Sinclair chose a course he thought might bring us into contact with the German Fleet. Stan Clarke studied his ASV (Air to Surface Vessel), which was a new piece of equipment he had, like radar. It gave off a blip if you were near an enemy ship. But he probably had no more than a few seconds to warn Tommy Lee that we were near something big.

Suddenly we came to a clearing in the cloud, where Tommy Lee could see what lay ahead for himself. In the turret at the back I couldn't see what we had almost bumped into and perhaps that was just as well. A thick wall of metal, the hull of a huge German ship, one of the big three, and it was only a kilometre away. We'd never come up against anything so colossal before, and the battle cruiser – we thought it was the *Prinz Eugen* but it was identified years later as the *Scharnhorst* – might have been further away than it looked, due to its sheer size.

The *Scharnhorst* was 770 feet long with a beam of 98 feet and stretched nearly 100 feet into the sky from the deck. She weighed 32,100 tons. We were going in anyway. In an instant Tommy had lined us up at the correct angle of attack, just 70 feet above the waves. He dropped our torpedo and Arthur Aldridge, the other pilot, must have released his too.

It was a split-second reaction, because if you got closer than 600 yards the mechanism on the torpedo didn't have time to arm it, so the explosive wouldn't go off on impact. Tommy had to press the button early enough to give that torpedo a chance – and he did. It's possible we were still too far away at that point to give ourselves the best hope of success, I don't know. We weren't going to hang around next to a deadly steel beast like that, just to see if our torpedo struck home or not. But before there was time to turn and head for home, we had to fly directly over the ship. You might think this was suicide, but it all happened so quickly. Having pointed the plane at the *Scharnhorst* to drop the torpedo, Tommy couldn't just veer away straight after release. That would have offered the Germans a nice belly shot and given them a bigger target to bring down. So Lee flew right over the German ship's bow, which only gave them a split-second look at our Beaufort's belly.

This was the moment I saw the ship for the first time. It looked massive; so big that for a moment it didn't feel like we were flying over this monster at all. It felt more like the thing was on top of us! But I didn't feel fear because I wanted to get involved; this was what I'd done all that flying for. This was my chance.

When the battleship's rear guns came into view from my turret, they weren't even being fired yet. How could I miss an inviting target like this? We were flying right over the deck of the ship towards the bows now. I'd waited months for an opportunity like this. I must admit, I did wonder what my little bullets could do against this great hulk of steel. But I was soon going to find out – and at least I had a better machine-gun than I'd started out with.

The VGO machine-gun, the one that required you to change the pan every 100 rounds, had been phased out by 217 Squadron a few months earlier. Now we had Brownings with ammunition belts and they were fantastic. I've heard people complain that the Browning ammunition belts were prone to jamming when you were in the thick of the action and blasting away intensively. It had never happened to me before – and I prayed it wouldn't happen now. I'd always thought the Browning was easy to fire. And now I could use it against the enemy at last. I didn't wait for any order from Tommy Lee to 'Open fire!' I didn't need telling.

I let rip all along the decks and heard the deadly purr I loved. Vvrrrrrrrr … The Browning sounded happy as she let them have it – much more rapidly than the old Vickers ever could. I really opened up with a series of long bursts, making sure the Browning spewed bullets exactly where I thought they'd be most effective. Vvrrrrrrrr … I gave that enemy ship a bloody good burst along the back end of the ship near the guns.

'There have to be men right there,' I thought. 'They must be manning those huge guns, even if I can't see the bastards. They're hiding themselves well but I know roughly where.'

Vvrrrrrrrr … 'There! That'll keep 'em quiet while we're turning!'

I couldn't see if I'd killed anyone, but it wouldn't bother me to hear I killed anyone that day. This was war. These ships were a threat to my country's freedom. I was going to give the Germans everything I had.

Better still, we were getting away. I'd bought us some time by spraying those decks to keep their guns silent. We had turned and it looked like we were through the worst of the danger. Miraculously, we'd attacked a steel monster with our tiny plane and we seemed to have got away with it. The torpedo hadn't struck home, because there were still no explosions coming from the German battleship, but I'd done my bit and now there was nothing else for me to shoot at. I almost switched off. I wasn't concentrating properly any more – didn't feel the need. Then it happened. Massive explosions sent our Beaufort upwards with an awful shudder. I heard screams from the front of the plane. Then much louder voices than usual. Then more screams.

I assumed the ship's guns must have woken up at last and they were giving us a right pounding. Were we hit? The screaming from the front continued. But somehow it didn't sound like a scream from physical pain; and besides, I didn't think the plane had received a direct hit yet. Then again, it might not take a direct hit to take us down, because huge vertical splashes were throwing our Beaufort about violently in what little air we had to fly in, just above the sea. If Tommy couldn't keep the plane level and a wing-tip touched a wave, then that would be enough to take us down.

I've always thought the splashes were created by shells from the enemy ship. I've always thought they were doing their best to put a shell right into us. Others have suggested that one German technique was to fire just under an enemy plane on purpose. They'd worked out that upward shockwaves could send an aircraft out of control. But a recent theory is that the splashes rocking our plane could have been caused by our own bombers, because their attack had been synchronised with ours to destroy these ships from a greater altitude.

Had Tommy Lee realised this was 'friendly fire', as it has become known? Whoever had laid on this nasty late surprise for us, it proved too much for our pilot. Remember, he'd been steady as a rock on operations until this moment. But then again he'd never been under fire before – none of us had. This was the first time it had ever really felt like we were in a war; and until a man is under fire, he cannot know exactly how he is going to react. Unfortunately for poor Tommy, he didn't take it well. When he wasn't screaming, he was yelling at John Sinclair, 'We'll bloody well get killed. Let's get the hell out of here or we're all going to die! Get me out of here!'

But Tommy was the pilot. He was the one supposed to be getting us out of there.

Still he went on. 'Bloody murderers! It's bloody foolish!'

Did he think his superiors had acted like murderers to send us out against these ships in our little planes? Or did he regard the Germans as no better than common murderers for trying to kill us? I only heard raised voices from the back, a general commotion which seemed to go on for ages. It was Sinclair who told me the terrible details later.

I still respect Tommy Lee to this day, he had been a very good pilot up to that point, I'm just sorry it happened the way it did. Like me, he thought we'd got away, he thought we had come through those terrible few seconds when you will either live or die during an attack on an enemy vessel. He thought he was in the clear and able to return to that girl of his against the odds. Perhaps mentally he let his guard down for a moment, and then all the horror of this shell or bomb attack poured into him. I'm no psychologist, all I know is that he started to crack up and Johnny Sinclair, with his limited previous experience as a trainee pilot, had to help him fly the plane while he got a grip of himself.

The screaming from the cockpit went on for a good five or ten minutes; until long after the shelling stopped. It wasn't something that happened over those few dreadful seconds when our Beaufort was being blown about and then quickly subsided. Even after the worst of the real danger was over, Tommy was still gone, lost in his own fear. Sinclair slowly brought him back to us, though. He must have done, because eventually the screaming subsided and our Beaufort stayed in the air. Sinclair must have helped him to focus on flying us home; reassuring him that the nightmare would be over for him, if only he managed to do that for us. With Johnny's help, Tommy got us all the way back to Thorney Island and landed us safely.

I never saw Tommy Lee again. We lined up in the intelligence office at Thorney Island for our de-briefing, and I noticed that Tommy wasn't there. I still wasn't quite sure why. Johnny Sinclair knew why and Stan might have done too. I'd been too far back in the plane to have heard as much as they did as Lee went through his terror. I didn't know for sure that the RAF would never let him fly again, or that we'd be left without a pilot. When I asked where Tommy Lee was, Sinclair just told me, 'He's gone LMF.' He gave me more of the details later.

He had been taken away and branded 'LMF' – Lack of Moral Fibre. It was the RAF's way of telling you that you were a coward, even though it took far more guts than the average man possessed just to get in the plane and fly a sortie against the enemy in the first place.

He must have fought his panic to bring us home too; otherwise I wouldn't have lived to tell the tale. There was bravery in what he did. It can't be easy to turn the tables on your fears and overcome them after they have run riot. He cracked up for a while, but he had put himself back together again for long enough to preserve us all.

Tommy was just one of many whose mind rebelled quite naturally against the idea of dying horribly. The RAF was suffering 3,000 cases of nervous breakdown each year during the Second World War – and that comes from the official medical report at the end of the war. That means every four months 1,000 RAF men cracked up. Every single month, 250 RAF men lost their minds, temporarily or otherwise. That's more than eight RAF men having a nervous breakdown for each day of the war, if you take the average number. What does that tell you? Young men were under severe mental pressure and didn't always have the strength to withstand it. Did that make them cowards? I don't think so. Tommy Lee wasn't alone in reaching his breaking point. And even though his limit came on the first day he really had to stare death in the face, he had already taken much more stress than some RAF boys had been able to withstand.

Here's another startling statistic: 1,000 of those 3,000 annual RAF nervous breakdowns happened to men who hadn't even reached the theatre of war yet. They were at operational training units, where casualties were high. Perhaps they saw friends crash and couldn't take any more. Tommy had been through that and done five months of ops before suffering his meltdown.

I've told the truth about what happened because it happened and I think it should be highlighted as one of the realities of war. It was certainly one of the key moments in my war. But no one's got anything to be ashamed of; Tommy did his best and until then it had been more than good enough.

Sinclair recounted those moments of chaos when we got back to the sergeant's mess. The more I heard, the more I thought about how terrible it must have been for Sinclair too. He was the navigator, down in the nose at the very bottom and very front of the plane, so he probably suffered the worst of the shockwaves from any shells, bombs or vertical splashes. In addition to that trauma, he had to deal with a pilot who was going to crash the plane and kill us all if he didn't pull himself together. There was no doubt about it, Sinclair had helped to save our lives and it was a miracle we had made it back to base. The strange thing was, if Sinclair had suddenly cracked up instead of Tommy, I wouldn't have been so surprised. As I've mentioned, I'd always found him a bit cold and insular. But Johnny's lack of emotion, the public schoolboy's stiff upper lip, seems to have done the trick in this particular case.

I'd kept quite calm too, considering. Perhaps I was under less stress in the turret at the back – though I definitely wasn't in any less danger. My boxing had already taught me to keep control of my emotions when I was under pressure. So I never felt great waves of fear when we were on operations. It was all about doing a job and reacting to what was around you. That kept fear at bay for me. Extremes of emotion were no good for you while you were operational. Looking back after it's all over, that's when you get more of a sense of what feelings were lurking under the surface.

It had been nerve-wracking to take off from Manston to head for the German fleet without a fighter escort. It had been exhilarating when I fired at the enemy decks. And of course I'd been worried when those massive upward splashes threw the plane about on the way out. But I never got scared enough to allow my emotions to dictate to me.

Big mood swings could be dangerous. The more level-headed and emotionally balanced you kept yourself, the better.

People ask me what I was feeling at key moments. The truth is, not a lot. You're focusing on what is going on around you; you're making the best decisions you can, you're facing the challenge. Feelings come later. Looking back, when I think of what we went through in a Beaufort, I frighten myself just thinking about it.

At the time though, we didn't want to think about too much at all – it was definitely time to have a beer. But one of my best drinking buddies, Bill Carroll, hadn't made it back. He had been in Tommy Carson's plane and they were missing. First Jonny Foster, now Bill Carroll. I felt rotten about what had happened to them. As was our habit though, I took the money Bill had left in his little crate of possessions and had a drink for him with it. It had been decided among the boys in the squadron that we wanted our mates to have our money if we were lost. Otherwise someone might pinch it; someone who hadn't even been through the same dangers.

So there I was, drinking quite quickly, swapping stories about the sheer size of the German ships we'd taken on, and then I felt a tap on the shoulder. It was Bill Carroll. 'Drinking away my money?' he asked me. I must have looked as though I'd seen a ghost.

'Sorry Bill,' I said. 'Thought you …'

'Well, the least you can do is to buy me a beer too, seeing as it's my money!' he laughed.

I bought him a beer and gave back what I'd taken. I was too delighted to worry about the embarrassment. We all thought he'd gone in the drink but here he was, alive and kicking. I could have given him a hug but I didn't. That wasn't our style. But everyone was happy to see him return.

Bill was late because Tommy Carson had gone out again, having failed to find the German fleet the first time. He wasn't the only crew to attack twice. We couldn't have done that, and perhaps it was just as well. The whole thing had been fraught with danger and the casualties were high for very little reward. The overall results from the Channel Dash were not impressive. The *Scharnhorst* received some damage from a mine dropped in front of it, but other than that the Germans went through the English Channel, round Holland and back to home ports in Germany relatively unscathed. The RAF lost forty planes and not a single torpedo hit home. Ours had missed, Arthur Aldridge's had missed after running alongside Tommy Lee's … everyone had missed.

It sounds stupid, but the fact that the ships were moving could have been part of the problem. We had been taught to come in from the side and try to hit a ship in the middle. But all our practice targets at Abbotsinch and everywhere else had been static. A torpedo coming in from the side at a fast-moving ship can easily miss. When the Beaufort pilot is under extreme pressure from enemy fire and you add more human error into the equation, you're hardly likely to be successful from that angle. I was no expert, but the disappointing results spoke for themselves.

Questions were quickly asked about the failure, including why the Beaufort torpedo squadrons were held back for so long. We had been taken out to the plane and then taken straight back again for lunch at Thorney, you'll recall. It had been confusing, to say the least. The Air Ministry admitted that the torpedo attack had been delayed so that it could be synchronised with Wellingtons dropping bombs from above just a few seconds earlier. If all had gone to plan, the German ships could have been hit by the bombers and then we could have sneaked in during the chaotic aftermath to finish them off. But something like that requires split-second timing. Such a plan is almost ridiculously ambitious in the fog of war.

Sadly, it appears that Tommy Lee's wartime flying career was ended by the sheer shock of friendly fire. There was an immediate knock-on effect for his crew. In the days after the Channel Dash, I felt naked. I was part of a crew without a pilot. It felt very peculiar and it was on my mind most of the time. I was worried about it and Stan Clarke was worried about it too. We both knew the score. If we were taken on by a new, inexperienced pilot, then we would be in even more danger next time.

We'd also lost our old Commander, Taylor, who'd moved on after the Channel Dash. And of course we had lost our own pilot, Tommy Lee. Then we were told that 217 Squadron's new CO had arrived. He was a pilot and he would be taking over a new crew. And who should that pilot be, but Wing Commander Paddy Boal, who had been in charge at Chivenor during training!

Boal had been given a good long rest at Chivenor after his first tour of duty and now he was ready for a second tour. The charismatic Northern Irishman was a pilot without a crew. We were a hardened, experienced crew without a pilot. It didn't take Boal long to work it out. Who did Paddy Boal choose as his crew? Us!

We were really pleased, Stan, John and I. Privately we considered ourselves to be one of the crack crews. And we thought it reflected well on us that we had been chosen. If the new CO had picked us out, or we had been allotted to him by those in a position to help him decide, we must be perceived as one of the best crews on the squadron by others too!

We also thought it increased our chances of survival, because we hadn't been given to a novice pilot. So many of those blokes didn't survive their first mission because they were trying so hard to impress without knowing how best to do their job and stay alive. Boal knew the ropes, his nerve would be steady, and it looked like a great combination.

For all I knew, if we got on well enough, he might even give me a lift back to Braunton the next time we had a spot of leave, and I'd finally get to see my Sylvia again. By an extraordinary coincidence, Boal and Sylvia lived in the same road back in Braunton!

That tantalising prospect of a reunion with my girlfriend was quickly dispelled. Sylvia and Braunton were left far behind for now, as if belonging to another life once more, because the squadron was moved from the South Coast of England all the way up to Scotland. In fact, we were shifted about as far up as you can possibly get! First we went to Leuchars outside Edinburgh, then up to Skitten near John O'Groats.

Something fresh was brewing. The RAF had taken a serious blow to its pride during the Channel Dash and now it was looking to save face. Churchill wanted a success against German shipping, and there would be opportunities off the coast of Norway.

Even if we'd stayed down south, I don't think I would have been offered that lift to Braunton, somehow. I felt a little disappointed that Wing Commander Boal didn't really take the opportunity to speak to us or get to know us. As an officer he was in a different mess and so there wasn't the automatic bonding we'd enjoyed with Tommy Lee, who had been a sergeant in our mess. All the more reason, I thought, why he might make the effort to speak to us all at length at some point. It never happened.

Maybe he wanted to keep his distance because he was the Commander and couldn't afford to get too friendly with us. Or maybe his mind was so full with his extra responsibilities that he just didn't think of it. Even so, it felt odd.

6

SUICIDAL

We thought we were as far north-east as you could get in Britain, but we were soon put right on that score. There was talk of being moved from Skitten right up to the Shetlands, the nearest possible islands to Norway. There was a remote air base in the Shetlands called Sumburgh. At the end of the first week of March 1942, we were on our way in poor weather.

When we reached Sumburgh, we found it was even more desolate than we expected, with the horrible sound of squawking seagulls a constant noise in the background. There wasn't much on Sumburgh apart from our air base. There weren't many people living up there and it was hardly surprising. Even so, Sid Knight and I scouted around outside the air base to see what we could find at the few buildings we could see beyond the perimeter. We were quite determined and resourceful and we found what we were looking for – a farmhouse that was prepared to sell us a few eggs. That was a bonus and a bit of a morale-booster as we did our best to make ourselves at home on this rocky Shetland outcrop.

We knew we wouldn't be hanging around for too long on a place like this and presumed there was some sort of flap on, some special target. Someone had mentioned there might be some big German ships up there somewhere – some of the ships that had been causing all the trouble for our merchant shipping. We soon found out why we were there and the reality was even worse than we had imagined. Not long after we reached Sumburgh we were called into a briefing. Wing Commander Boal wasn't taking it because 217 Squadron had joined up with planes from 42 Squadron. There were more of them than us, so it was their Wing Commander, a dapper thirty-year-old called Mervyn 'Willy' Williams, who stood up in front of us and began to speak.

'Our target is the *Tirpitz*,' he said. That in itself was enough to get our attention. The *Tirpitz* was by far the biggest monster left in the Kriegsmarine's fleet. She was the surviving sister of the *Bismarck*, and it was probably just as well I didn't know her precise size or firepower at the time. The *Tirpitz* was a killing machine, designed to eliminate any threat with ruthless ease. She was 823 feet long overall, with a beam of 118 feet. She weighed 42,900 tons, but the most fearsome thing about her was her cannons. The *Tirpitz* had four pairs of 38cm (15-inch) guns – and if you took a shell from one of those, you'd know about it. If you flew at the *Tirpitz*, you'd also have six pairs of 15cm (5.9-inch) guns aiming at you. If you dodged these, you'd have to get past eight pairs of 10.5cm (4.1-inch) guns, whose shells could still deal a fatal blow to you and your plane. There were twelve 2cm (0.79-inch) guns ready to spray bullets in your direction too, but you almost certainly wouldn't get close enough for that to matter. The *Tirpitz* had no less than fifty-eight additional guns designed to throw up a terrifying wall of flak, through which it would be almost impossible to pass.

The only comfort – if you could call it that – was that the *Tirpitz* couldn't use any of its eight torpedoes on us. We only had one, but at least when it came to torpedoes, we were at an advantage. The question was this: if you were faced with 106 sources of potentially deadly fire from the ship, what chance were you going to have to make your single torpedo count? And those 106 ways to die excluded the additional power of the escort vessels and fighter planes that would shield the *Tirpitz* by throwing everything they'd got at us.

Did we still think we were in with a chance of doing the *Tirpitz* some damage? Of course! We were young men, full of confidence and belief in our own indestructibility. Besides, the *Bismarck* had been sunk the previous summer, hadn't she? So did we think our bosses had taken leave of their senses when they decided to make the *Tirpitz* our target? No ... not at this early stage of the briefing, anyway. The objective itself didn't come as a big shock to me. I didn't hear the word '*Tirpitz*' and think, 'Well, that's it then, we've had it.' But this was going to be a tough one, there was no doubt about it. Any aircraft that came up against the *Tirpitz* were going to be very lucky indeed if they came away in one piece. I just thought we'd be the lucky ones, because I always thought that if anyone was going to be shot down, it would be someone else, not us. That went for any mission – even this one. So as far as I was concerned, we were going to have a go at the *Tirpitz* and come back again.

Churchill was under no illusions, though. He considered this ship to be such a threat to the Allies that he felt it necessary to throw whatever he could against it – whatever the cost. He'd made that clear when he'd written to the Chiefs of Staff Committee on 25 January 1942 – even before the Channel Dash disaster made a success of some kind even more imperative.

The *Tirpitz* had been lurking in the same area at the end of January as it was now. Churchill had explained, 'The presence of "*Tirpitz*" at Trondheim has now been known for three days. The destruction or even crippling of this ship is the greatest event at sea at the present time ... the entire naval situation throughout the world would be altered.'

Despite Churchill's impatience, nothing had happened in January, or indeed February, except the more obvious humiliation of letting the *Scharnhorst*, *Gneisenau* and *Prinz Eugen* slip through. That trio was safe by now in their German ports, so the *Tirpitz* represented our big chance to salvage some pride for the RAF.

She had been spotted again by a reconnaissance plane from the aircraft-carrier HMS *Victorious* on 9 March. The *Tirpitz* had brushed aside an attack by twelve Fairey Albacore planes, dodging the torpedoes and shooting two aircraft down. Could we do any better? What the pilots thought of the mission, I don't know; but we all just listened to Wing Commander Williams, pilots and crew together. We wondered how this daring strike was going to be done.

'We're going to attack her as she tries to enter Trondheim Fjord on the Norwegian coast. Some of you will be carrying mines to blow any protective nets around her. Some will carry bombs. Most of you will carry torpedoes. The mines will be dropped first, then bombs, and finally the Beauforts armed with torpedoes will go in to sink her. Between us, we men of 42 Squadron and 217 Squadron, we will do just that – sink her. By doing so we will remove the greatest threat to Allied shipping that remains. We shall write our names in history.'

I sat and listened and waited for what might come next. The more important a mission was, the more the commanders were prepared to risk in terms of loss of human life and planes.

To his credit, I suppose, Williams didn't hide from the problem created by the distances we'd have to fly. He couldn't really, because the pilots all knew the range of the aircraft they flew.

'Men, I should tell you that the fjord is a long way from here and you will not have enough fuel to return.'

What? Hang on a minute. What exactly are we being told here?

'Once you have used your weapons and cleared the area, you will face two choices. One: to fly across to Sweden and find a place to land there. For this reason, one man in each crew will be given some money in Swedish krona. The Swedes are officially neutral, as you know, but they should be friendly to any of our crews who make contact with them. It can only help to have some money to pay for any assistance they offer. We have a Legation in Stockholm which can arrange for your return to Britain.'

It all sounded quite exciting until we thought about it more carefully. So we were supposed to fly over the mountains between Norway and Sweden, probably in poor visibility, then just find an airfield and land? Was it as simple as that? Or did Williams expect us to crash-land in a field, or maybe bale out and parachute down into the welcoming arms of some Swedish villagers somewhere? It sounded a bit tricky. So what was the second option?

'Two: to fly back along the course you would take to return to Sumburgh, if you had enough fuel. We will have rescue boats positioned along that course and we will calculate where you are likely to run out of fuel. When you come down into the sea, we will pick you up as quickly as we can. Good luck men. Be ready.'

We'd be ready but was he serious? We'd lost some blokes just a few days earlier, when one of our planes had gone down in the North Sea just off Scotland. A local fishing boat had come to its aid. By the time that boat got there, within about twenty minutes, all the airmen were dead from exposure. If they didn't pluck us out of the water within about five minutes on the way back from Norway, we would be dead too.

Then it began to dawn on me. Williams didn't really expect us to survive this attack on the *Tirpitz*. It was a one-way trip, a suicide mission, and these plans for survival were just designed to offer us some sort of slim hope – hope that wasn't really there if we thought about it. It was a strange feeling, to realise that; but you had to do your duty.

No one complained. No one got up and tried to pick his plan apart. We were airmen in the Royal Air Force; we'd been given a job to do and we were going to do it. I don't remember feeling afraid because I had my usual attitude – someone else would be shot down, not me. Whatever the dangers, I was always going to do a trip and try to make it a success. That was everyone's attitude. No one went around trying to spread doom and gloom. We had our private thoughts about what we were being asked to do but we didn't start squealing about it. We were the Wing Commander's crew; we weren't going to tell him the raid wasn't realistic. We could have been up on a charge if we'd shown anything that could be construed as cowardice. We could have been branded 'LMF' like they'd done to Tommy Lee. Then we would have been cleaning toilets for the rest of the war. True, we'd have been alive at the end of it but we didn't think like that. We were young men and we wanted to show we had the bottle to do what was asked of us. So we all waited and we were all ready to pounce when we got the green light from our superiors. We were going to do the job we were asked to do, whatever our chances of survival.

There was plenty of time to think about it, though, because the briefing came two days before we manned our aircraft for the mission. When the orders finally came through and we realised the waiting was over, to a man we were on the tarmac in our Beauforts at 0600 hrs, itching to take off. I'd been chosen to keep hold of the money if we made it over the border after taking on the *Tirpitz* in Norway and in my pocket was £30 in Swedish krona.

The signal to take off was a green flare. I just wanted to get in the air and get it over with. When that flare went up, we were going to take off from this desolate island and fly to almost certain death in the thick flak of the *Tirpitz*, though I still had a feeling deep down that I might survive the raid, and I was ready for the flare. I was ready for the mission. Finally the flare went up and lit the dark sky … but it wasn't green.

'Wait a minute. This flare is red.' We all knew what that meant. The mission had been aborted. It had all fallen through at the last moment. Suddenly we all felt really flat. The excitement had gone, replaced with disappointment that nothing was going to be done. Ask any airman. If you're told something has to be done and you're going to do it, then the whole thing is aborted without warning, it is always a flat time. You feel a bit of a disappointment, however outrageous or dangerous the mission would have been.

Why had the trip been called off? It turned out that the *Tirpitz* had stopped short of where we had planned to intercept it, due to bad weather. It had gone into the safety of Narvik instead. The bloody Germans had used the weather to get the better of us again. But how did we know all this? Apparently, we owed our lives to the code-breakers at Bletchley Park, because they knew all the movements of the German ships as soon as their radio traffic came through. They couldn't just act on this information though as that would give the game away and let Hitler know they'd broken Enigma, so they had to send an observer plane over Narvik to make the Germans think they had a lucky visual on the *Tirpitz*.

A few days later, the *Tirpitz* escaped further down the Norwegian coast to Trondheim, where we had been briefed to attack her. She used the cover of more terrible weather to get there. Some Halifaxes and Lancasters tried to attack the *Tirpitz* anyway at around this time. Four were shot down, one crashed into the sea after running out of fuel and another crashed into the cliffs on a fog-shrouded Sumburgh. Once inside the port, the *Tirpitz* was safe and we never got to have another go at her. The strategic consolation was that the *Tirpitz* was contained somewhere it couldn't do much damage to the Allies. The human consolation was that the suicide mission was off – and we had all lived to fight again another day.

Willy Williams stayed on Sumburgh and attempted a fresh strike on a convoy off the Norwegian coast on 20 March. Three Beauforts failed to find their targets and ran into trouble in icy cloud as they tried to return to Sumburgh. Ice in a carburettor could be fatal; and it very nearly was for Williams. He lost speed as he approached the Sumburgh runway, landed on one wheel and collapsed the whole undercarriage. Then his plane skidded out of control and crashed into the Flight Office, catching fire. For Williams and his crew, it was a race against time to get out of that plane before the torpedo they were carrying exploded. In truth, Williams should have jettisoned that torpedo over the sea, before he tried to land at all. Mercifully he and his crew won their race and avoided the inevitable explosion – but the Flight Office was blown to pieces.

This sort of brush with death wasn't unusual. If we'd stopped to think about it, we'd probably have had to come to the conclusion that we were all living on borrowed time. I didn't bother thinking about it. What was the point? We were living on the edge and we might as well get used to it.

On one particular day, though, things didn't feel quite right. We'd flown back down as far as Leuchars, it was the morning of 1 April and there was a suspicion we were being lined up as the April fools. We'd heard about what had happened and were worried about the possible consequences. But what could we do as we prepared for the strike? We couldn't go to the Wing Commander and tell him we were worried about the state of our pilot. The pilot in question *was* the Wing Commander – Paddy Boal, DFC.

Word quickly went round that the boss had enjoyed himself rather too much in the officers' mess the previous night. He'd always enjoyed a drink, Paddy – that was common knowledge – but this time it sounded like he'd gone too far. He'd been up until the early hours, teaching his fellow officers how to dance an Irish jig, to a lively tune called 'The Siege of Ennis'. The booze had been flowing freely and Boal had almost drunk the mess dry.

None of us was perfect, far from it – we all liked a beer in the sergeants' mess just as much as some of the officers liked a drink in their own mess – but when you were the pilot, everyone depended on you. As the gunner in my little turret at the back, people might look to me if we were attacked by enemy fighters. I'd have to do everything I could to get them off our tail. But even if I was blasting away for all I was worth, it would be the pilot's positioning of our Beaufort that would save us as much as my aim and anticipation. Similarly if we were going to hit a convoy, it was the pilot who had to pick a ship and fly straight at it, just 50 feet above the waves, before rising another 20 or 30 feet to drop his torpedo at just the right range. It was the pilot who had to check we were between 1,000 and 600 yards from the target, so the torpedo could do its worst. He had to be clear-headed to make all those decisions in a few split seconds. So the three of us on Boal's crew were all thinking the same thing: how could the Wing Commander be sufficiently clear-headed to do his job properly, the day after a night like that? Even if we flew in the afternoon, he might still be hung-over, his brain still a bit cloudy.

You always tried to have faith in your pilot, though my own faith had already been shattered when poor Tommy Lee had cracked up on the Channel Dash. Had we really been so lucky when Wing Commander Boal had arrived and adopted us? Boal, supposedly so warm and genial, still hadn't said more than a few words to any of us. Each time we went out to the aircraft he was silent, just kept himself to himself, and only communicated to run through the pre-flight checks with us.

I hoped the stories of the night before were exaggerated. The trouble was, we'd given up exaggerating long ago on 217 Squadron. Real life-and-death situations were so common now that there was really no need for exaggeration any more. There was no room for bullshit in this kind of environment, because shit hit the fan every other day, sometimes when you were least expecting it. So it seemed highly unlikely that the stories of Boal's drunkenness had been made up to give us a scare.

At least we hadn't been called into a dawn strike. The Wing Commander really would have been incapable in the early hours.

It was early afternoon by the time we received confirmation that we were going after an enemy convoy, which had been sighted off the Norwegian coast. At least it was far enough south to give us the range to return to our Scottish base that evening. Nice of our superiors to give us a chance of survival this time! We could be thankful for small mercies, and the latest weather forecast was another of them: clear skies nearly all the way to Norway, turning to low cloud just as we reached the coastal area. If accurate, that forecast might suit us quite nicely.

It was time to stop thinking about issues out of our control. We headed to the aircraft and found the Wing Commander there, aloof as usual. We looked for any signs that he might not be fit to fly, but he masked whatever hangover he had well. We weren't the sort of people to refuse to fly with Boal, not unless he was staggering around singing nonsense. The silence, the distance between Boal and his crew, told us nothing. But it didn't reassure us either. Once I'd climbed into the turret – requiring the usual contortions – that was it. Whatever happened now, I could only do what I could do. The rest was down to others.

At least Wing Commander Boal wasn't flying alone. He'd be leading the other two Beauforts – piloted by Pilot Officer Stevens and Flight Sergeant Morgan – into battle. Perhaps we'd all get away with it, though statistically it was more likely that one of the three planes wouldn't be coming back. Today, knowing what I knew, the two-in-three chance of survival might have seemed too generous. You tried not to think like that, though. Better think positive.

Some leave had to be coming to me soon, and I knew exactly what I was going to do with mine. I wanted to head for Devon to see Sylvia; I longed to do that so much more than I wanted to go back to London to see my family and friends. Love does that to you. And I reckoned it *was* love, even though she was still only a teenager. I was only a young man in my early twenties, she was old enough to love me, and I wanted to be with her. But first I had to get back from this strike and a few more afterwards.

The Beaufort's turret was familiar and reassuring. My parachute was strapped to my front – something of a sick joke when the most dangerous part of the mission usually came when we were less than a hundred feet above the waves. Some smart work with the guns might help keep us in the air. We took off at 1615 hrs and flew out over the North Sea. Once I saw we were clear of land below, I fired a few bursts from my Brownings. I had to know they were working when there was such a strong chance we'd meet the Germans again that day. The vibrations I felt from spitting hundreds of shells into the blue skies told I was ready for action.

The weather forecasters were right. It was a beautiful spring day until we neared Norway, heading towards Stavanger Fjord. Then we disappeared into low cloud. Boal flew at about 1,000 feet to avoid the waves he could no longer see, while navigator Sinclair and wireless operator Clarke continued to feed him information. Stan must have got some blips on his Air to Surface Vessel (radar) and told Boal – unless of course what happened next was just an extraordinary coincidence.

We turned, came down through a clearing in the clouds, and suddenly there they were. A convoy of German ships just below – nine of them. We had to strike quickly – but the seconds were ticking by. I couldn't hear the conversation at the front of the plane. I didn't hear Sinclair single out the biggest ship for Boal to target and implore him to get on with it. I didn't hear Boal's casual insistence that he wanted to take a closer look at the convoy before he settled on a target for his torpedo. I couldn't hear Sinclair's tone become more urgent, even desperate, as his angry pleas were ignored. What I did hear was a sound like furniture breaking, a strange sound. But in the heat of the moment I thought nothing more of it, because I was looking for something to shoot at. I couldn't see the ships any more, only sky. Then I realised it was because we'd gone into a steep, sudden dive, to get right down to wave level and drop the torpedo. I wanted to shoot at something, I wanted to help. My fingers were on the trigger of the Browning, desperate to press. But I couldn't see anything worth hitting – only the murky clouds above. The frustration would soon pass, I knew that much, because you couldn't dive like this for very long. We were flying faster and faster, and Boal hadn't had much sky to play with in the first place. You had to level out for the torpedo to be dropped effectively, so the Wing Commander would do that any moment now. The plane was starting to shake, and we were still accelerating. I stayed fairly calm as usual. We were going into battle; this was Boal at his most aggressive; this is why he'd won a DFC.

In fact, the Wing Commander was dead. He'd taken a shell right through him as he dithered and disagreed with his navigator about the target and the need for urgency. The sound of the breaking furniture had been the impact of the German shells hitting us. Even when we'd still been up in the clouds, the German ships had heard us coming. When we'd shown ourselves, they were ready. Only the swiftest, sharpest reactions from the pilot would have given us a chance to drop our torpedo at the ship Sinclair had singled out, and then get clear of the flak before it became lethal.

As I looked for targets and held my nerve, I didn't know that Boal had taken his last drink, danced his last jig the previous night. I didn't know we weren't going to level out, or that the plane was out of control. Perhaps it was just as well that I didn't have a clue what was going on. Within the next few seconds, everything would become clear enough.

7

BEAUFORT DOWN

I woke up in the freezing water. At least it felt like I was in the water, but I was still in my turret. What was happening? My turret was starting to fill up with icy water, so we must be in the sea. The wings lay broken on the low waves, but wouldn't stay above them for long. Though I had to get out, something stopped me temporarily; nothing physical, just a pathetic sight which left me spellbound. Our pigeon floated past my turret, still in its bright yellow cage.

We always carried pigeons. They'd been known to save lives in the recent past. If you managed to release them in time, they could fly home and their owners could glean vital information just from examining the state they were in. The owner would then contact the RAF and offer their best guess as to how long their precious pigeon had been flying. The squadron could marry that information with the probable flight-path of whichever plane the pigeon had come from, and plot a likely position where the plane had come down. This may not sound very scientific and it wasn't. But sometimes it worked, and there had even been cases of pigeons decorated for bravery.

This particular pigeon, which I'd collected back at Leuchars just a few hours earlier, was going to have to be brave – but not because it needed to steel itself for any long flight which might result in our rescue. It was stuck in its cage, I was stuck for the moment in mine, and I watched helplessly as pigeon and bird cage sunk beneath the North Sea waves. Still in a daze, I felt sad for the pigeon. Then I realised that blood was pouring from my head, and I'd go the same way as the bird if I didn't do something quickly.

As if to drive home the danger I was in, I saw our dinghy pass my turret as it drifted clear of the crash-site. Our navigator, John Sinclair, was already in it. How on earth had he managed that? Either he had pulled the toggle under the wing to release the dinghy himself, which would have been a very nifty piece of work, or it had come away and inflated automatically on its own. What I didn't know was that he'd managed to reach that dinghy even though he'd sustained serious injuries to his legs. The impact of the crash, combined with the shrapnel created by the shells which had killed Boal, had left him in quite a state. He'd shown great determination to haul himself out of the water because he must have been in a lot of pain.

And I knew that I had to get out and join Sinclair in that dinghy if I was going to live. Would my body enable me to do that? What sort of a state was I really in? Beside me in the turret I noticed a metal plug, which was attached to the guns. It had been squashed and distorted beyond recognition. Had my head hit that plug? How broken was I, aside from the gash in my head? I'd soon find out. Looking up, I could see that the top of my turret had been sliced right off by the impact of the crash. My escape route had been made for me, if only I could heave myself clear. The freezing water was already making me feel numb, as was the shock of the crash. But it's amazing what you can do when your life depends on it. I unclipped myself – mercifully my safety belt hadn't been crushed by the force of plane meeting sea into something that couldn't be released. I lunged for the top of the turret, aided by the rising water, and launched myself clear, inflating my Mae West as soon as I met the outside sea.

That's when I saw my good friend Stan Clarke, bobbing up and down in the water with a strange expression on his face. No wonder he'd wanted to avoid working in the turret. 'When I'm in the turret Moggy, I always feel like I'm about to fall into the sea,' he'd confided to me a few months earlier. That feeling he'd had about falling into the water one day, maybe it was a premonition. Now his worst fears had come true. He was such a great swimmer though, much better than I was, so I knew he'd be able to make the dinghy before me if he set his mind to it.

'Swim for it Stan!' I shouted, pointing at Sinclair and the dinghy as they drifted slowly away from us. I began to do just that, because there was no time to hang around. Five seconds later I turned to check on Stan's progress, and saw that he'd disappeared beneath the waves. That odd expression he'd had on his face told me something now. He'd been too badly hurt to tell me any more; and he was too seriously wounded to strike out for the dinghy. Poor Stan. It was too late for me to save him. He was gone.

Now I was angry. The bloody Germans, why had they chosen our plane to shoot down? How dare they? They'd got Stan and he was lost forever. They weren't going to get me too, so I swam like hell. I used all the anger and every last bit of strength I had in me, and saw I was getting closer to the dinghy.

'Keep going!' Sinclair shouted, which gave me enough encouragement to swim some more. 'You can make it!'

What Sinclair was really thinking, he told me later, was that even if I did make it, I was probably already a dead man. What was all that sea doing to my brain? The water was flowing into a great big bloody hole in my head, and he didn't see any way I could survive that.

Luckily I couldn't see any of this happening; but when I finally reached the dinghy, I realised I had a serious problem. The sides of that dinghy were so high that I couldn't climb aboard. How the hell had John managed to get in? Didn't the designers realise that anyone trying to get into a dinghy under these circumstances might not be feeling at their strongest, and would require assistance? I tried several times to climb up and in, but I just slipped hopelessly back down into the sea. Was it going to be like this? Was I going to drown right next to the dinghy, with John Sinclair's legs too messed up for him to be able to give me any help?

Once again I'd underestimated John, though I sensed he might only have the strength for one big heave. He grabbed me by my parachute straps. Perhaps that bloody parachute was going to come in useful after all. With a seemingly superhuman effort, Sinclair didn't just pull me up and into the dinghy, he pulled me right across to the other side of the damned thing, so that the clips from my parachute hooked onto the rope which ran round the side of the vessel.

This unlikely turn of events left me in fresh danger; face down in a dinghy which was filling with water at the bottom, unable to move. Oh God! Now I'm going to drown in the dinghy. Sinclair couldn't shake me loose. I turned my head to one side whenever I could, to breathe air not water. I was surviving, with the odd splutter, when I heard the engine of a small boat. It had to be the Germans, coming to gloat, ready to finish us off. Before they did that I was going to take the chance to let them know what I thought of them.

Perhaps it was the sheer sense of outrage over what they had done. But the words left my mouth in a loud, defiant yell.

'We're British, you bastards!'

That's what I shouted and that's what we were. How dare these Germans bring us down and take lives?

A big German sergeant closed in, boarded the dinghy and then lifted me clear, as though I was some kind of rag doll.

'*Keine Angst, kleiner Mann,*' he said to me almost gently. It meant 'Don't worry little man.' Then he added, 'Which one of you just shouted at the top of his voice?'

I wasn't going to hide what I'd done or blame John Sinclair for my own words.

'I did! It was me!'

I said it with all the defiance I could, suspecting these might be my final words on earth.

'Good lungs!' That was his reply. He didn't even pay me the compliment of being offended at being called a bastard.

'Good lungs for such a small man,' he added. 'Very good! But for you, little man, this war is over now.'

So what were they going to do? It was about 6.30 or 7 p.m., a lovely sunny Norwegian evening by now, but I was bloody freezing. Was this the last sunshine I'd ever see? Were they going to shoot us? No, they really were rescuing us. How bizarre was that? But I knew we wouldn't be going home, not for a very long time – if at all. No point in looking ahead. The first thing I wanted was to stop shaking, which was proving impossible. Maybe I'd have more chance once we were on board one of the ships we'd been trying to destroy.

Later I learned we'd targeted convoy number 838, which was on its way from Heligoland to Kristiansand South. To be precise, there were eight German ships and one Norwegian ship. There was also a Danish ship bound for Esbjerg, which had detached before our attack. We'd found the main convoy at 57° 57'N, 08° 15'E. But our biggest problem had been the three patrol boats protecting them – flak ships, essentially. Among these was Vp 802, named the *Sagitta* and commanded by Leutnant zur See Moritzen. This was the vessel which had wasted no time in shooting us down – and it was also the one which had rescued us.

Once we were on the *Sagitta*, the Germans realised they had to help us stop shaking too, now that they'd gone to the trouble of bringing us on board. So they took us to their engine room, the hottest part of the ship, and a place run by an engineer called Chief Mechanician 2nd Class Zapf. They gave us Schnapps and blankets, though they didn't offer much in the way of medical treatment for John's legs or my head. The Schnapps did help though, and they treated me very gently. Although the shaking did not entirely go away, it did subside.

Sinclair looked over at me and warned the Germans, 'All the sea water must have gone right into that hole in his head.'

The Germans weren't too worried. Instead they searched me and found the £30 worth of Swedish krona in one of my pockets. They didn't ask me why I had that money, fortunately. But they did bring a picture of a Beaufort and asked us to confirm that this had been our plane.

'*Nein!*' John and I answered sharply. It must have been obvious we were lying, because the Germans went away laughing.

We were heading for Kristiansand and an uncertain welcome. A beautiful spring evening on the Norwegian coast had been made for happier occasions than this. It soon made way for a cold Scandinavian night. Temperatures plummeted. We waited nervously to see what would happen to us. The local occupying force, it soon became clear, were going to be far less friendly than the German sailors we'd been trying to sink.

By the time we were taken off the boat at Kristiansand, it was midnight and bloody freezing. John Sinclair could hardly walk because of his legs and I was starting to shiver violently again, but the German soldiers who took charge of us showed no compassion at all. They left us in the back of an open-top estate car while they went away to ask their superiors what to do with us. We must have been out there for an hour as the temperatures dropped even further, and we shivered more and more violently. The soldiers eventually returned with what looked like a senior German officer. By this stage we were desperate to get into the warm somewhere. It didn't happen. The officer, who was called Oberleutnant Engelhardt, had us driven through the freezing night, across Kristiansand to a smart-looking apartment block. Engelhardt ushered us out and I thought things might be looking up.

But then poor John and I were ordered to climb some stairs without any assistance. The state John was in meant I had to carry him on my back up several flights of stairs. At least my head had stopped bleeding – which was hardly surprising because my circulation had probably frozen up completely. It looked like the effort might have been worth it when the officer knocked on an apartment door that was clearly familiar to him, and an elegant blonde woman opened it to greet him.

The woman was a little too old for me and John to find her attractive. We were more interested in what we could see behind her – a beautifully lit, cozy apartment, perfect for getting warm and surviving the night. Though we waited hopefully to be invited in, it soon became clear that wasn't going to happen. The woman was no more pleased to see us than Engelhardt had been on the quayside. Then I realised from his apologetic tones what was happening. They'd arranged a date for that very night, and because we'd been shot down that romantic liaison had been ruined. They weren't going to have the fun they'd been looking forward to; and it was our fault.

After giving his explanation and doing all he could to pacify his lover, Engelhardt turned us around, ordered us back down the stairs and out into the back of his freezing car again.

The chill hit us and cut me to the core. I wasn't sure how much of this we could both take. But the tour of Kristiansand by night still wasn't over.

Next we were taken to a hotel, which we were told was the local headquarters of the Gestapo. John and I should have been terrified. For all we knew, we were about to face torture or even execution but we were so cold we just wanted to get inside, whatever fate awaited us. The officer handed us over to two guards and left us, probably wondering whether there was still time to make it up to his lover that night.

We quickly realised the two guards weren't Gestapo or SS because they didn't have the right insignia or attitude. They were too friendly to be either – they even made us a hot drink and it tasted wonderful.

We didn't get a plush hotel room to sleep in – that would have been asking for too much – but a lot of the hotel's rooms had been turned into cells, bars over the windows and we were led into one of these and given a blanket each. That was all we needed to survive.

Back at 217 Squadron's base, they had realised by now that we weren't coming back. I didn't realise it at the time, but the news caused an extreme reaction in one of my best pals. Apparently Sid Knight, my fellow Londoner, just said: 'That's it.' He had looked around the dormitory, which was becoming increasingly empty. He was sad for me and he didn't rate his own chances of survival in the long run either. He went LMF straight away – before what had happened to me could happen to him too. They made him clean toilets, that sort of thing, for the rest of the war. He accepted his fate at first. He knew it was better than what had happened to the crew on my plane. He wrote to my parents during the war and couldn't wait for peace to break out for all our sakes. While he'd been operational on 217 Squadron, he could easily have been killed several times over. If that red flare hadn't gone up in Sumburgh, he probably would have been. The thought of me being shot down was the last straw for him. He couldn't have gone on after that, he said. I didn't hold it against him that he'd packed it in, far from it. We've all got our limits. Needless to say our friendship endured.

While Sid was quitting at Leuchars, Johnny and I were close to our limit across in Norway, too. Our broken bodies must have been totally exhausted, because before we knew it we were waking up and it was light. The hole in the top of my head was covered in what felt like dried blood. Presuming that it was this that had stopped the flow, I thought I'd better leave it like that. Sinclair was in worse trouble because he was still in a lot of pain with his legs.

I peered out of the window and saw scores of Norwegians going about their daily business. There was a lot of ground outside the hotel, like a big playground, and around it there were railings. One or two Norwegians were lurking just beyond these railings. These young men weren't all that far away from our windows and they were acting as though they had a death wish. Remember, this hotel was inhabited by the Gestapo. If we could see them, the Gestapo could see them too. But one of these Norwegians still made a 'V-for-Victory' sign when he knew we had eye contact. This brave young man, someone I'd never seen before let alone met, was apparently putting his own freedom at risk, just to try to raise my spirits. Did he know I was British? He must have done. It was a simple gesture but it was moving too. He wasn't the only one. Other young men started making the V-for-Victory sign too. They were a very courageous lot.

I wondered how we could take advantage of the sympathy and potential help we'd clearly find if we made it out onto the street. Maybe there was an underground movement that could help me get back to Scotland by boat. If people helped me hide, they could find the right resistance contacts and send me on my way. It had to be worth a try, we couldn't just give up.

So I came up with an idea. It wasn't a very original one, but I thought it might work just the same. There was no chance that John could escape with his legs in that sorry state, and no one had even bothered to attend to them yet. But I was mobile enough to make my getaway, given half a chance; and Sinclair could still have his uses.

'John, you fake being ill and make some noises to get a guard in here. I'll stand behind the door and hit him once he's inside. Then I'll be out of this place and into the street before anyone can stop me.'

'What about me?'

'You can't even walk mate, never mind run,' I pointed out.

'No I don't mean that,' he replied. 'What are they going to do to me if you escape?'

Shit. I hadn't thought about that. John had a point, too.

'Moggy, if you beat up a guard and go tearing off, they're going to take it out on me. You know they are.'

He was right. The Gestapo hadn't seemed interested in us so far. If I tried to get away that might change everything. Though I was desperate to escape, I just couldn't do it to John. Blast his injured legs. It wasn't his fault and I knew we had to stick together. It could have been me in that state instead of him. It was frustrating, but for now I was going to have to take whatever was coming to me.

Even so, I decided something then and there. I was never going to stop thinking about escape. Not until I was finally free.

Johnny told me what had happened on the plane. Boal had ignored his advice and flown us right into the guns of the ship that shot us down – the *Sagitta*.

Sinclair explained, 'I pointed out which ship to go for, but he changed his mind and was veering around and stuff. He wasted time. Then he got it.'

Had the Wing Commander been trying to ensure that he aimed his torpedo at a German ship, instead of a Scandinavian one they might have forced to join their convoy? If so he paid a terrible price for his mistaken belief that we could just hang around like that until he was satisfied. Johnny reckoned Boal had been hit straight through the seat, probably by a shell, and been killed more or less instantly. Because poor Stan was sitting so close to Boal – the radio compartment had been just behind the pilot's seat – he must have been hit at the same time and was already fatally wounded when we struck the water.

★   ★   ★

The telegram, addressed to my war-veteran father, 'Mr G. Mayne,' duly arrived at my parents' house – 44 Mundania Road, East Dulwich, London – on 2 April 1942.

It read:

DEEPLY REGRET TO INFORM YOU THAT YOUR SON 1253284 SGT MAYNE M.G. IS MISSING AS THE RESULT OF AIR OPERATIONS ON 1ST APRIL 1942 LETTER FOLLOWS ANY FURTHER INFORMATION RECEIVED WILL BE IMMEDIATELY COMMUNICATED TO YOU PLEASE ACCEPT MY PROFOUND SYMPATHY = AERONAUTICS LEUCHARS +

With all the 'regret' and 'sympathy', it was as good as telling my parents I was dead. They said a letter would follow, and it did, the very next day. It was from Flight Lieutenant H.B. Leeming, Adjutant for 217 Squadron. He signed it 'for the Wing Commander', though of course the Wing Commander was dead.

The letter, again only addressed to my father, read:

Dear Mr Mayne,

I deeply regret to confirm the telegram that was addressed to you yesterday, stating that your son had been reported as missing. Will you please accept the deepest sympathy of myself and the air crews of this Squadron.

Your son was a wireless operator/air gunner of an aircraft, piloted by S.M. Boal, D.F.C., the Squadron Commanding Officer, which left this aerodrome during the afternoon of Wednesday, the 1st April to carry out an attack against enemy shipping in the North Sea. The aircraft failed to return from this sortie, and no communication was received from it, nor is there any other news of it. It is possible that it was forced down by enemy action or by engine failure; in either case, if the aircraft was forced to alight on the sea, its crew could possibly have escaped by dinghy, to be picked up by shipping or washed ashore.

A hope therefore does exist that your son may have been taken prisoner of war. It has been our experience in the past that information concerning prisoners of war has been received through the auspices of the International Red Cross, and if any information is received concerning your son, I shall be very happy to inform you at once.

Your son had only been serving with this Squadron for a few months. He was very keen to take his part in this Squadron's effort to defeat the enemy, and we are all very sorry to lose his services.

Yours faithfully …

There was another letter that day from the Air Commodore, whose signature I never did decipher. I've still got the letter though and I can only imagine my father's feelings when he open yet another heartbreaking communication and had to read it to my mother.

Dear Sir,

I regret to confirm that your son, No 1253284 Sergeant Maurice George MAYNE of No 217 Squadron, Royal Air Force, is missing, the aircraft of which he was the air gunner having failed to return to its base on the 1st April 1942 after an operational flight.

This does not necessarily mean that he is killed or wounded. I will communicate with you again immediately I have any further news and would

'Profound sympathy from the RAF.'

be obliged if you, on your part, would write to me should you hear anything of your son from unofficial sources.

May I assure you of the sympathy of the Royal Air Force with you in your anxiety …

As such letters go I suppose the last two were quite nicely put. But those words again: 'regret' and 'sympathy'. It was a coded warning to expect the worse, even if the letter made it clear that all hope was not lost. They mentioned 'anxiety'. That word probably failed to do much more than skim the surface of what my parents were feeling.

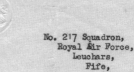

No. 217 Squadron,
Royal Air Force,
Leuchars,
Fife,
Scotland.

Reference:
217S/2061/89/P1.   3rd April 1942.

Dear Mr. *Inaigue*,

      I deeply regret to confirm the telegram which was addressed
to you yesterday, stating that your son had been reported as missing .
Will you please accept the deepest sympathy of myself and the air
crews of this Squadron.

      Your son was a wireless-operator/air gunner of an aircraft,
piloted by Wing Commander S. M. Boal, D.F.C., the Squadron Commanding
Officer, which left this aerodrome during the afternoon of Wednesday, the
1st April to carry out an attack against enemy shipping in the North Sea.
The aircraft failed to return from this sortie, and no communication
was received from it, nor is there any other news of it. It is possible
that it was forced down by enemy action or by engine failure; in either
case, if the aircraft was forced to alight on the sea, its crew could
possibly have escaped by dinghy, to be picked up by shipping or washed
ashore.

      A hope therefore does exist that your son may have been taken
a prisoner of war. It has been our experience in the past that information
concerning prisoners of war has been received through the auspices of the
International Red Cross, and if any information is received concerning
your son, I shall be very happy to inform you at once.

      Your son had only been serving with this Squadron for a few
months. He was very keen to take his part in this Squadron's effort
to defeat the enemy, and we are all very sorry to lose his services.

        Yours *faithfully*.

                          HB Leeming F/L
                  Flight Lieutenant, Adjutant,
   fr W/Comm No. 217 Squadron, Leuchars.

Mr. G. Mayne,
44 Mundania Road,
East Dulwich,
London, S.E.22.

'It's official. I'm missing and my father receives the bad news.'

8

INTERROGATION

No letters, no phone calls. Sylvia didn't know what had happened, but she knew that something was wrong. She was doing her best to carry on and had taken a part-time job at a big house just outside Braunton, looking after a young boy, whose father was a kindly soldier called Colonel Payton.

Sylvia recalls:

I was upset one morning when I hadn't heard from Maurice for a while. Colonel Payton appreciated his workers and he didn't like to see any of us down in the dumps. So when he saw me so upset, he asked me what was wrong.

I told him, 'I haven't heard from my boyfriend for weeks and I've got this feeling he may have been shot down.'

He said, 'I'll see what I can do. I'll try to find out.'

And I'm sure he did do his best to find out, but he couldn't get me any information. That was a very bleak time. Week upon week of agony for me. It was horrible. Waiting. Just waiting.

Over in Norway I knew I was still alive but I too was waiting – to discover my fate. The local Luftwaffe officers barged their way into our hotel room and told the guards they were taking us over to their local headquarters. Nobody stopped them. They took us to their Mess and gave us Schnapps. We became separated, John talking to one group of officers while I talked to another. They were all very nice blokes, although one did lead me over to their portrait of the 'Führer' and told me what marvellous eyes Hitler had, which was a bit strange. They all thought Hitler was great but I just told them that Churchill was greater.

The Luftwaffe officers kept us for a while and then they took us back to the Gestapo hotel, where we were moved into a tiny little cell, to be looked after by elderly Luftwaffe men from the lower ranks. Perhaps they were trying to tuck us right out of the way this time, where the Gestapo wouldn't find us. They made us some custard and one of them wanted to chat.

'War – no good. Hitler – no good,' he told me with a smile. If any of the Gestapo had heard him, he could have been shot on the spot.

'Churchill, no good,' he added. I couldn't be bothered to disagree. Then he pointed at himself and also at John and me.

'You! Me! Vee good!'

I was still so angry with the Germans for shooting us down that I wasn't keen to include this guard on any list of good people, even after his kindness. But he hadn't been the one to put us in this condition. And deep down I knew what he meant. We were all just normal people caught up in the war Hitler had started. (Why he was blaming Churchill I wasn't quite sure. But I was in no state to debate the point.) It struck me how the lower ranks in the Luftwaffe were different in their outlook to the officers – especially towards 'Der Führer.'

After a week in Kristiansand, we were taken away again. We weren't given any warning when we were suddenly driven to an airport. We weren't told where we were going but we landed in Denmark an hour or two later. We didn't go into Copenhagen, staying instead at Kastrup aerodrome. The Germans began to question us there. I still wasn't worried because I felt we were still in good hands at that stage. The Luftwaffe seemed to be pretty fair so far. They weren't short of questions, though. An officer I hadn't met before asked me for my parents' names and my squadron commander's name. Did I know anything about him? They already knew he was down, that much was obvious. I still didn't tell them anything about Paddy Boal.

Funnily enough, I don't think they ever mentioned the word torpedo, or asked for any details about the Beaufort aircraft. They were more interested in the squadron and the people in the squadron. They asked what my job was and I told them I was a gunner. They didn't ask me if I'd ever fired on German ships; and I was glad they didn't, because I'd fired on the *Scharnhorst* as ferociously as I could during the Channel Dash.

We only stayed in Copenhagen a few hours and I still hadn't really been subjected to a bad interrogation. I was put on a Junkers 52 aircraft to Marburg, a German university town near Frankfurt am Mein. From there it was only a short train ride to 'Dulag Luft', which was the Luftwaffe's interrogation centre, situated in Oberwesel, near Koblenz. This place was a bit scary at first. The first thing they did was to take all our RAF things away from us, including our flying uniform. They searched each uniform so thoroughly that they even examined the buttons. In the meantime those clothes were replaced by a perfectly clean Czechoslovakian army uniform. I wore those Czech clothes all the time at the Interrogation Centre, trying to prepare myself for anything they might throw at me.

The building was very clean and had a beautifully neat office. The scary thing was the worry at the back of your mind about what they might do to you to get the information they wanted. We'd all heard horror stories. I'd read about torture.

Our own superior officers had warned us about it too. When the possibility of capture had come up during training, the RAF lecturers had warned us to say as little as possible, but not to give false answers. Give them your name, rank and serial number and leave it at that, because there were cases of men who had begun to talk a bit and then been targeted for torturing, in order to get even more out of them.

It didn't look like this place was Gestapo-run, but you never knew when the Gestapo might turn up – and the prospect of torture never felt far away. The level of aggression during each interrogation depended on the officers involved. To my relief, the first German officer who questioned me had a packet of 'Players' not a pair of pliers. He offered me a cigarette and chatted away to me quite happily. This approach became a regular occurrence, but it could be quite surreal.

One day he came in and said, 'I've just been talking to the crew of another of your aircraft we shot down. One is the pilot of a Mosquito and the other is his friend. We can't get anything out of the pilot because he just says he is a very "tour Scot". I thought I knew what "tour" means – is there another meaning to this word?'

I said, 'No, I don't understand what you mean.'

'Tour,' he repeated.

I just looked confused, because I was.

This went on for two or three days and it was driving them mad. 'He is very "tour". What is "tour"?'

'I don't know, really!' I insisted. I was getting as frustrated as they were.

It only dawned on me much later that they were referring to the word 'dour', and this Mosquito man was a typically 'dour Scot'. They probably never did get it.

One or two interrogators were aggressive, whereas most were extra kind and crafty. I didn't shout back at the aggressive interrogators but they never got much out of me. In the main the Germans were very pleasant to me at the Centre, so nice that they might even have got a little bit more out of me than I'd originally intended. But they still claimed I wasn't giving them enough information, and that's why they were keeping me. They told me all the others from my batch had gone on to Stalag VIIIB, the designated POW camp, and I was the last one left because I hadn't answered their questions as well as the others had.

'If you would just sign this form,' they told me, 'you can get going too. It is only a basic form so that the International Red Cross has your details.'

'I'm sorry,' I told them as politely as I could, 'but my superiors told me that I mustn't sign any form.'

This carried on for a few more days. 'Are you going to sign the form today?' they asked.

'I've told you, I can't do that,' I replied. 'I've told you my name, my rank, my serial number. I've tried to be helpful.'

'But you haven't told us the name of your C/O.'

'No,' I said, 'because I'm not allowed to do that.'

'Doesn't matter!' they said. 'We've already got that name. We shot him down with you, didn't we?'

It was true but I didn't say anything.

'How are your squadron going to get on without him?'

'There are many great people in my squadron,' I said.

'Just one last question and you can go. Who trained your navigators?'

He put that question with a hint of a slightly mocking grin on his face, as though the Germans were distinctly unimpressed with our navigators.

'I don't know,' I said. 'I'm not a navigator.'

Staying off the military stuff, that was my main aim. Get out of there before you tell them anything useful. They had asked where I lived, where I was born, what school I went to, that sort of thing. I didn't mind answering that, because it didn't strike me that it could be of any use to them.

'Can you remember any of your masters' names?'

I thought that was a peculiar question to ask, but I answered it anyway, because again I thought it was harmless.

'Mr Chipperfield was one,' I said. Mr Chipperfield stuck in my mind because he was very presentable, nice-looking, not an athletic type but someone who still took the boys for sport. I remembered him because when he took us for cricket, he'd keep his coat on and bowl underarm at us. Not exactly the ideal preparation for matches against other schools, but he was so nice to us we didn't mind. Besides, he used to put some wicked spin on those underarm balls, so they weren't as easy to deal with as they might sound.

Of course, the details of Mr Chipperfield's bowling action would have been completely lost on the Germans, who didn't know one end of a cricket bat from another. If I was able to confuse them, so much the better. Though I'd been shot down, my morale was good. Down but not out, you might say.

Looking back, I suppose they could have used little details like those memories of Mr Chipperfield as a back-story for one of their spies but that didn't cross my mind at the time, so I just answered what I felt was harmless. It still seems more likely they were just loosening me up with casual conversation, before asking me about the squadron and the names of the people on the squadron. That's what they really wanted to know. I said I couldn't remember names like that because I was only a young lad. I was giving the impression that I was of very low intelligence. I was only a gunner; I didn't know anything about it. I took the attitude that I was a bit thick and didn't mind admitting it.

A whole group of downed airmen had been taken to the Interrogation Centre but I was kept on about ten days after the original lot had been moved on. Johnny Sinclair went on to Stalag VIIIB before I did. I think they kept me where I was because I wouldn't give them any names from the squadron. So I was stuck there until the next lot had come in and been questioned too. When they finally got fed up with me, I was allowed to go on to the prison camp.

By the time we were ready to go, Stalag VIIIB at Lamdsdorf had been described to me as a horrible place. It was right over towards Silesia, where Germany had invaded Poland and pushed back its border. Lots of the guys said VIIIB had a terrible reputation. They said it was one of the worst because there was almost no food on that border, whereas in other parts of Germany food was more plentiful. Of course we didn't know about the concentration camps or the slaughter of the Jews at that stage, so our idea of what constituted the worst possible place couldn't be compared to the hell that some poor souls were to suffer in German captivity.

When I finally reached the prison camp, I realised how massive it was, like a huge circle around a central parade ground. There was a tremendous number of British soldiers packed into huts in a compound on the other side of the camp to us. They had been captured in France years earlier – when the British Expeditionary Force was overrun and only part of it had escaped at Dunkirk. These were the men who hadn't got out in time but managed to survive. There were about 50,000 of these army lads when you counted up all the different units, so no wonder the place was so big. The POWs mostly worked, many of them doing jobs in the camp. Others were selected for work parties which did things outside the camp. They were taken out to the local town, where they had all types of compulsory work to do. When they weren't working, the army lads seemed to be free to wander all over the place.

The camp Kommandant seemed nice enough when he gave us the usual talk about obeying the rules and not bothering to try to escape. He was tall, ex-Kriegsmarine and didn't seem to lose his cool, even when one of the new prisoners gave him some outrageous lip. When the Kommandant passed among our men with two guards, some clown shouted out, 'Hello sailor, where's your winkle-barge?'

Instead of ordering the culprit into the punishment cells, the Kommandant spoke in quite a withering tone as he put the man straight using plain facts. He gave his prisoner a brief history of his distinguished career in the German navy before he had taken charge of the camp. He looked at the prisoner with an air of triumph, as if he had won the argument with ease, then simply moved on. It was better than a rifle-butt to the head. The Kommandant just seemed to want to be respected as a serviceman, the same as everyone else who was there.

'He could be worse,' I thought.

But that was before I found out what could happen if you really stepped out of line; and before I realised that prisoners could become easy targets for reprisals, if their captors were looking for revenge for any perceived injustice. Even if your Kommandant wasn't one of the worst, he still had to obey orders from higher up. And some of those orders could be very malicious indeed.

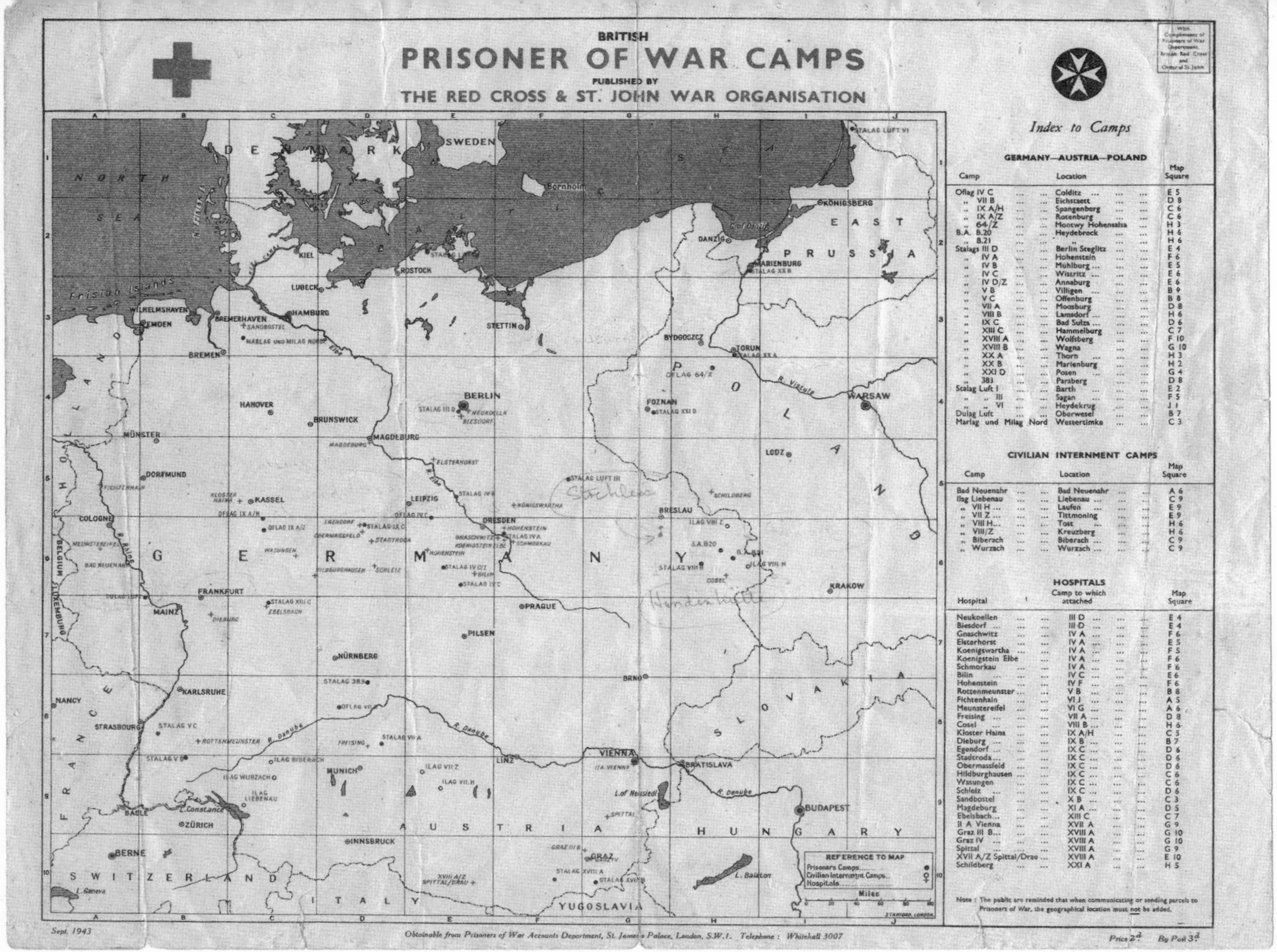

map shows
the locations
of POW camps
in Nazi-held
territory.'

BRITISH
PRISONER OF WAR CAMPS
PUBLISHED BY
THE RED CROSS & ST. JOHN WAR ORGANISATION

Index to Camps

GERMANY—AUSTRIA—POLAND

CIVILIAN INTERNMENT CAMPS

HOSPITALS

REFERENCE TO MAP

Prisoners Camps.
Civilian Internment Camps.
Hospitals.

Miles

Obtainable from Prisoners of War Accounts Department, St. James's Palace, London, S.W.1. Telephone : Whitehall 3007.

Sept. 1943

None of this was clear to a young, newly arrived air gunner in a huge camp. For now I just took in my surroundings and tried to keep my head down until I knew how things worked there.

Like I say, everything seemed to be built around this massive parade ground. There were enough buildings to make up a village, or even a town. The British soldiers were on one side, more central than us to the parade ground. On the other side was a compound with barbed wire all the way round, absolutely covered, it was. That was the RAF compound and where I was going to live. There were about a thousand of us packed into eight barracks inside the wire.

We were put in stone barracks that had been used in the First World War, so they were pretty uncomfortable. The beds were in blocks of twelve, three high. The windows had no glass in them. There were shutters, which the Germans seemed very proud of, and those shutters were left closed during the day. The draft came through though, which was nice enough during those early days because it was the start of summer. But I knew it was going to be a lot worse in winter, so I was sharp enough to get myself a top bunk just under the ceiling, because I knew heat rises.

I had a lovely pair of flying boots – soft black leather, much better than anyone else on the squadron had. You could whip the top section of leather away if you wanted to – depending on how much air you wanted to reach your feet. You could pull that top section back round behind the boot, making the front look like an ordinary shoe. The stitching had been designed so that the boot stayed in one piece but had all this flexibility. Those boots were my pride and joy and I was already looking at them as my future escape boots. But the Germans took them away from me at Lamsdorf. They gave me clogs instead. Clogs! I couldn't believe it at first.

Not that there was much walking to be done. We were locked in all day and there was never any entertainment those first weeks. But with a hundred blokes in each barracks, it didn't take me long to realise that there were all sorts of things going on if you looked hard enough; all sorts of sub-groups … including an Escape Committee.

There were no officers in a Stalag. If you were an officer you went to an Oflag. Everyone in Stalag VIIIB was a non-commissioned officer or 'NCO'. But that didn't mean we weren't able to organise ourselves into various groups to get things done. And what I wanted to do most of all was to escape.

Unfortunately the Germans couldn't allow the RAF to go out to work. Too risky, they'd decided. In the earliest days of the war, the captured RAF boys used to be taken out for a walk through the woods near the camp on Sundays – all very nice and civilised. The Germans had soon stopped that, because by the time they got back from those Sunday strolls, there were dozens of RAF lads missing! No coincidence that the letters 'raf' are to be found in the word 'crafty'! In the end the Kommandant had issued a definitive ruling – the RAF were not allowed outside the camp in any shape or form. And that rule was still being enforced when I got there. We were proud of it in a way, though it didn't improve our chances of escape.

Next door to us was another compound, this time for the Canadians, who were good lads. But strangely the New Zealanders were right over on the other side of the barbed wire, along with the army. I'd get to know the Kiwis very well in the end, and with good reason, too. They were allowed out of the camp to work, which was always worth bearing in mind if you were looking for a way home.

At first things didn't seem as bad as I'd been told. Being over near Poland, it was true that the food was very poor. In fact we heard that even the local population was starving. Having your food cut drastically can be a big shock to the system. I probably suffered less than most because I wasn't a big eater anyway. Even so, not eating properly would take its toll on me too, over time.

My parents still didn't even know I was alive, let alone whether or not I was eating properly. Sylvia didn't know anything had happened to me at all, though she feared something terrible. She didn't know my parents so she'd heard nothing.

About ten days after I'd gone down, my father wrote back to Flight Lieutenant Leeming of 217 Squadron in Leuchars, asking for further information.

He asked after Stan Clarke and Sid Knight, because he knew they were close friends of mine, had met Sid in the past and Stan at my twenty-first birthday party a few months earlier. Perhaps one or both of them could write to my father, to let him know what, if anything, they'd heard? It would be nice to have some contact from them at such a difficult time, anyway.

What my father didn't know, of course, was that Stan Clarke was dead and Sid Knight was about to be sent away from 217 Squadron in disgrace, for refusing to fly after I was shot down.

Flight Lieutenant Leeming wrote a handwritten note to my father on 13 April. Again, it has survived.

Dear Mr Mayne,
Thank you for your letter. I am sorry to say there is no further news I can give you regarding your son.

Sgt Knight, 'Sid,' in your letter, is going to write to you, but the other, 'Stan,' was one of the crew which was lost.

I will let you know at once if any further news [sic] and can only hope with you that it will be good news …

But there wasn't any news. Not for days. Then, finally, there was a breakthrough – from the most unlikely of sources. My cousin Joyce Mayne had come over from Australia to get married. She was part of a dance troupe called the 'Breezy Babes' and was quite a character. She heard Lord Haw-Haw, the German propaganda

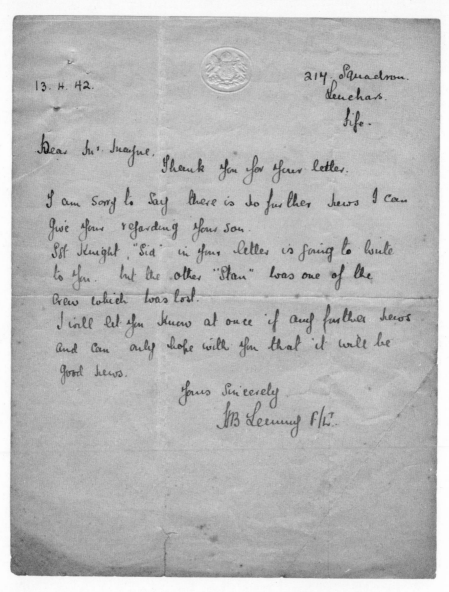

13. 4. 42.

214. Squadron.
Leuchars.
Fife.

Dear Mr. Mayne,
Thank you for your letter.
I am sorry to say there is no further news I can
give you regarding your son.
Sgt. Knight "Sid" in your letter is going to write
to you. but the other "Stan" was one of the
crew which was lost.
I will let you know at once if any further news
and can only hope with you that it will be
good news.

Yours Sincerely,
HB Leeming F/Lt.

'No news is bad news. My family are left in torment, waiting to know if I've survived.'

broadcaster on the radio; and he had mentioned that I was a prisoner of war. I suppose Lord Haw-Haw did us a favour in a way.

Joyce wrote to my father. (Joyce Mayne had never even met me but she had met my parents.) The letter – short, sweet and written from '39, Island Wall, Whitstable, Kent' – survives to this day:

Dear Uncle George,

Just been given out on German wireless station.
Sergeant Maurice Mayne
Prisoner of War.
We are so glad he is safe.
Did you know?
Love Joyce Mayne (Baker)
PS Enclose wedding photo. Got married March 31st.
PPS Will write and tell Roy [her brother, my cousin] that Maurice is safe.

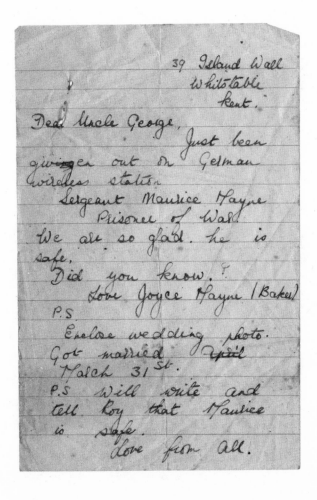

'Unlikely source! But now my family learn I'm alive.'

Like many British citizens, Joyce Mayne (Baker) enjoyed listening to Lord Haw-Haw – even in the first month of her marriage. You might wonder why they liked listening to a man whose only aim was to spread Nazi propaganda in Britain. But he had a very resonant voice and you couldn't help listening to him. He'd say kind things to ordinary working class British people sometimes. Not to government figures, of course. In fact, he would gently tell the British people about the wicked things their government was supposed to be doing. That way he would try to create a split between the British wartime government and those who might be suffering during the war. It was poisonous stuff but it also made for very attractive listening. From Whitstable the reception was crystal clear when Lord Haw-Haw gave his broadcasts from the Continent. So Joyce was listening to him carefully that evening and just as well. Lord Haw-Haw's words were wonderful news for my family that night.

On 21 April the Air Ministry sent a telegram to my parents to explain that they too had heard Lord Haw-Haw's broadcast, though they thought it should be taken with a pinch of salt. Mum and Dad kept that telegram. It read:

YOUR SON SGT MAURICE GEORGE MAYNE WAS MENTIONED IN A GERMAN BROADCAST 20TH APRIL 1942 AS BEING A PRISONER OF WAR STOP. THIS INFORMATION SHOULD BE ACCEPTED WITH RESERVE PENDING OFFICIAL CONFIRMATION STOP. ANY FURTHER INFORMATION WILL BE IMMEDIATELY COMMUNICATED TO YOU.

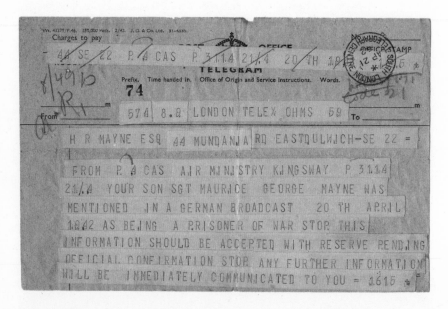

'Cautious optimism. The Air Ministry seems to have heard a similar broadcast.'

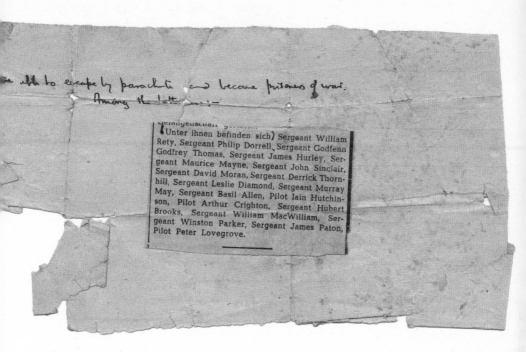

...ble to escape by parachute and become prisoners of war. Among the list were :—

> (Unter ihnen befinden sich) Sergeant William Rety, Sergeant Philip Dorrell, Sergeant Godfenn Godfrey Thomas, Sergeant James Hurley, Sergeant Maurice Mayne, Sergeant John Sinclair, Sergeant David Moran, Sergeant Derrick Thornhill, Sergeant Leslie Diamond, Sergeant Murray May, Sergeant Basil Allen, Pilot Iain Hutchinson, Pilot Arthur Crighton, Sergeant Hubert Brooks, Sergeant William MacWilliam, Sergeant Winston Parker, Sergeant James Paton, Pilot Peter Lovegrove.

'Newspaper confirmation that John Sinclair and I have become POWs.'

Then a German newspaper printed my name along with sixteen others, preceded by the phrase '_Unter ihnen befinden sich_' ('among them are').

The list included John Sinclair, though he was in a different hut, having arrived earlier than me. I didn't see much of John from that moment on. He made his friendships and I made mine. We'd never been close, though I never forgot that he had helped to save my life.

9

TIES

I tried to introduce myself to the Escape Committee as quickly as I could. An unsmiling British pilot called Lawrence was rumoured to be on the Escape Committee, and he happened to be on the same table as me for meals. I spoke to him, though he gave me the impression he might only be able to help me indirectly. The idea was that you never knew quite who the Escape Committee people were, because it was all supposed to be a secret.

In the end they came back to me – or at least one of their representatives, called Ken 'Tex' Hyde did. My good fortune was that Hyde was also on my table for meals, so contact came easily enough. 'Tex' took me into a corner at the back of our barracks, discreetly put a plain-coloured shirt and civilian jacket on me and then took my photograph. One day soon he was going to put that photo on some fake German identification papers.

You may wonder how on earth they had managed to get hold of a camera … so did I! It turned out that Hyde was a former Royal Canadian Air Force photographer – and a very resourceful bloke he was too. He had put the word out about what he needed and one of the army lads out on a working party had got hold of a camera. He soldered it into a metal drinking canteen to smuggle it back through the German checks. Unfortunately the canteen leaked and weeks of secret repairs were necessary before the camera was in working order again.

Hyde wasn't short of help. The good thing about a lot of men being thrown in a POW camp was that a variety of skills could be called upon. So a watchmaker fixed the corroded shutter with his skilled fingers, an optician worked on the lens, and finally all 'Tex' Hyde required was some film and chemicals for developing pictures.

Civilians on those work parties were bribed with coffee and cigarettes – and here in Upper Silesia it wasn't as though people were particularly loyal to the German cause. Finally Hyde had everything he needed.

So I'd had my photo taken and the papers were to be printed up on a German typewriter obtained through similar underhand means. If a camp guard seemed a bit on the weak side, or had a greedy streak, or just seemed to sympathise with the prisoners, socially skilful people gently went to work on him to try and get what they wanted. Guards of Polish extraction felt much less loyalty to Hitler and were often good value. What I learned in time was that you really could get just about anything you wanted; everything except for freedom. If you wanted that, it was a question of 'get in the queue and wait your turn'. One problem; it was a very long queue.

Prisoners were flocking into our camp, not least because I think another camp somewhere was closing, and that meant the numbers at VIIIB were swelling fast. As you can imagine, every other bloke wanted to escape. I was just one of many. You couldn't operate independently. It was explained to me that I'd risk compromising better-organised escapes if I suddenly lost patience and tried to do something hasty by myself. So there was no alternative; you had to fall in line and wait for the call. The camp was going to be my world for the foreseeable future, so I might as well get used to it.

At least my parents were going to receive confirmation of where I was before I tried to escape! On 11 May they received the following communication:

A TELEGRAM FROM THE INTERNATIONAL RED CROSS QUOTING GERMAN INFORMATION STATES THAT YOUR SON SGT MAYNE IS NOW A PRISONER OF WAR IN GERMANY AT DULAG [sic] LUFT LETTER FOLLOWS.

You had to be grateful for small mercies in Stalag VIIIB. Little things helped me from the start. I'd had that basic education in German back at school in Paddington, so it didn't take me very long to get quite good at speaking and reading the language. Things in the camp didn't seem quite as alien to me as they might have done to other new people, who had more trouble adapting. But that wasn't true right across the board, because no one could really feel at home in a place like that.

What I found difficult at the start were the toilets. They were round the back of the barracks, just the other side of our little parade ground; and they were ghastly places. We called them the 'forty holers' because that's all they were – forty holes. There were four rows of ten. When you first became a POW and went to the toilet in the camp it was just so embarrassing. You went to the forty holers and found that the back part of you was being seen by blokes in the next row. My God! Ghastly! You just had to get used to it. In time this became no more than a crude part of daily life. That's the trouble with prison camps. You just get crude generally.

I didn't know it, but statistically I was probably safer where I was. So many Beauforts were getting shot down that you were lucky to survive a tour. In May it was the turn of Wing Commander Mervyn 'Willy' Williams. The man who had nearly sent me to my death on that *Tirpitz* suicide mission showed that he still wasn't afraid to take on the giants of the German fleet. The *Prinz Eugen* had been ordered from Trondheim to the Baltic port of Kiel for repairs, and that gave the RAF another window of opportunity to sink her. Wing Commander Williams led six Beauforts in two waves and headed up a much wider attacking force. But the wall of flak proved virtually impossible to avoid.

His record shows:

On the night of May 17th, 1942, he led a force comprising Beauforts, Hudsons, Blenheims and Beaufighters in an attack on Prinz Eugen. Despite intense defensive fire from the cruiser and four escorting destroyers, Wing Cdr Williams led his force into the attack with great courage and determination. Unfortunately, he was shot down during the engagement and is a prisoner of war. He always displayed inspiring leadership.

Williams won a DSO for his action, during which the lives of the other three men on his crew were lost. Like me he was picked up by a German ship. Unlike me, he was taken to an Oflag – initially, at least – so our paths didn't cross.

On 30 May 1942, I managed to write to Sylvia for the first time since being shot down. I addressed it to 'MISS SYLVIA WEST, EXETER ROAD, BRAUNTON, N.DEVON, ENGLAND.'

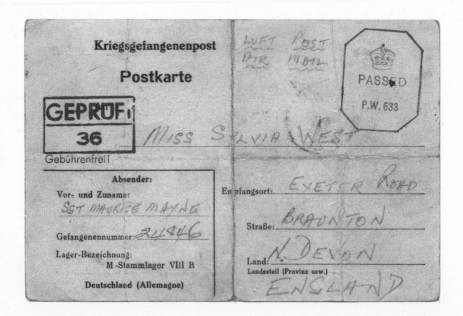

The letter-card was marked 'LUFT POST' – 'AIR MAIL' – it too survives, along with all my other letters to her. It read like this:

MY DEAR SYLVIA,
AT LAST I'M ABLE TO LET YOU KNOW WHERE I'VE FINISHED UP, SO YOU CAN SEE THE REASON WHY YOU HAVE NOT HEARD FROM ME FOR SUCH A LONG TIME. SOMEHOW I MANAGED TO ESCAPE WITH MY LIFE BUT FOUND MYSELF A PRISONER OF WAR. DO PLEASE WRITE TO ME. MY ADDRESS IS:-
SGT MAYNE 245846 PRISONER OF WAR, M.STAMAILAGER VIIIB, DEUTSCHLAND. I REALLY AM LONGING TO HEAR FROM YOU SYLVIA. I'M AFRAID THAT'S ALL I CAN SQUEEZE IN NOW, CHEERIO, LOVE MAURICE.

It was one thing for me to send this, another for it to arrive. More than a week later, when Sylvia had still heard nothing from me for months, she determined to discover my fate. So she wrote to the War Office to try to find out once and for all whether I was dead or alive. It was most unlike me not to be in touch, she explained. We had been together for a year and this had never happened before. Please could they at least tell her if I'd been shot down and killed, she implored.

Kriegsgefangenenlager   Datum: 30. MAY 1942

MY DEAR SYLVIA, AT LAST I'm ABLE TO LET YOU KNOW WHERE I'VE FINISHED UP. SO YOU CAN SEE THE REASON WHY YOU HAVE NOT HEARD FROM ME. FOR SUCH A TIME. Somehow I MANAGED To ESCAPE WITH MY LIFE BUT FOUND MYSELF A PRISONER OF WAR. DO PLEASE WRITE TO ME. MY ADDRESS is :- SGT MAYNE 24846 PRISONER OF WAR. M.STAMMALAGER VIIIB. DEUTSCHLAND. I REALLY AM LONGING TO HEAR FROM YOU SYLVIA, I'm AFRAID THATS ALL I CAN SQUEEZE IN NOW. So CHEERIO. LOVE MAURICE

Form No. 6.

Any further communication
on this subject should be
addressed to—
The Under-Secretary of State,
The War Office,
London, S.W.1,
and the following number
quoted.

THE WAR OFFICE,
LONDON, S.W.1.

11 . 6 . 19 42 .

~~Sir,~~ *Madam*

I am commanded by the Army Council to acknowledge the

receipt of your letter of *8 . 6 . 42 .*

on the subject of *the whereabouts of*

Sgt. Mayne R.A.F.

and to inform you that it has been forwarded to *the*

Under Secretary of State

Air Ministry. Kingsway W.C.2

to whom it should have been addressed in the first instance,

and who will give the necessary instructions for a reply to be

sent to you.

I am,

~~Sir,~~ *Madam*

Your obedient Servant,

3118. Wt.19228/6220. 30M. 6/40. Wy.L.P. Gp. 853. J.5149.

She wrote to the Record Office for the Royal Air Force in Gloucester on the same day, to find out if they knew anything. If they couldn't tell her what had happened to me, could they at least give her my home address in London, which must be on their files, so that she could contact my parents to see if they had been told anything?

In mid-June she received the following stuffy, officious and totally unsympathetic reply:

Madam,

I am commanded by the Army Council to acknowledge the receipt of your letter of 8.6.42. on the subject of the whereabouts of Sgt Mayne R.A.F. and to inform you that it has been forwarded to the Under Secretary of State, Air Ministry, Kingsway, WC2, to whom it should have been addressed in the first instance, and who will give the necessary instructions for a reply to be sent to you.

I am, Madam,

Your obedient Servant,

P.J. Griff

Sylvia had to endure another month of agony. My letter from the POW camp still hadn't arrived. She kicked herself for not having asked me for my home address in the first place, but then again she'd known I was hardly ever going to be there because I was based all over the place. Wherever I'd been, I'd always written to her, so why did she need to know where my parents lived? We were young and positive; it had never occurred to us that we would need to make plans for a worst-case scenario.

Finally, on 4 July 1942, the following letter arrived at Sylvia's house, from the RAF Record Office in Gloucester. It survives to this day.

Under the heading '1253284 T/Sgt. Mayne, M.G. – R.A.F.' a pen-pusher for the Air Commodore wrote:

Madam,

With reference to your letter dated 8th June, it is with regret I have to inform you that the above named airman was reported missing on the 1st April, 1942, and is believed to be a prisoner of war.

I would further add that it is contrary to the regulations to disclose the home address of the airman …

Despair and then hope in the space of a few words. 'Regret … missing … prisoner of war.' Didn't they know what that careless arrangement of words could do to a person? In Sylvia's case, though – and very luckily for me – they stirred in her something that would never die.

More than seventy years later, she recalls:

From the moment I heard the terrible news that Maurice was missing, my feelings deepened somehow. 'Believed to be a prisoner of war.' They weren't

Telephone No. : SPRINGWELL (GLOUCESTER)..........2306/7   RECORD OFFICE,

Telegraphic Address :

RECORDS TELEX, GLOUCESTER.   ROYAL AIR FORCE,

Any communications on the
subject of this letter should   GLOUCESTER.
be addressed to :

AIR OFFICER i/c RECORDS,

Address as opposite,   Date..........4...July...1942.....

and the following number
quoted :—   Cld/1253284.

Your Ref. :...........

1253284 T/Sgt. Hayne, M.C. - R.A.F.

Madam,

      With reference to your letter dated 8th ult.,

it is with regret I have to inform you that the above named

airman was reported missing on the 1st April, 1942, and is

believed to be a prisoner of war.

      I would further add that it is contrary to

regulations to disclose the home address of the airman.

                     I am,

                      Madam,

                          Your obedient servant,

                          for Air Commodore,

                          Air Officer i/c Records,

                          Royal Air Force.

Miss Sylivia West,
Exeter Road,
Braunton, Nrth. Devon.

sure, so I still didn't know if he was dead or alive, but I just thought 'Oh God, I want him home again.' I'll never forget it. I felt a loss and the feelings came over me. I wished he had come to see me in those months before he was shot down. But I remembered what we'd had and I wanted him home again, so we could be together. Of course at that time I didn't expect it to take as long as it did. The waiting became endless.

The irony was that, just a few days later, my letter arrived in Braunton from Germany, confirming that I was alive and well.

1 Fine footballer! Maurice 'Moggy' Mayne (front row, far right) is only about 12 years old here but already a trusted member of his local football team.

2 Maurice's father George survived the Somme and the rest of the First World War.

3 Not out! Talented Maurice is only
15 when he plays for a winning adult
team called Old Vauxonians.

4 Boys to men. Maurice and his
brother Ken before the war.

All kinds of rumours were rife about what was going on in the war – and which RAF squadron was doing this or that. I did hear from a fresh batch of RAF prisoners during the summer of 1942 that 217 Squadron had gone to Malta. My friends were said to be having a rough time of it on the Mediterranean island, which was bombed all the time. And when the Beauforts went after the German ships carrying fuel and arms to North Africa, the casualties were very high.

For all that, I was still envious. Would I rather have been risking my life as a free man on Malta, fighting the war to defend my country, or be penned up in Lamsdorf doing nothing? For me it was no contest. I would have preferred Malta, even after I learned later that most of the original members of 217 Squadron from my intake had died on Malta. I would have taken my chances. I never thought I would be the one to die, remember?

One day in August 1942, Douglas Bader turned up in the camp. This RAF pilot was a living legend because he had lost a leg, yet he had continued fighting the Luftwaffe in the air with the help of a false leg. Even after being shot down he was still trying to escape, with the help of a new leg the British had sent him, apparently with Luftwaffe permission! In fact, Bader had escaped so many times that he was about to be sent to the infamous Colditz Castle for the rest of the war.

In the meantime he had been brought to Lamsdorf and managed to get permission to come and visit all the RAF lads while he was there. Everyone had heard of Bader and his legendary exploits, including me, so there was quite a lot of excitement in the camp when the word went round that he was coming to see us.

I was sitting at a table playing Ludo when he came into our barracks. He sat down with us and asked us, 'Are you making plans to escape?'

'Yes, I'd like to escape sir,' I replied, though my turn hadn't come yet.

'Good man!' said Bader, before moving on to the next table.

I'd be lying if I said that Bader was a particular inspiration to me, because he wasn't. The man who inspired me more was a Canadian called Sergeant Hubert Brooks, who'd been shot down in a Wellington. He and the rest of his surviving crew had come into VIIIB in the same batch as me and were all on my table at mealtimes. 'Brooksy' was as determined to escape as me, and the Escape Committee must have noticed that. We waited to see who would be first in their queue.

I just wanted to get back to Sylvia before she fell in love with someone else. As it was, I didn't even have a photograph of her, because I hadn't been carrying any when we were shot down.

On 16 August 1942, I wrote to Sylvia:

I only wish that the photos I had of you were with me here in this prison camp. They were so nice and I thought such a lot of them. Perhaps, Sylvia, when you write, which I pray you will do, you can send me one or two of yourself to keep me company. When I come back to England, and I hope that day isn't far off, I want to see your pretty face first of all – that is of course providing some other lucky chap hasn't won your heart by this time …

I hadn't heard from Sylvia, it had been a year since I'd seen her and there'd been a long period during which I couldn't contact her. I didn't know if she'd been enjoying another summer romance in Braunton with someone else.

A couple of months or more after we arrived at VIIIB, on 19 August, the Allies launched a raid from Britain, crossing the English Channel to hit Dieppe on the coast of France. We heard a bit about it, because Ken 'Tex' Hyde didn't just have a camera – he had a little radio too. Hyde had got hold of the crystals he needed for this homemade contraption. But a makeshift aerial had to be placed in a specific position outside so that he could get a good reception. I volunteered to climb out of the window and lay at the barbed wire with this aerial, so the boys inside could try to hear some news from the outside world. We'd pick up the British news sometimes, though we didn't realise at first that a lot of it was propaganda.

An ex-school teacher called Bill Routledge, who was good at shorthand or speed-writing, would jot down what we heard as fast as he could. The next day he would write it up, and we would compare that account to the German version of the news, which we would get from the copy of a German newspaper, nicked and brought back into the camp by one of the army lads who went out to work in the town. Someone from another barracks might also have been listening to the German news on a different radio, and we could match all that against our own radio report. We'd study the conflicting accounts of a battle or raid like Dieppe, having prepared them for examination. And then we'd work out what we thought was actually true. As RAF men, what we noticed in particular was how the numbers of aircraft shot down in a battle always varied sharply between the British and German accounts. We came to the conclusion that the true total was usually something in between. We'd write up our own story for people to digest, using our own educated guesswork to determine what had actually happened.

In the case of Dieppe, so much detail was coming out from the German side about Allied casualties, and so little firm detail from our own side – except that the raid was deemed to be a 'daring success' – that we suspected the Germans were the ones telling the truth. Our side was being economical with that truth and the BBC was being wonderfully positive, with nothing firm to back up their grand claims.

In reality the Allied raid on Dieppe had been a bit of a disaster, with more than half the 6,000 Canadians involved having been killed, wounded or captured. The British tried to report it as a triumph, not concentrating too much on the terrible casualties. Indeed, Winston Churchill argued later that Dieppe 1942 had been an important step in the long build-up towards the full-scale invasion that would come in 1944. He wrote, '… until an operation on that scale was undertaken, no responsible general would take the responsibility of planning for the main invasion.' It was true that the Allies learned from some of their mistakes at Dieppe, but in many people's eyes that didn't justify the raid; the human cost was too high. At the time we shook our heads sadly at the German reports of all those losses. But we never thought the raid would impact on us in any way.

We knew that the Canadians had been heavily involved in Dieppe and that they had taken some Germans prisoner. Then we heard a disturbing anecdote. The Canadians had been escorting these Germans back to their landing craft to take them back to England, where the plan was to get more information out of them. Suddenly one of the Germans had yelled out. He seemed to be trying to alert some of his mates in a unit he knew was positioned nearby. He was probably begging them to come and shoot the Canadians and free the prisoners while they still could. One of the Canadians shot this noisy German before he could give any more of the game away. That was the account that reached us, and we believed it.

Yet the Germans believed there to have been numerous atrocities at Dieppe, not just this one isolated and understandable shooting. Apart from captured Allied battle plans, revealing their intention to shackle all German prisoners caught, there were some far more extreme reports which had reached Hitler. Those reports told of several German prisoners washing up on the Dieppe shores after the Canadian withdrawal, all those bodies with their hands tied. Hitler was incensed, and responded by ordering that all Canadian prisoners be shackled in his own POW camps.

You would have thought the Canadians, who were in a compound just across from us, would have got the worst of the backlash in Stalag VIIIB. The Germans had captured about a thousand Canadians from the *Windsor Scottish* (Montreal). Maybe they did have it bad, but all I know for sure is that the Germans also started taking reprisals against us in the British RAF compound.

Before, we'd been able to walk about between barracks during the day, chatting to prisoners housed in neighbouring huts. That was denied to us now. We were ordered into our own barracks and told to sit on the floor, about a hundred of us. The first thing they did was to tie us up with sisal, our hands bound tightly in front of us. This cheap, coarse string hurt a lot, but you couldn't complain, because there were guards walking up and down quite menacingly.

The RAF had played a supportive role at Dieppe, along with the Royal Navy but the RAF hadn't committed any atrocities as far as we knew, so the German decision to victimise us was hard to fathom. 'Allies shooting German prisoners' – that's as much as the Germans needed to hear, apparently, before they decided to take it out on us too. What we didn't know was that the Allies had since responded in kind to Hitler's order to shackle Canadian POWs. British and Canadian authorities had then ensured that all German prisoners in Canada were shackled too. That had probably made us more vulnerable to reprisals. It also led to an uprising by German prisoners in Canada, as the backlash for Dieppe continued. It was all getting a bit pointless, this tit-for-tat shackling. It seemed unnecessary, looking back.

Each person will have his own opinion as to whether the Dieppe raid was worth it. But any long-term lessons learned at Dieppe were of little consolation to us, as we continued to be shackled all day in Lamsdorf. Our wrists soon developed sores as our skin rubbed and chafed against this coarse string. We sat there feeling miserable, ignorant of the wider political games being played by Hitler and our own side.

We felt a sense of injustice. As far as we could see, we were only being targeted because the Germans wouldn't allow the RAF men to go out to work, because they reckoned the desire to escape was more prevalent in us. We were no use to the Germans as non-workers, so they felt they could do what they liked with us.

That ordeal of having our hands tied by sisal lasted for about three weeks. After that things became even worse, because the string was replaced by tight handcuffs. That was really uncomfortable. Can you imagine trying to go to the toilet with your hands tied? You could just about wipe your bottom but it needed a feat of contortion before you could do the job.

If this was the way we were going to be treated from now on, we could kiss goodbye to any dreams of freedom. The shackling went on for about eight weeks. It was hell. Finally the International Red Cross got wind of what was happening and they came to take a look. They didn't come into our barracks, but they may have visited our camp and they definitely knew what was going on. Bravely they insisted to the Germans that the pressure on our wrists was eased a bit – and that led to the introduction of chains, which were put on to link the cuffs. That meant more space between our bound hands. Although we were still cuffed, you had to be grateful for small mercies.

'Tex' Hyde took a photo of a man in these latest cuffs, loosened by the chains. He looks very miserable but believe me, these were the better shackles. Every night, a guard came in and took the chains off, so that we could at least climb onto our bunks and sleep in some kind of peace.

Gradually we were able to get up to our little games. We found a way to release the shackles during the day, too. Someone realised you could use the keys from sardine tins to undo the cuffs. We'd put them on again in time for the Germans to come and take them off each night. As time went on, more and more sets of chains went missing – including mine. I hid my chains away in my mattress, because you never knew when you might need them.

Eventually the anger about Dieppe seemed to subside, both the Germans and Allies were ready to relent on the shackling of prisoners, and further intervention by the International Red Cross gave everyone an excuse to take things back to the way they had been for prisoners before Dieppe. All we knew of course was that the cuffs suddenly came off one day, and we were back to living as normally as prisoners can live.

We didn't bear a grudge against the Canadians. In fact the longer the war went on, the closer we got to them. We used to shout messages across to their barracks at night, and vice-versa. Whatever they did in Dieppe, there must have been a good reason for it if you ask me.

Once the shackling was over, we could catch up with our mail. And what a wonderful surprise awaited me. Sylvia had written back! Not once but twice! Joy and relief swept over me when I read her first letter. She hadn't deserted me in my hour of need. She was sorry to hear that I was a prisoner of war but relieved I hadn't been killed. She still had feelings for me. She said she loved me. There was still hope for us … more than hope! The second letter was just as tender.

On 13 September 1942 I wrote back:

My Darling Sylvia,
At last I'm able to write and tell you that last week I received two very welcome letters from you and they had only taken three weeks to reach me. Unfortunately my outgoing letters are being restricted now as also are the incoming ones. Still Sylvia if you don't hear from me for long periods please don't worry at all about me. I'm always thinking about you and I know you think of me too. I've spent the whole of this summer in this prison camp but in spite of that I've been able to appreciate the glorious weather we've been having here. Just like that lovely spell we had when I was with you in glorious Devon. My word Sylvia that summer I spent with you was the best I've ever had in my life. Still I do hope you and I are going to have lots more in the future. And as soon as this damn war is over dearest, the future will become most important to us – I wonder if you'll like to live in London?!
Well, darling as you see I must finish now but I'll write as often as possible.
Cheerio my darling
All my love,
Maurice
xxx

Sylvia wasn't sure about a life in London, because she wrote another letter to me asking, 'How would you like to live down here in Devon and become a farmer's boy?' When I read those lines, I almost felt engaged to Sylvia already. I hadn't proposed and she hadn't accepted; but from the moment she suggested I settle down in Devon as a farmer's boy, it felt like we belonged together and we were going to spend our lives together. Not that I did want to settle down in Devon as a farmer's boy; but any way to be with Sylvia was worth considering.

Sept. 13th 1942
STALAG VIIIB

My Darling Sylvia. At last I'm able to write & tell you that last week I received two very welcome from you & they had only taken three weeks to reach me. Unfortunately my outgoing letters are being restricted now as also are the incoming ones. Still Sylvia if you don't hear from me for long periods please don't worry at all about me. I always am thinking about you & I know you think of me too. I've spent the whole of this summer in this prison camp but in spite of that I've been able to appreciate the glorious weather we've been having here. Just like that lovely spell we had when I was with you in glorious Devon. My word Sylvia that summer I spent with you was the best I've ever had in my life. Still I do hope that you & I are going to have lots more in the future. And as soon as this darn war is over dearest, the future will become most important to us — I wonder if you'll like to live in London?! Well, darling as you see I must finish now but I'll write as often as possible

Cheerio my darling
all my love
Maurice
x x x

The problem was that I couldn't be with Sylvia, because I was locked up in Lamsdorf. She was free; she was only eighteen years old, a pretty girl who loved nothing more than to go out dancing. What could I realistically expect of her? No prisoner of war could be totally sure that his sweetheart would wait forever. And I voiced my insecurities to Sylvia in a letter on 11 October 1942.

> … Of course dear it's my heartiest prayer that you'll never tire of waiting for me, but of course should anyone else come along then I'd always wish you the best. But I don't want that to happen. I need you so badly, Sylvia. I'm sure it won't be long before I'll be with you again …

If only I'd been right.

Though she never stopped supporting me, to an extent Sylvia felt she had to live in the here-and-now. I could hardly blame her really. All these decades later, she can explain her attitude in her own words.

> I probably wrote to Maurice about once a week. I wrote when I felt like it and when I wasn't out dancing. You didn't expect me to stay at home, did you? When you're young you can't sit at home and mope, can you? I wanted to enjoy myself. He used to go out with other girls before he was shot down; and in the same way there were a couple of different blokes who were interested in me, too. Like I said before, you go to the village hall, you have a dance and you say 'shall we meet tomorrow?' It was nothing serious, but I didn't tell Maurice about any of this when I wrote to him in the camp. I didn't feel the need, because I knew deep down that if he did manage to get home it was going to be Maurice all the way in the end. That was the way I waited for him, that was the way I knew I could be there for him. My heart never belonged to anyone else and the longer he was away, the deeper my feelings became for him.

Getting home consumed my thoughts every day. Until I had the answer, the situation would continue to tear me apart.

10

LIFE AND DEATH IN STALAG VIIIB

To fight the frustration of captivity, any sort of resistance to the Germans was satisfying. Perhaps in those naïve days we didn't fully realise how potentially deadly the games we were playing might have been, if they had turned sour.

You couldn't stay cooped up forever and my attitude was this: if there were reasons to risk a little bit of excitement, particularly at night, I was up for it. A couple of times at night I went out through the window of the barracks. If you remember, the camp was like a huge circle around the parade ground. The army and their huts were on the far side, the RAF and the Canadians were on the near side. In between were masses and masses of barbed wire. Beyond that wire and nearer the army barracks were some allotments, where the Germans used to grow their food.

I decided one night to go out and raid their allotment, along with two friends of mine – 'Mac' William and Dougie Fletcher. Between us we carried a thing called a Kaubel, which was like a big pot with a top and handles. We had to climb through our own compound's barbed wire first and get out of there. Then we had to go across the main centre of the camp, where there was a lot more barbed wire. We'd never have been able to do that if it wasn't for the teams who worked constantly on the barbed wire to keep a secret way open. They cut doors in this mass of barbed wire and remembered exactly where they were, maintaining the opening at every opportunity. You could pull the gates in the barbed wire open, but then you had to remember to close the door to leave the barbed wire exactly where it had been before. That way the Germans never got suspicious.

That wasn't the end of the challenge. All the time at night the searchlights were going round, probing for any trouble. If they shone in your direction, you had to stand perfectly still, whatever you were doing. Otherwise the shadow cast behind you – which was enormous sometimes – would move and they would see that. You might have thought they'd spot the big shadow of a human being anyway, but it wasn't like that. All kinds of things could cast a shadow like a person. The guards in the tower, with their machine guns at the ready, only knew a shadow was really a person if it moved. As long as there was no movement, the guards didn't suspect anything was untoward, and raised no. So we had to stand absolutely still; your life might depend on it, though to young men it just felt like a fun game. In fact, we did get the giggles, and then we became desperate not to let our sniggers create any noticeable movement in our bodies, which wasn't always easy. Finally the clueless searchlight passed.

We got away with it and reached the allotment, where they were growing cabbages, very nice cabbages too. We pulled them out by their tops and dropped our prizes into the Kaubel. After that we went after some carrots, and then some tomatoes, and on it went like that. Sometimes you couldn't even see what you were lifting out of the ground; you just pulled it up and dropped it into the Kaubel. We took it back to the barracks as quietly as we could, where some of the lads had stoves lit and waiting. They were fired by some of the wood we'd taken from the beds. In the end it got so we couldn't take much more wood from the beds, otherwise the bunks would have collapsed!

The Germans didn't know about our homemade stoves, which was handy. These improvised stoves were called 'blowers'. They had a handle to turn on the outside which you wound as fast as you could to work a fan inside them which put oxygen through the fire you'd lit. We shoved everything we'd nabbed with the Kaubel straight into the cooking pot with some water, and put it on the stove. We chucked in anything left over from Red Cross parcels that we thought might add to the taste too. Fan, fire, bowl; three simple components to help make a treat. In no time at all our ingredients would be heated. And by about midnight we'd have a tasty soup to enjoy, with each man filling his own 'Dixie' – tin pot – to share in the little feast.

Great nights, those! The soup tasted all the better because we knew we'd got away with it and got back at the Germans in the process. Of course, if we'd been caught red-handed, then what we'd done would have been regarded as a serious crime. We'd definitely have been thrown in the punishment cells for a good few months at the very least. Would we have been shot for repeat offending? Possibly.

I dare say that the Germans soon discovered that some of their vegetables were missing. But the beauty of it was that the British Army had been detailed to look after the German allotments. So if there were any punishments dished out, it was the army that copped them – something which pleased us RAF blokes no end! With no possible proof of the true culprit, the Germans wouldn't have gone overboard with their punishments. We knew we weren't sentencing British Army men to execution, but we might have caused them a few problems for a while.

The letters from Sylvia kept coming. She'd been pulling out vegetables too – but from what she told me in those letters, her work sounded a lot harder than mine. By now she was working for the Land Army on what had been a bulb farm before the war. The government hadn't wanted to bankrupt a good business, so they let the farm continue to use a few fields for their flowers. All the rest were converted to vegetables, and that's where the Land Army's efforts were usually concentrated.

Sylvia did her best to make me feel part of her daily existence. She recalls:

I sent Maurice letters telling him about daily life in the Land Army, what I was doing. We were out in the fields, digging potatoes, that sort of thing. We were pulling cabbages and dealing with all kinds of veggies. We used to have to handle the cauliflowers in winter, and they'd be so cold they made our hands numb. We'd take them off to market too, we'd always be busy.

The contribution of young women such as Sylvia to making sure Britain's population had enough to eat shouldn't be underestimated. It was back-breaking work but there was a terrific team spirit among the girls who mostly made up the Land Army. I enjoyed hearing about what Sylvia and her friends had done each week, but what I wanted to receive from Sylvia most of all was a photograph. She worried I might not even recognise her, because we hadn't seen each other for eighteen months. She was sure her appearance must have changed a lot in that time. On 21 November 1942 I wrote to reassure her on all counts:

My Darling Sylvia,
You know I'm always thinking of you and even talking of you and longing for the time when you'll be mine for ever. By the way Sylvia, don't forget to send me some snaps of yourself. I want some of you more than anything else. I'm sure you couldn't have altered much since I saw you last, and even if you have I'm certain you must be looking nicer than ever. Sometimes I get rather low in spirits here but as soon as I think of the future we're going to have together I buck up considerably. I'll take the opportunity now of wishing you a very happy Xmas dear and if I'm too late for that I'll wish you an even happier New Year. Goodbye for now sweetheart and God bless you.
All my fondest love,
Maurice xxx.

Though I tried to sound upbeat, the harsh reality of winter in Eastern Europe was starting to bite. A week later I wrote to Sylvia, 'It's very cold here now and I believe it's going to be colder still.' That decision to grab a top bunk the previous spring had proved to have been a very wise move. The top bunks were warmer, and any little improvement was welcome. Although we were given a woollen blanket to help us survive, that biting wind kept coming through the shutters and reached every part of the barracks. We cursed the Germans for removing the glass in the windows. But some clever blokes had put little homemade emersion heaters up in the ceiling, hooking them up to the light bulbs by a wire to feed off that electricity. The Germans never noticed them up there, because the beds were piled so high and so close to the ceiling that they probably didn't even have a clear view of what was up there. Those little heaters undoubtedly helped us to survive. The Germans had never provided us with any heating at all. How they thought we were supposed to survive in temperatures way below zero, I don't know. Perhaps they hoped we wouldn't.

At least I found the clogs I'd been given were warm, cozy and surprisingly practical. I found I could run and even play football in them eventually. The stoves were a godsend too. The colder it became, the more we appreciated them. You could make anything on them – even porridge if you had the ingredients. This secret supply of hot water meant you could drink coffee and tea to warm yourself up, if you could make something taste like either.

Christmas was coming and I wrote to Sylvia on 20 December.

I knew the letter wouldn't arrive until the following year, but I wanted to put my thoughts down on paper anyway.

> … I do hope everything in dear old Braunton is going along smoothly. Christmas is only a few days off now and we're going to make the best of it in spite of our surroundings. But I'm confident Sylvia that by this time next year I'll be back with you, making our plans for our Christmas together.

I had to think positively. It was the only way to survive, because Christmas can sometimes make you reflect on who you've lost and who you're missing most.

In that same letter, I added:

> I'll remind you that I'm ever so anxious to have some snaps of you here, so do please send some off in case you haven't already done so.
>
> Incidentally, I don't think I've told you before but poor Stan (do you remember him?) was killed when we were shot down in the sea. I was terribly sorry to lose him like that …

You couldn't let depression set in; you had to keep going where you were. The simplest of things made a Christmas in captivity more bearable. A British bloke with fair hair came round with a choir. He'd organised it in another barracks and they must have been practicing for the big day, because they were good. That

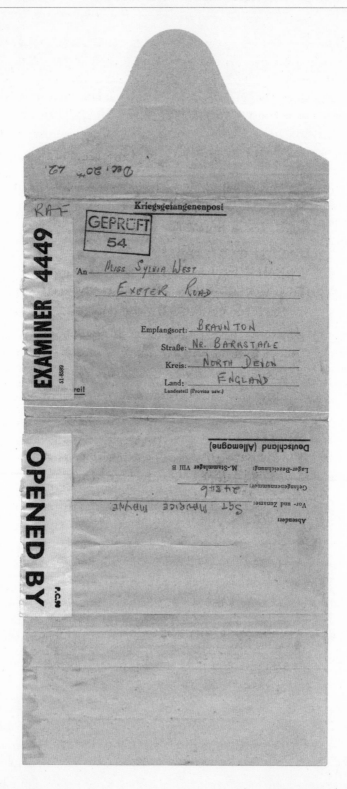

Dez. 20." 42.

RAF

EXAMINER 4449

51-8589

OPENED BY P.C.90

Kriegsgefangenenpost

GEPRÜFT
54

An Miss Sylvia West

Exeter Road

Empfangsort: Braunton

Straße: Nr. Barnstaple

Kreis: North Devon

Land: England

Landesteil (Provinz usw.)

reil

Deutschland (Allemagne)

Lager-Bezeichnung: M.-Stammlager VIII B

Gefangenennummer:

Vor- und Zuname: Sgt Maurice Mayne 24506

Absender:

20th Dec. 1942

My Darling Sylvia. I do hope by now dear that you have received at least some of my letters & cards to you. My mail as you most probably know is limited but I have been writing to you about twice in every three weeks. How are things with you Sylvia? I do hope everything in dear old Braunton is going along smoothly. Christmas is only a few days off now & we're going to make the best of it inspite of our surround- -ings. But I'm confident Sylvia that by this time next year I'll be back with you making our plans for our Christmas together. Once again dearest, I'll remind you that I'm ever so anxious to have some snaps of you here, so please do send some off in case you haven't already done so. Incidentally, I don't think I've told you before but poor Stan (do you remember him?) was killed when we were shot down in the sea. I was terribly sorry to lose him like that. Although I've been away from you for such a long time Sylvia it doesn't make a bit of difference in my love for you. I do hope you find it the same. No matter how long I'm here I shall always love you dearly & you will always be in my thoughts. Look after yourself dear. Remember me to all at home
All my fondest love to you
Maurice
x x x

choir stood at the entrance to our barracks and sang carols for us. It was a nice touch and reminded us of our humanity.

What I didn't know was that Sylvia had sent me a Christmas parcel. I never did receive it, because we weren't allowed parcels, except from next of kin. I'd forgotten to warn her about that rule – and I could only apologise when I found out what had happened. The Germans did let me have her Christmas card. In February. Bloody Germans. Bloody war.

I heard that some of the blokes were having money sent to their loved ones as part of the back-pay the Air Ministry owed us. It sounded almost unbelievable, the notion that we could shower people with money back home, while we were trapped behind barbed wire in Germany. But it turned out to be true!

How did I get the money? I used the International Red Cross mail, which was marvellous. I wrote to the Accounts Department at the Air Ministry. You might have thought it was impossible to do that, while you were a prisoner of the enemy, but I did. I told them I wanted them to send some of my pay to loved ones. The Air Ministry being the Air Ministry, they wrote back to me in the POW camp, sending me the appropriate form to fill in. I did so, and the Air Ministry took care of the rest through RAF Pay Command, sending the money I'd authorised to my parents and Sylvia. That was at the beginning of 1943.

Sylvia remembers how taken aback she was:

A cheque suddenly arrived for £20. That was quite a lot of money in those days. There was no accompanying letter from Maurice. The Air Ministry just said, 'From Maurice Mayne.' I wanted to buy something lasting with the money that would remind me of him when I looked at it, so I went out and got myself a gold watch. I've still got it, even if it doesn't work any more!

Hubert Brooks escaped from the camp in early 1943. My mealtime companion was there one moment and gone the next. Now I knew who had been ahead in that Escape Committee queue! I have no idea why he was fast-tracked and I wasn't. Perhaps they thought he had more chance of being successful. Maybe he told the Escape Committee what he was planning on doing once he got beyond the wire. It involved going back to war almost immediately – and the war always took priority. But how did he get out?

It turned out 'Brooksy' had swapped identities with a New Zealander called Fred Cole. We never saw Brooksy again, so we assumed he had made it! In a way he had, though he had no intention of heading for home and safety just yet. I learned later he had very quickly made contact with the Polish underground instead; he fought shoulder to shoulder with them, even became the equivalent of a colonel, and helped to kill hundreds of Germans as part of the Polish Resistance. It would have been inspirational to some of the lads if they'd known. But I didn't need any inspiration like that and I wasn't desperate to fight in any resistance unit either. I just wanted to get home. Any escape route I could find, I'd take it.

In the meantime, trivial events in the camp took on a huge importance. The Germans decided to allow a football match between English and Scottish prisoners to be played. It was billed as 'England v Scotland', as though it were a full international. Unfortunately the Scots won 1-0, a result which we English vowed to avenge sooner or later. There was plenty of ribbing from the Scots about that victory. They wanted to get maximum enjoyment out of it, so they never tired of reminding us. At moments like that you could almost forget where you were, if only for a few hours. But the camp had a dreadful way of reminding you where you were, just when things seemed more bearable.

By 1943, we were sometimes allowed to walk around between the barracks, free and easy. It was a new privilege; it hadn't happened the previous year, when we were only allowed to exercise in our own compound. I was walking around like this one day, milling with the crowds of RAF, army and navy lads, all taking the chance to have a chat to each other. As we took our exercise and enjoyed some rare, wider social interaction, something dreadful happened. Suddenly a little piggy-eyed German pushed past me, a short chap. In true rifleman style he went down on his knee, which looked ominous and very dangerous with all these British servicemen in front of him. I was only about 10 feet behind him and I didn't hear him call out any sort of warning. There was no 'Halt,' no '*Hande hoch*,' nothing. He pointed his rifle swiftly at his target, fired one shot and hit this British bloke in the back. The poor man fell like a stone, seemingly killed instantly. He never moved or uttered a sound again.

I didn't have time to bump into the German to spoil his aim. If I had, someone else could have been killed, someone who hadn't done anything at all. It all happened so quickly.

This German was a very sharp-eyed soldier and he had clearly been given specific orders: look for a certain, wanted man and if he found him, shoot to kill. Shoot on sight, even if the target was moving among the crowds. We never knew why this was deemed necessary. The Germans were generally fine if you stuck to the rules, but they could be savage if you stepped out of line.

They might have been looking for this British man for some time. In VIIIB there were lots of blokes who tried to hide away after committing what the Germans perceived as a crime against them, either in the camp itself or in the town. When these hunted men knew the search for them was at its most intense, they would hide in little underground holes. There were all sorts of tunnels and caves because the camp had been there for ages. It had been a POW camp during the First World War, so who knows what little hiding places had been left behind from those years? Then of course our army boys had been there for a long time during this war too. Let's just say the lads weren't short of places to hide wanted men.

If the Germans captured such 'outlaws', they were put in a special compound after they were found guilty – and they nearly always were found guilty, whatever the circumstances. These compounds were packed tight with Allied servicemen who had fallen foul of the German law.

But the bloke they'd just killed obviously hadn't wanted to give himself up easily. You might think that he must have murdered a German or raped one of their women to deserve instant execution like that. But he may have done nothing worse than hitting a German officer, or found a way to go out with one of their women. Who knows, this poor prisoner might even have done nothing worse than steal a loaf of bread. I never did find out what he'd done, but German justice in this case was instant and final. Unfortunately, he'd either been flushed out of his hole, or he'd decided to come out and make use of the unusual crowds to move unnoticed into a safer place. Who knows, the Germans might even have allowed us all to mill around together that day precisely because they knew the wanted man would see it as an opportunity. All the guards must have been ordered to keep an eye out for him. Sadly the man who spotted him first, this piggy-eyed German, was a great shot. Not that he looked pleased with himself for bringing his man down so ruthlessly. In fact, after he had administered that brutal justice, he suddenly looked frightened. He realised where he was – in the middle of a big crowd of British blokes – and he had just killed one of us. He could easily have been overrun, and he knew it, so he got out of there quickly, before shock could turn to anger among the lads.

The British prisoners wrenched a door off one of the huts and carried this poor man away for medical attention in the sick barracks. It was pointless though because he was obviously dead. He'd probably been dead even before he hit the ground.

It shook us a bit, that terrible killing. I also realised that the Germans at our camp were just as good shots as the Germans who had shot us down on 1 April 1942. As a gunner, I couldn't help admiring the marksmanship, because he had fired from quite a distance. If he hadn't been such a good shot he could easily have hit one of the other lads milling about, because there was a hell of a lot of blokes walking around that day. It was still a terrible tragedy, but you couldn't afford to be soft. Not when a young German guard could come in, shatter the illusion of peace and take a life with one second of pressure on a trigger. I wonder what he thought of himself later. He was probably given some kind of commendation for his handiwork, though he might not have felt totally comfortable receiving it.

Some Germans enjoyed their brutal work more than others. One man who looked particularly pleased that he had been handed a role as a paid bully was Unteroffizier Kussel. This guard was nicknamed 'Ukraine Joe' by the Canadians, to reflect his country of origin. Kussel was a big brute, and he'd taken to the Nazi way of life like a duck to water. Tex Hyde took a big risk one day by taking a photo of Kussel through a hole in his battle-dress jacket. The Unteroffizier didn't spot the camera or hear the click and the photograph came out beautifully. Who knows, perhaps it was used against Kussel when the time came later to identify some of the worst of the German guards who'd worked in the camp.

Personally I hadn't thought Kussel was all that bad at first. He usually had a big smile on his face and I didn't initially interpret that smile as sadistic. But then I saw him at work some mornings, getting the prisoners out of bed. When it was freezing cold, you didn't want to get up as suddenly and as quickly as Ukraine Joe demanded. Kussel would march in and bark 'Raus, raus!' ('Out, out!'). If you weren't quick enough to obey him, he would hit you on the back of the shoulder with the butt of his revolver. One prisoner called Jake just didn't seem to have it in him to get up quickly. He took some fearful beatings from Ukraine Joe, who singled him out and victimised him just as all bullies love to do.

Correspondence from home was a welcome distraction from the brutality of the camp. On 20 February 1943 I wrote:

> I've been thinking a lot about our future lately Sylvia and the first thing that comes into my mind is the fact that I'd love you to meet me with my people at the station when I do finally arrive home. I'll write home to mum and dad and they can fix it with you for when that glorious day does come …

I gave Sylvia my parents' address. Poor Sylvia, how she could have done with that address the previous summer, when she'd been trying so hard to find out what had happened to me.

11

THE PROPOSAL

As the first anniversary of my captivity approached, Sylvia went to considerable lengths to make one of my biggest wishes come true. She recalls:

> I didn't have photos of myself just lying around, so I went to a studio so that a professional photographer could do some photos especially for Maurice. I wanted him to have a nice picture of me, so that he could remember me clearly and come back to me when he could.
>
> It cost a fair amount of my wages to do it, but I must have been able to afford it anyway. We used to get about 48 shillings a week. Our bosses said we ought to pay our parents at least one pound from that – 20 shillings. So I was left with the 28 shillings per month and the photos came out of that.

The pictures were stamped on the back by the Proctor – the Germans censored everything – but they left her beautiful face unblemished. I placed the best photograph in a frame I'd already prepared for it.

Sylvia wanted me to send her a photo too, which made me chuckle at the time. The only photo I'd had taken at that stage was by the Escape Committee – and I couldn't send her that one. Perhaps 'Tex Hyde' could take another secret picture if I asked him. In the mean time I wrote back gratefully:

> My Dearest Sylvia,
> Today I feel terribly happy and elated because I've just received a lovely letter from you enclosing two charming snaps. Oh Sylvia I'm so pleased to have them and so pleased to see that you are looking as fresh and as lovely as ever. Actually this letter should have gone home, for you know my mail is limited but I couldn't resist writing you again this week. So perhaps dear if you are writing to mum and dad (44 Mundania Road, E. Dulwich, London SE22 is the address) you would mention that this week I have received my third next-of-kin parcel

from them. I'm ever so proud Sylvia to hear of you working in the Land Army and we lads here think that you are doing the hardest work of the lot … Every day I'm with you in my dreams Sylvia, and each day cannot pass quickly enough for me for I'm longing so much to see you again. Be patient honey and soon I'll be with you forever. Cheerio for now sweetheart.

For you here's all my fondest love and kisses, yours always, Maurice xxxx

The thrill of having those photos with me on my top bunk never went away. Later I wrote to her again and said, '… Every time I glance up at your pretty face smiling at me from the frame, I wink at you dear and promise you a really happy and wonderful future …'

It was all very well talking about the future, but in the first week of May 1943, I tried to make something clear to Sylvia. It was something that had remained unspoken between us, yet understood for some time.

> … Of course Sylvia I'm taking it for granted that as soon as possible after I've arrived home, you and I will get married. How does that sound to you dearest? And if you feel optimistic about my being home soon, then I think Sylvia that you might start making a mental note of the things you and I will need for our home. I'm anxiously awaiting that day Sylvia, for I'm so terribly in love with you …

I'll never forget Sylvia's reply, because she wrote, 'If I'm going to marry you, I'd better know how old you are!' Sylvia had told her dad that she'd received what amounted to an official proposal from me.

He'd asked, 'Well how old is he then?' To her temporary embarrassment, Sylvia had been forced to admit that she didn't know how old I was because she'd never bothered to ask me. It had never seemed important, but of course it was an issue for the parents of a woman still so young.

So Sylvia asked me now, by letter, and on 7 August I replied with the following basic information for my new fiancée, grinning as I wrote, and hoping that the truth about my advanced years wasn't too shocking for the inhabitants of Sylvia's house on Exeter Road!

> … you asked me how old I was, for you weren't quite sure, so here it is. I am 22 now and will be 23 on the 26th December next. And now dear you'd better correct me if I'm wrong but I have the idea that you are nineteen now and will be twenty on the fourth of January next …

I hoped that would satisfy all concerned! But the fact that she hadn't known this basic information about me was a reminder of how little time we'd spent together

9th May 1943.

Dearest Sylvia, During the last week I have received another letter from you with the four charming photographs of yourself enclosed. Thanks a lot dear, they really mean a lot to me. To my great joy you are still looking as lovely as ever and only increases my anxiety to see you. Have you heard from Mum & Dad yet? I hope so because I've already written to them & asked them to write to you. Of course Sylvia I'm taking it for granted that as soon as possible after I've arrived home, you and I will get married. How does that sound to you dearest? And if you feel optimistic about my being home soon, then I think Sylvia that you might start making a mental note of the things you & I will need for our home. I'm anxiously awaiting that day Sylvia, for I'm so terribly in love with you. My people will give you any news that I might miss giving to you, so do keep up a correspondence with them won't you sweetheart. Give my love to all at home, to Betty & of course to Nan. Take care of yourself dearest. Heres all my fondest love,
Yours always
Maurice
xx

'A proposal of sorts!'

in the first place. If she didn't know how old I was, did she still remember clearly what I looked like? Fortunately I was now in a position to do something about that. That summer the Germans had surprised us by allowing us to have a group photograph taken, all of us looking as smart as possible in our uniforms, so that we could send copies back home.

It felt amazing to be doing this photography out in the open, with the official camp camera, instead of in secrecy with stolen equipment. Though I say it myself, I looked quite good. I'd been playing as much sport as possible that summer – though never my beloved cricket, because the surfaces weren't suitable. Sport and sun had helped our outward appearances, and of course the Germans wanted everyone back home to think they were so kind and hospitable that we were actually having fun in their 'hotel'.

We didn't have beaming smiles in the snap, we didn't want to give the impression we were in a holiday camp. We wanted people to remain concerned for us, while knowing we were still in reasonable shape.

I sent Sylvia a copy of the photo and pointed out which one I was, just in case she really had forgotten.

> … If you should have any difficulty in picking me out, I'm second from the right in the second row. How are things with you my dearest? I do hope you are still fit and well and still waiting patiently …

I wanted to buy Sylvia the kind of present a man usually buys his fiancée. So in that August of 1943, I asked the Air Ministry to send some more money to Sylvia. Then I wrote to her:

> … Through the Air Ministry I have remitted a few pounds to you dear, so that you can buy yourself a dress ring or anything else you require … I'm quite fit at the moment but just dying to see you, Sylvia …

I'm not sure why I used the phrase 'dress ring' instead of 'engagement ring'. I had the latter in mind, but perhaps I didn't want to scare her too much or make her feel that I was trying to make her my property. The problem was, that letter took many, many months to arrive.

It was so frustrating to be trapped where I was. Like most people, I tried to stay as cheerful as I could, in spite of it all. The better you adapted to your environment, the more chance you had to keep smiling. Everyone picked up some German, and the ordinary British Tommy wasn't averse to using some slang phrase he'd learned to communicate with a fellow Brit.

If you wanted to know the time, you might call out, '*Wie spat?*' – which, translated literally, means 'how late?'

Others would jokingly echo the question by yelling 'Fish paste!' – which sounded very similar to '*Wie spat.*'

Little things like that, touches of humour, helped pass the time and keep your spirits up. But we all knew we were papering over the cracks. And frustration was bound to boil over every so often.

Like many people, I had a fight or two in the camp. One time we were sitting around drinking this horrible blue mint tea, which could actually turn pink in the cup, when we started talking about the Greeks. There was trouble in Greece. They'd been invaded by the Italians and then the Germans but they were putting up a good fight by early 1943, a very good fight. They'd taken back some towns in the mountainous areas in the middle of their country. I'd heard about it and I was impressed. But the bloke next to me – whom I'll nickname 'Rainbow' for reasons that will soon become apparent – didn't like my opinion.

'Rainbow' was someone I knew quite well, but he stared at me and said, 'Bloody dirty greasy Greeks!'

I stood my ground. 'Don't say that, they're not that bad.'

Within a few seconds a trivial disagreement had provoked fighting talk. It got so bad that when I next said something he stood up to really have a go at me. In his hand he had a cup of blue tea. I saw this tea was coming towards me, so I whacked his hand and it went all over him. Then I followed up with a right and a left. Bang, bang! Both straight into his face. That was it. Over very quick.

Later in the morning we were doing our usual walk round our part of the camp for a bit of exercise, and I saw him. His face was already blue-black where I'd whacked him and starting to turn all the colours of the rainbow. He looked at me and I laughed and he laughed. Good old Rainbow. He didn't bear a grudge.

Letters could bring comfort when they arrived at the POW camp – but they could also bring sudden misery and despair. Some poor devils didn't get letters. But there were times when even they felt lucky. For letters could be like deadly weapons if they confirmed a man's worst fears. 'Dear John' letters, they were called – and they could do a lot of damage. It was very sad to see how some of the men just went to pieces for a while after they received a 'Dear John'.

One poor chap stays in my mind because he was so upset that he couldn't function. I think he got back to some sort of normality in the end, but it was a real struggle.

How did most cope? In a way you might find surprising. In the corner of our barracks of about a hundred men there were letters displayed, 'Dear Johns' from girls or women who had left their boyfriends or husbands.

'Dear So-and So … Unfortunately something has happened …'

Naturally the letters were very personal. They were meant to be private, but they became very public indeed. You might ask why. As if it wasn't bad enough to be sent a 'Dear John', as if private humiliation and heartbreak wasn't sufficiently terrible, the lads made sure that one man's darkest nightmare became the public property of all of us.

But when you think about it, there was a marvellous solidarity in the sharing of a man's private pain. It was something we did to ensure a man didn't disappear into his own hell without understanding from the rest. As the number of letters increased, it sent out the unmistakable message that victims of a 'Dear John' were not alone, that many women had let their men down in this way. It was a way of getting back at the girls. 'Look what that old bag has said!'

It could happen to any of us – and we all knew it. However confident a man was in the stability of his relationship, it only took one horrendous letter to destroy the life you had known or hoped to build back home. Having said all that, I never thought that Sylvia would send me a 'Dear John' letter. Perhaps it was the sheer quality of the short time we'd been able to enjoy in each other's company. She knew we'd had something special and she believed, as I did, that it could be like that again.

In the meantime though, we were in different worlds, and we just had to live with it. I'm not going to pretend that was always easy to handle. The late summer of 1943 was tough for me emotionally. I admitted to Sylvia on 28 August, 'I'm missing you an awful lot dear, sometimes this long wait almost gets me down, but I'm always praying that it will be over soon.'

I clung onto the idea of marrying Sylvia. On 18 September I wrote, '… I don't know how you feel about it Sylvia, but if you still love me when I return I'd like to get married as soon as possible …'

But Sylvia was out having fun, dancing … with other men! A week later, after I'd received another of her letters, I decided to reply carefully but honestly:

> … I was so glad to see you almost won a waltz competition, but strangely enough felt very jealous of your lucky partner. Silly of me, I suppose. Oh, perhaps it won't be long now darling before you and I will be going to all the dances together. Have you my photo yet Sylvia?

There was a wartime song called 'Who's Taking You Home Tonight?' and it kept going through my mind, almost tormenting me. The lyrics went something like this:

> Who's taking you home tonight, after the dance is through?
> Who's going to hold you tight, and whisper, 'I love you, I do'?
> Who's the lucky boy that's going your way,
> To kiss you goodnight at your doorway,
> Who's taking you home tonight?
> Darling it's plain to see,
> I'm pleading, please, let it be me …

But it couldn't be me, so I might as well have changed the final lines to, 'Darling, it's plain to see … it's not me, it's not me …'

I craved intimacy and privacy for Sylvia and me to reaffirm the bond we'd had. But I didn't even have privacy for myself. I've already told you about the 'Forty Holers'. Let me give you another example. I was picked to play football for the RAF against the army. It was regarded as a big deal but I didn't have any football shorts. Until then I'd played in casual trousers – 'slacks' we called them. Someone told me that a bloke in another barracks had a spare pair of shorts. I sought this chap out and asked him if I could borrow them. He said I could, then gave me the grubbiest, dirtiest old pair of shorts I think I'd ever seen. Still, beggars can't be choosers, so I put the shorts on and played soccer.

The very next morning, I had terrible itching down in a certain area. The chap in the bed next to me was a dentist, which gave him a basic medical knowledge of matters other than teeth.

He said, 'What's the matter with you?'

I said, 'Oh, I've got this terrible itching!'

He said, 'Alright, let's have a look.' Then a few seconds later he said, 'Oh, dear.'

That's when he turned to the rest of the barracks and shouted back up to a hundred blokes in there with us.

'MOGGY MAYNE'S GOT CRABS!'

It was so embarrassing. I was off to the camp doctor after that – a German – and he cured me of my embarrassing problem in no time.

* * *

Friendship is a beautiful thing. I had good friends writing to me from back home and one of them was Sid Knight, the RAF man who had gone LMF when I was shot down. He had been supportive to my parents when time allowed and I appreciated that. They had supported him too, since it was tough to live with the stigma of being in the RAF when you'd refused to fly any more. Sid had wanted to join the code-breakers, so that he could continue to contribute to the war effort, but he'd been turned down. If he couldn't be useful he wanted to be allowed to return to his old job in civvy street instead. He was still fighting an uphill battle.

On 21 July 1943, Sid had written to my parents:

Well since I saw you last I have had some leave and spent it very quietly in Wiltshire, as I'm afraid I am feeling very fed up with life in the RAF since I had to leave the Squadron, and most certainly since Maurice has been away. So all I am hoping now is that the firm are successful in obtaining my release for me …

I have written to Maurice and will be writing again during the next week. I hope you are still hearing from him regularly.

Well what do you think of the position of the war at present? Things certainly seem to be moving faster these days don't they? But still not as fast as I would like to see them moving …

Please forgive me for writing such a dull letter but that is how I have felt since I was turned down on the Code and Cypher Course …

To be branded LMF was never going to be good for a man's career. But what I liked about Sid, apart from the fact that he wrote to me whenever he could, was how sensitive he was to what my family was going through – especially after my younger brother Ken went to war too. Ken had been in the Home Guard but had since joined the Hussars. They eventually joined up with the Inniskillen Dragoon

'My brother Ken in army uniform with camera.'

Guards in the Tank Corps. Sid so desperately wanted the war to end, for all our sakes, and before any harm could come to Ken.

You can feel Sid's compassion in the letter he wrote to my parents later that year, as well as a keen eye for analysis of the wider war:

> ... I'm sorry to hear that Ken has now left you to go into the Army. I can well imagine your feelings, and the comfort he must have been to you both in Maurice's absence, and I sincerely hope he will be back with you again before very long.
>
> The news is still steadily moving, and now with the capture of Sicily I can well foresee Italy giving in, in the very near future, and it will be the most sensible thing they have done since our fall at Dunkirk, although I suppose they still think that they can hold out, but still time will tell ...

Time was something I had in abundance. Almost any development, large or small, was welcome to relieve the boredom. About eighteen months into my time at the camp, a German officer came into our RAF compound and began demanding to see 'Moricky Minor'. It took the lads a while to work it out; but this was the way the Germans pronounced my name – Maurice Mayne.

'He wants Moggy,' someone said, and they had little choice but to lead the man to me.

I wondered what I'd done and what was going to happen to me. Then the officer – who was dressed in this beautiful green German uniform – pulled out an envelope and gave it to me. I opened it in his presence, wondering if there was bad news from home. But in the envelope was camp money – special notes in circulation at Lamsdorf. He explained it was the equivalent of the £30 in Swedish krona that the Germans had taken off me just after they'd shot me down. His duty done, the German duly left.

I could hardly believe it. The camp money was pretty useless in itself because we really had nowhere to spend it. There were no facilities or treats worth spending it on at all. But it did tell you about the German sense of honour, at least among certain elements of the Luftwaffe. It was a strange old war, I thought. One moment a German was shooting dead a fellow Brit right before my eyes; the next moment an officer was seeking me out to make sure the Germans weren't perceived to be 'welching' on their debts.

If you thought about it all too much, it would drive you mad, so I just tried to take each day as it came, while all the time telling myself that I would be free one day to spend my time in the company of the people I chose.

The frustration of captivity was reaching an intolerable level. I'd had that tentative contact with the Escape Committee almost as soon as I'd reached the camp. Now, eighteen months later, I was still no closer to escaping. I knew only too well that the world didn't revolve around me, but when was it going to be my turn? Why the delay, when Brooksy had come in at the same time as me and he was long gone? You knew the Escape Committee would come to you when they were ready, but I was getting impatient – and that's only human nature.

Then I went down with jaundice. Just about everything turned yellow. The only thing that wasn't yellow was my urine, which had turned the colour of darkish beer. An added problem was that I didn't want any food. You might say I was in the right place, because there wasn't much food around. But if people were preparing food of any kind, I just had to get away from them – that's how ill I felt.

The Germans took me down to their little hospital by the main gate and gave me arsenic. They weren't trying to finish me off. Arsenic is best known as a poison but in small quantities it can counter illness and help to make you feel better.

On 12 October I wrote to Sylvia, 'At the moment I'm in hospital dear, but don't worry over me, it's nothing serious.'

Within a week or so, the arsenic had done its destructive work. It put paid to my jaundice, but thankfully not me. I started to feel better, though it would take a month before I was discharged from hospital.

Sylvia didn't know for ages, because a massive delay had built up on my letters home. She still hadn't even received the letter I'd sent her with the photo from back in August! At the same time she was being asked out to dances like any other young, pretty girl; and she was what I wasn't – free.

When I wrote to Sylvia on 23 October 1943, it was hard to hide my anxiety.

Darling Sylvia,
I haven't heard from you for a little while now but am expecting to do so in a day or so. How are things with you dear? I hope everything is OK? Am still in hospital but will be out any day now. Write often dear won't you?

Even when you tell yourself you have nothing to fear, doubts creep in. Even in the most secure of men, the significance of silence can play on the mind, magnifying horribly.

12

MEET THE FAMILY

It's funny how life can change in the space of a week or two – even when you haven't been anywhere or done anything. By 6 November, my spirits had soared, thanks to that wonderful, caring girl who kept supporting me from little old Braunton in Devon. I couldn't wait to thank her.

> My darling Sylvia, this week has been a great one for me. I have received several letters from you this week plus the one enclosing the snap of you and the girls in working dress. My word Sylvia dear, you certainly are looking brown, fit and well!

Sylvia had sent me a group photo of her with thirteen girlfriends from the Land Army. She put an 'x' on her legs and then wrote on the back, 'that's me "x", just in case you didn't recognise me!' Those words were another reminder of just how long it had been since we had actually seen each other.

Sylvia sent me more group photos of herself with all her young Land Army girlfriends. 'Some of the girls. S x' was the simple message on the back of one. Needless to say, the pictures went down a storm in the camp. The boys could look at the other girls and pick out their own favourite – though they had to watch what they said if they were admiring my girl!

By the time Sylvia finally received the photo I'd sent her months earlier, it was almost November. At about the same time she received the money from the Air Ministry, because my request to them, sent in August, had been delayed in the post, too.

Sylvia can tell you what she did with the money. She knew it would please me no end. 'The second time Maurice sent me money I went out and bought a ring. It wasn't exactly an engagement ring, but we were sort of engaged anyway by then.'

This was probably the second key moment in our long-distance courtship. The dazzle of the dances back in Devon were one thing, along with the dashing young men passing through Braunton, but by wearing my ring she was saying that nothing could beat the summer of 1941. And now she had a photograph to help her remember me too, until I could be there in person.

Sylvia swapped opinions with my mother on how I looked, because she knew I'd sent my mum a copy of the same photo. Since Sylvia and I were engaged, she wanted my parents to know what she looked like in her work environment, too. So she sent them a photo of herself, with her Land Army friends.

Exeter. Rd
Braunton
Nov. 19th
/43

Dear Mrs. Mayne,
Was pleased to receive your letter last week. & to know you are all keeping well these strenuous days.
During this past three weeks or so, I have been most fortunate, & received three letters, three cards & also a photograph, the same no doubt as you had. Maurice doesn't look any different to me; perhaps; a little thinner if anything, which I'm sure we dont really mind; as long as he is in the best of health.
I am enclosing a snap for you of some of our girls

Sylvia was also wondering whether it was time to introduce herself in person. I'd been telling her – and my parents – to do this for months, but somehow the get-together had never happened. Now, at last, she was ready.

Dated 19 November, her bold letter went like this:

2/

that we had taken during our
working hours. I expect you
will recognise me in my jumper;
don't you think we look a
happy crowd?

We are hoping at Xmas to
get some leave, so my friend
& I thought of coming to London
to spend a few days, & I should
very much like to come & make
your acquaintance if convenient;

I'm sure Maurice would be
delighted to know that we had
met.

So hoping to hear from
you again soon,

Kind regards to all,

Sylvia.

Dear Mrs Mayne,

Was pleased to receive your letter last week and to know you are keeping well these strenuous days.

During this past three weeks or so, I have been most fortunate, and received three letters, three cards and also a photograph, the same no doubt as you had.

Maurice doesn't look any different to me; perhaps a little thinner if anything, which I'm sure we don't really mind; as long as he is in the best of health.

I am enclosing a snap for you of some of our girls that we had taken during our working hours. I expect you will recognise me in my jumper; don't you think we look a happy crowd?

We are hoping at Xmas to get some leave, so my friend and I thought of coming to London to spend a few days, and I should very much like to come and make your acquaintance if convenient; I'm sure Maurice would be delighted to know that we had met.

So hoping to hear from you again soon.

Kind regards to all,

Sylvia.

My mother wrote straight back to say they looked forward to meeting Sylvia when the time came. Meanwhile my father, veteran of the Somme, was busy winning a battle on my behalf. He was a great one for taking up an issue with the authorities if he believed in the cause. And this was a cause he felt strongly about.

In theory I could have changed camp in 1943 – and given some of the things that were going on, you probably think I was mad not to jump at the chance. But in the end I asked my father to help see to it that I didn't have to change camp. There was a suggestion from the Air Ministry that selected NCOs should be sent to officer-only POW camps and become 'batmen' to the officers. There was even a little extra pay in it for those who succumbed to the pressure to do so.

I was selected to go to an Oflag but I wasn't in favour of doing that at all. To hell with it! Bad enough being a prisoner of war, let alone waiting on some bloody officer hand and foot to make sure his shirt collar was pressed perfectly! So I wrote to my father to explain the situation and I made my feelings clear. I wanted to know what my rights were.

A long conversation followed between my father and the Air Ministry about that. For their part, the Air Ministry suggested the idea might not be a bad thing, because we prisoners might get better treatment if we were batmen to the officers. But my father represented my feelings well, and in the end, on 26 November 1943, he received the following letter on behalf of the Air Ministry's Director of Personal Services:

TELEPHONE:
GERRARD 9234
Extn................

Any communications on the
subject of this letter should
be addressed to :—
THE
UNDER-SECRETARY
OF STATE,
and the following number
quoted :— T.6050/43.P.4.Cas.B.

Your Ref. ....

AIR MINISTRY

(Casualty Branch),

73-77, OXFORD STREET,
W.1

26 November, 1943.

Sir,

      I am directed to refer to your letter
dated 12th October, 1943, and to inform you
that the International Convention for the
treatment of prisoners of war provides that
non-commissioned officers may be compelled
to undertake only supervisory work unless
they expressly request remunerative occupation.

      There is no reason why a non-commissioned
officer should not work as a batman if he is
prepared to do so although he cannot be
compelled to undertake such duties.

      It is hoped that this information will
assist you in replying to your son.

      I am, Sir,
      Your obedient Servant,

      for Director of Personal Services.

G.R. Mayne, Esq.,
  44, Mundania Road,
    East Dulwich,
      London, S.E.22.

'Victory! My dad has won his latest battle.'

Sir,

I am directed to refer to your letter dated 12th of October, 1943, and to inform you that the International Convention for the treatment of prisoners of war provides that non-commissioned officers may be compelled to undertake only supervisory work unless they expressly request remunerative occupation.

There is no reason why a non-commissioned officer should not work as a batman if he is prepared to do so although he cannot be compelled to undertake such duties.

It is hoped that this information will assist you in replying to your son …

Success! 'Cannot be compelled'! I didn't have to go and be a servant to an officer if I didn't want to go! I would have refused to go anyway – and I didn't meet anyone else who wanted to go either – but it was nice to have the blessing of officialdom for my decision to stay where I was for now.

As Christmas approached, I was in high spirits again and tried to convey how I felt to my girl back home. If we stayed strong now, we could have as many happy Christmases together as we wanted.

You have no idea how much I'm looking forward to our wedding day Sylvia. When I come home I shall have plenty of money for you and I to be married straight away and then I shall do everything I possibly can to make you the happiest girl in the world …

Sylvia was going to be in my home for part of the Christmas holidays that very year. I just wasn't going to be there with her. If I'd known about this before Christmas, I'd have found the notion both agonisingly frustrating and positively beautiful at the same time. She wrote to my mother on 12 December to arrange her visit. Fittingly she was going to bring Eileen, the friend she'd been with when I'd met her on the street in Braunton for the very first time.

Dear Mrs Mayne,

Many thanks for your letter of the 25th. Sorry I haven't written before but it wasn't until this weekend we knew when our leave commenced.

My friend and I are both very thrilled to know we are coming to stay with you.

We shall be travelling on the 29th and should arrive at Waterloo station about 2.15 (the train leaves here at 8.35).

Our leave doesn't start until the 24th and as travelling facilities are restricted during the days 23 to 28 we are unable to come sooner, as we should have liked.

I have received a card from Maurice within the last fortnight, but it was a long time coming, just over four months, so I hope to hear again soon.

This isn't a very long letter but I shall be seeing you soon and will tell you all the news then, hope you are well, will close now with kindest regards,
Sylvia.

Knowing none of this, I wrote to Sylvia on Christmas Day and said, 'I am praying that this will be my last Christmas away from you darling.'

As that letter went off on its long journey to Braunton, my parents and fiancée finally met. And it was a great success. Apparently my mother told Sylvia, 'I knew it was serious right away when he came back at Christmas, 1941 and he told me, "Mum, I've met this girl." It was just the way he said it.' Two years later, there she was.

When I heard that Sylvia had stayed with my parents, I felt so happy. It was wonderful to know that my loved ones had got together for the first time. Any boost to morale was helpful after Christmas, as I continued to recover my strength.

Sylvia continued to strengthen her relationship with my parents and she was already like family for them. She wrote to them again on 11 January, enclosing an aerial photograph which included the house where I'd first spotted her, a face looking out of the window. By now American forces were building up their strength in Devon, ready for the day when the Allies would finally invade the European mainland. Braunton was changing, the war was changing.

What hadn't changed were the postal delays from the camp to Britain. It meant that much of the news Sylvia and my parents were digesting was over two months old. Of course, if I'd been ill and got better again this could work to my advantage in terms of minimising worry back home. Sylvia had begun to understand this.

Dear Mr and Mrs Mayne,
Here's a few lines as I promised expect you have received my card by now it just shows part of the main road. I put a cross on our house to give you an idea where we live, it's rather a nice view out over isn't it? I believe it shows a part of Instow and Appledore, two little seaside villages.

Well we are just getting settled down to our quiet life again, it's been raining now for the last few days, so everything is in an awful mess, it's so terribly muddy, with all these American lorries here, not a bit like London.

Yesterday I found the letter from Maurice which I mentioned to you about coming out of the hospital he wrote the same day he was discharged and that was dated Nov 6th so by this time he is, I expect, back to his usual self again.

We have found Braunton very dull since returning from the town life. Saturday we went down the village to do a little shopping but instead of spending an afternoon looking around, inside an hour we had been in nearly every shop. As you see it doesn't take us long to go over our small village.

Haven't had any more news from Maurice; have you heard lately?

This is all the news for the time being; it's much nicer writing to you now that we have met; when I wrote before, I found it rather difficult sometimes; didn't quite know what to write about.

Kindest regards to all,

Love,

Regards from Eileen,

Sylvia.

2.

Tho' rather back aching bending over the rows, wish I could send you some but we are not allowed to have them, we have some wild double daffs growing down our own orchard they are just in bud now but when they come out a bit more I'll send you some, if you would like them.

Some how Eileen & I always have something to say about London during the day usually wishing we were up walking around the shops, last saterday we received our polyfoto's from Holdron's they turned out lovely I've enclosed one for you; I've sent Maurice some about six stuck on

P.T.O

Time was passing, and still I was no nearer to making good the escape I'd mentioned to Douglas Bader. What was going on? There had been recent talk of me escaping with Willie Routledge, the ex-school-master who'd been so good at jotting down the German news that he could do it as quickly as their newscaster could speak. We'd been thrown together at meal times and he'd mentioned that he was keen, but I didn't share his enthusiasm for a double act. I liked Routledge and I was friendly with him. We'd even had our photo taken together by Tex Hyde and his secret camera at one stage, a picture which survives to this day. But Hyde and I were so different that the idea of escaping together didn't really appeal to me. He was too distinctive somehow, too tall, a big strong chap, too obviously British-looking, too noticeable in every way, including his personality.

Eventually I became evasive when the question of escape came up, because I wanted to go on my own. This probably didn't please him too much, and maybe I should have sat him down and told him straight, to avoid any confusion or disappointment. But he took the hint soon enough – and he couldn't really complain. When you're going to risk your life doing something, you have the right to decide how you are going to do it. I didn't really want to rely on anyone but myself. I felt my best chance of slipping through was to go it alone. If I was going to fail, I'd only have myself to blame. So once that was decided, I was back to wondering when it would be my turn.

I was desperate to be active again. The boys in the camp imagined our women, working hard in fields and factories to contribute to the war effort, while we did nothing. It was tough to take, however proud of them we were. Another of Sylvia's letters, dated 31 January, arrived at my parents' house at the start of February 1944, and she detailed some of the work she'd do in the Land Army.

Dear Mr and Mrs Mayne,
Here I am again with a few lines hoping it finds you well; I have just got over a cold; so I'm feeling fine now.

Received a card from Maurice last week saying he is fit and well and hopes to see us soon.

We are quite busy these days at the farm working in the green houses, picking daffodils. They really are beautiful to see just one mass of yellow, not a very nice job picking them tho'. Rather back-aching bending over the rows, wish I could send you some but we are not allowed to have them, we have some wild double daffs growing down our own orchard they are just in bud now but when they come out a bit more I'll send you some, if you would like them.

Somehow Eilieen and I always have something to say about London during the day, usually wishing we were up walking around the shops. Last Saturday we received our polyphotos from Hodgson's they turned out lovely. I've enclosed one for you; I've sent Maurice some about six stuck on a piece of paper. I'm having some enlargements so when they are ready I shall send one to him.

Well for the time being I'll close with kindest regards to all.

Love,

Sylvia

PS Received a letter from Maurice today quite well and fit.

I wanted to try to speak to the Escape Committee again, to find out what was going on. And as far as I was concerned, the human face of the Escape Committee was my Canadian friend, 'Tex' Hyde, and a grim-looking Englishman called Lawrence.

One day Lawrence seemed to sense what I was about to ask him, because he said to me, 'You'd better get yourself ready. It's still up to you, of course, but your time is coming, probably next month. The plans are coming along nicely. We're going to get your new papers ready. But are you ready?'

'Yes of course, sir.'

They had given me a set of 'papers' – which actually consisted of just one sheet – many months earlier. It was an 'Ausweiss' – a travel pass, the most precious document you could get. But now they kept their promise and made a much better set of papers for me. The plan was for me to pose as a Belgian electrician working his way through Germany. Hyde had given me some unpronounceable Flemish name, and gambled on no German official trying to speak Flemish to me. Our understanding was that very few Germans knew Flemish, so the choice was logical. If they suspected I was British, they might well try to call out to me in English to see if I could be tricked into responding, or at least gauge whether or not I had understood. We'd been warned about that when we first joined the RAF, because we were given a short lecture about what to expect if you became a prisoner of war and wanted to escape.

'Beware of tricks,' they'd told us when we'd been training at Chivenor. But I was prepared to bet the Germans didn't have any tricks waiting for me in Flemish. Just in case they smelt something fishy, I was going to take a series of trains towards the North Coast of Germany, as if heading there almost by chance. All the time, of course, my intended destination would be a specific German port called Stralsund. This had been chosen for me by the Escape Committee because it was considered small enough to have remained free of the most stringent security checks on people passing through. Once there, I could take a boat to neutral Sweden.

'Still planning the same route?' he asked.

'Yes, sir.'

'Mind if I come and talk to you a bit later?'

'No, sir, that's fine.'

When he did come to have a private word, he chose to climb up onto my top bunk, just under the ceiling, for our little chat.

'Do you remember where Stralsund is and how to get there?' he asked.

I knew by now, alright. They'd briefed me before, which was just as well, because otherwise I wouldn't have had a clue.

When he produced the new papers, I began to realise how the delay in getting me out of the camp had worked in my favour. This time they'd come up with a really marvellous set of papers, consisting of two or three sheets of really detailed forgeries – superb work. The printing on them was absolutely perfect – genuine German print.

I thought, 'This Ausweiss will fool anyone!' I couldn't fault the work they'd done for me.

He'd said nothing yet about what the escape itself would entail. Then he broke the news: I'd have to swap identities with some army chap, so that I could start to leave the camp regularly as part of a work party. Then I'd have to find a way to slip away entirely, before the whole ruse was discovered. To do the initial identity swap, I'd have to get out of our compound and into the army one to make contact with the other man.

This didn't seem beyond me. I'd been out of our compound in secret several times before, of course, to steal the Germans' vegetables. I hoped that kind of previous experience would help me when the time came. My moment to get out of all this madness had nearly arrived.

For some, who had no such hope and perhaps no loved ones writing to them from home, the madness was inescapable. Some people lost their minds completely, others to lesser degrees. One bloke sought his escape in religion, which you might think was admirable. But the change we saw in this man didn't look healthy at all. He just tuned out, stopped seeking solace in the normal daily contact with people who had been his friends. Instead he started walking about as though he were a priest, looking up at the sky, lost in what he perceived to be some personal dialogue with God. Now, there's 'good-religious' and then there's 'barmy-religious'. This bloke had gone barmy as far as we could tell, though he seemed serene enough in his own little world.

Two other chaps were very, very good friends. As pals they shared everything together – they were practically inseparable. But for some reason or other, they fell out one day and started punching each other. That wasn't so unusual in the camp, but the next thing we knew, one of them was dashing over towards the wire and had begun to climb it. The other one quickly followed, and before we could stop him he was on the wire too. They must have known they wouldn't have time to climb over the top before the Germans got them. They must have realised it was like committing suicide, rushing the wire like that; but some people reached the stage where they'd just had enough. I'll never know if the second man was trying to save the first, or just didn't want him to die alone. But the Germans didn't waste any time at all; they were both shot straight away and died up there on the wire. It was just one of the many sad things that happen in prison camps when people reach breaking point.

I'm convinced that people who were getting letters from home were more likely to survive. I had my darker moments, but the letters kept me sane. Letters had become my comfort, the best part of the world I inhabited, so I'd landed a job in the perfect place. I'd managed to get a job working at the camp post office. You'd sort all the mail out from each bag, while keeping a lookout for anything which might improve your situation. One day I saw a pile of blank letters which the Red Cross had sent for us to use. I snaffled some of them because they'd give me one last chance to send letters to people before I risked my life escaping. Sylvia was first and foremost in my mind and of course she had piles of letters after that, because I wasn't sure when I'd be able to write to her again.

At last it was time to sneak out of our compound and make contact with the soldier whose identity I was going to take. His name was Private Len Murray and he was a New Zealander from Te Kuiti. He'd been captured on Crete, like most of the men in his compound. He wasn't in very good health apparently, so he knew he couldn't escape, even if he wanted to. The next best thing for him was to help someone else to escape. And at the same time he could give himself a rest from having to work for the Germans, along with the rest of the New Zealanders. The break might help him to get better, or at least slow his deterioration.

I had to get across to the New Zealand barracks to meet him and seal the deal. Then I was going to stay with the Kiwis, never to return to the RAF barracks. And he was going to come back in the opposite direction to stay with the British. It was all as simple as that, apparently – the first step to freedom.

I didn't say goodbye to anyone, because the swap, like the escape, was all going to be done quietly. I didn't explain anything to Bill Routledge, who might still have been harbouring hopes of going with me. If he had objected, it could have caused a problem, and I had enough on my plate without having to explain myself to him. It was better if the first time Bill Routledge knew for sure that I'd gone it alone was when he realised I wasn't in the RAF compound any more. Then he'd know not to ask too many questions, but to get on with his own life and make his own plans for escape if he could. (That's exactly how it turned out, because I heard later that Bill did escape, but only got a couple of streets before he was caught by Hitler Youth members. At the risk of sounding unkind, that rather supported my own decision to leave him behind when it was my time to go. Bill and I met up after the war, he came to my parents' home in East Dulwich, and he quite understood my reasons.)

The Escape Committee showed me where the latest gates had been cut in the barbed wire and I began to crawl through, stopping when the searchlights settled unknowingly upon me. After I'd stayed still in the blinding light, it moved on and so did I. Doing this on my own took a lot more nerve than when I'd been with mates hunting for those vegetables. This time it was no laughing matter. My freedom depended on the success of this effort. So I felt jubilant when I got through all the barbed wire and reached the New Zealanders' compound unnoticed by the Germans.

A sergeant from New Zealand was standing at the barracks door, watching me approach with some suspicion.

'Hey Kiwi,' he said, 'Where you goin'?'

'Join the boys, you know?' I said as casually as I could. But he was blocking the way.

'Where d'you come from?' he asked.

I thought I had a good Kiwi accent for a Cockney, so I held my nerve. 'Tikawidi,' I said.

'Tikawidi? Where's that?'

'Just across the bay.'

'Just across the bay where?'

'Wongarui.'

He looked even more suspicious. 'Wongarui?'

'I mean Wongaray.' This wasn't going well.

'What are you? RAF?'

The game was up. 'Yes, RAF,' I admitted.

'OK, go on, your secret's safe with me,' he smiled.

At the very first step, my escape plan had been rumbled. But at least he'd let me go into the barracks and join the boys – and a nice crowd of blokes they were, too. There were actually all sorts in that barracks, not just Kiwis but Canadians too.

I asked to meet Len Murray. But when I saw him, I had a shock. I was expecting him to look like me or at least be the same build. But he was tall – much taller than me. And he looked nothing like me at all, except that we had similar colour hair. Surely that wasn't going to be enough to make this work? How could one man be mistaken for the other? But there was no turning back for me now; and Len Murray was ready to be escorted through the barbed wire in the opposite direction, aided by a guide who knew all the gates and ways through to the other side of the camp.

'I'm looking forward to putting an RAF uniform on,' he said with a smile. He'd always thought we RAF blokes looked smart; but my uniform probably didn't look very smart by the time he got it on. That uniform had been through quite a lot in its time.

My first identity check as Len Murray was approaching, and I felt nervous about what was going to happen. It was also the first time I'd gone out with the New Zealand work party. A young German soldier was looking at each of our bits of photo ID. I looked nothing like Len Murray, but the guard was checking everyone through quite quickly. Would I get away with it? I steeled myself to show no hint of how I was feeling. The German guard glanced at the photo and then at me … and he waved me through, as easily as that.

I walked out of the camp gates for the first time in nearly three years. Unfortunately, because there was no obvious way to break free of the work party, I was going to have to come back through those gates again later that night, and several times beyond that. I was tantalisingly close to freedom, yet even now I had to be patient, or I would ruin everything.

13

A HINT OF FREEDOM

I wrote to my mother in Len Murray's name, telling her that Maurice Mayne might be home at any time. She wrote to the Red Cross to ask what it meant. They told her not to say anything about it, because it looked as though I was going to be on the move – probably all part of an escape. They were very savvy, the Red Cross. They used to get messages in and out using the numbers on food tins sometimes. Anyway my parents had their hopes raised and they wrote to Sylvia to explain that some sort of escape might be on the cards.

From Sylvia's reply on 3 March you get a sense of the anticipation in the air.

Dear Mr and Mrs Mayne,
Well I must say when I received your letter last week I was thrilled to bits; it was exciting news wasn't it?

Up to now I haven't had any more letters from Maurice but as you say I don't suppose we shall hear now for some time. I must thank Mr Mayne for his letter, it was very nice of him to write to me.

Last weekend we had a couple of days off but we didn't go anywhere special, just to the shows and dances that were on.

I don't think it did me any good as it left me with a cold. Yesterday I was home from work also today. Don't suppose I shall go back this week now.

Well we are having some grand weather down here a little windy but quite sunny.

Hear you have had some big raids on London lately, hope you are both OK. Must say I'm glad I wasn't there …

… Cheerio for now,
Love
Sylvia.

Exeter Rd
Braunton
March 3rd

Dear Mrs & Mr Mayne:

Well I must say when I received your letter last week I was thrilled to bits; it was exciting news wasn't it? up to now I haven't had any more letters from Maurice but as you say I don't suppose we shall hear now for some time. I must thank Mr Mayne for his letter it was very nice of him to write to me.

Last week end we had a couple of days off. but we didn't go any-where special just to the shows & dances that were on.

Sylvia recalls:

It was the excitement of knowing that Maurice was going to try to get home to us. It didn't cross my mind that it was going to be very dangerous and he could even get shot trying to reach me. We were just thinking positive, believing he could do it, that he was coming home.

Sylvia didn't expect to hear from me while all these escape plans were being laid – but she did anyway. That's because I'd also written to her as Len Murray. The letter took a few weeks to arrive, as usual. Looking back, Sylvia remembers how intrigued she was.

> There was no explanation about a change of identity. I simply got a letter from 'Len Murray'. I could see it was Maurice's writing and his mother had warned me about 'Len', so I realised that something was going on.

Everyone had to be ready for my escape and the silence that would follow for a while. But if Sylvia stopped writing to me as Maurice in the main camp, some sharp-eyed German's suspicion might yet be aroused. I hinted at this too:

> My darling Sylvia here's another line from me dear and this time you'll find me away from the lager and in a working party. Please carry on writing to Maurice at the main camp, and drop me a line very occasionally. Please, don't worry over me Sylvia dear. I'm in the best of health. Keep writing to mum and dad and they will give you all the latest news. Anyway darling I'm still terribly in love with you and think of you every day and night. Don't ever think I've forgotten you, honey, although it's so long since we've seen each other … There's very little more I can say now, so before I close, I'll send you all my deepest and sincerest love. Remember me to Eileen and all at home.
> Goodnight my sweetheart,
> All my love,
> Len xxx.

We 'New Zealanders' used to march out of the barracks every morning to a peculiar area called Hindenbürghutte. This zone was quite a way from the camp, and it was full of factories. This had all been part of Poland before the war. But the Nazis had just marched in and changed the names hurriedly from Polish to German, without any obvious degree of imagination. They used heroic names of their own to crush the original identity of the area.

The Nazis used this industrial hotbed to make all kinds of things, including armoured trains. We had to work there and I was put on a site digging very deep holes for a pile-driver. I was very good at making it look as though I was very poor at doing something. Even digging in very, very sandy soil was apparently beyond me. As they dug down the hole, they'd put in flat-boards and platforms on the sides – all the way up to the top. The blokes at the bottom would scoop the sand up to the next platform. And the chaps on that platform would throw it up to the next platform. That's the way they got the earth back to the top.

But when they put me on it, things were a bit different. I had a long-handled spade, a pointed spade. I dug soil and pretended to throw it up to the next platform, without ever quite managing to do it. Perhaps I had that innocent sort of face, but 'Jerry' couldn't quite work out why I couldn't get it up there. Instead of going up to the next platform, the earth fell right back down below me, often all the way to the digger at the bottom.

The German boss tried so hard, he even came down and grabbed the shovel in order to try to show me. And the word he used always stayed with me. He said, 'Oopla!' as he propelled the soil up to the next level. 'Oopla!' That should have improved my technique, as far as he was concerned. It didn't cross his mind that I might not want to work with the Germans; that I was just there to find a way to escape and leave their God-forsaken country forever.

I looked at him very seriously, as though I was giving his 'Oopla' catch-phrase full consideration, as if it would help me to get it right at last. And then of course I made a fresh mess of it, just as I'd been doing all along. He just couldn't understand why I couldn't do it, and yet it still didn't seem to cross his mind that I was doing all this on purpose. It was just a little sleight of hand I was using, one that you couldn't really detect or blame, but one that proved decisive in securing my complete failure as a human digger for the Nazi war machine. In the end this man, who had tried so hard on my behalf, decided that even the finest kind of 'Oopla' tuition wasn't enough to transform someone as stupid and uncoordinated as me into a decent worker. Sadly, reluctantly, as though it represented a personal failure on his part, the foreman pulled me out of the dig, and I was ushered away in search of something that even I couldn't be dumb enough to get wrong.

On 5 March 1944, I sent Sylvia another note as Len Murray:

Darling Sylvia,
Another line to keep you informed of my welfare, etc. Don't ever worry over me honey will you? There's no need for it at all. I'm very fit at the moment and am getting fitter every day. Owing to the change of camp my mail to you and yours to me may be delayed. But it will catch up in due course.
All my sincerest love for now dear,
Ever yours,
Len xxx

Stubbornly, the Germans still gave me a digging job. This time it was just a trench to this pile-driving place. And we were given a massive incentive. We were told if we could finish digging our own respective part of the trench by twelve o'clock, we could go home early. The trench didn't have to be very wide, but it had to be about 3 feet deep. Everyone else got to go home early, having successfully completed the digging of their part of the trench. Not me. I was still digging away uselessly, as though a shovel were entirely alien to me. I dug down little more than a few inches, I made a complete fool of myself, but they didn't throw me in the cells. They just decided I was an idiot who couldn't give a good account of himself if he tried.

Despite my best efforts, they did get this pile-driver installed, and some scaffolding went up so they could put the finishing touches to it. I responded by pinching the bolts whenever I could, throwing away any component I could get my hands on, and generally being the best little saboteur I thought I could be. It was a risk, because in theory I could have been thrown off the work party entirely. That would have denied me the freedom to finalise an escape plan, because I wouldn't even have been allowed to leave Stalag VIIIB. But fortunately the Germans never credited me with the intelligence to have been useless or disruptive deliberately. And they must have wondered how I'd ever been selected for combat, given that I couldn't control my own body in any helpful or meaningful way.

To them, I probably didn't seem to have the sense I'd been born with. One time I didn't even have to fake it. Instead of walking on a path, I chose to walk on some soft, springy grass next to the path. It felt nice under foot at first; then it became a bit spongy … and then boggy. My feet were starting to sink quite low in the grass and I wondered why it was so soft. I looked down and saw my boots were a strange kind of orange.

'You dirty man!' a German guard yelled.

Then I realised what I'd done. Right opposite the factory they had huts which were toilets. The toilets were holes. When they were full up, they moved the huts along. What had been left there was like a natural fertiliser, so the grass had grown. I'd really put my foot in it this time – quite literally. They hosed down my boots until all the mess was gone. Nice of them, really. Or perhaps they just didn't like the way I smelt.

I was working with the New Zealanders for more than a month before I found a way to escape. It wasn't me who spotted it. Someone from the New Zealand work party had heard about it; and since they knew I was all geared up to escape and had the right papers hidden away, they took me round the back of some warehouses to have a look. I couldn't believe what I saw. The Germans had piled up some earth – and they'd done it right next to a wall. Some of the free workers must be using it as a short-cut to get out of the complex and get home as quickly as possible. Why couldn't I do the same? Over the wall there must be a street waiting below. I didn't know where that street led to, but I was going to find out. When the time was right, I was going to climb up that mound of earth and drop down over the wall to freedom.

On 19 March 1944, I wrote to Sylvia again. It was my way of telling her that I was going to try to escape very soon.

My Dearest Sylvia,

When letter time comes each week, it brings me very close to you, dear. All the things I've been thinking throughout the week flash through my mind, but I can never get them all down on paper. Anyway sweetheart I spend most of my spare moments thinking of how wonderful you are and the times we are going to have together. As each week passes by, I find I love you more and more, and this period of waiting becomes more unbearable than ever. Please don't ever worry over me darling. If you ever do have cause to worry, just write home and they will put you right. Remember I will always love you Sylvia and no other will ever be able to spoil it. I'm anxious to be home soon, but then of course so is everyone here. Anyway perhaps our prayers will soon be answered. Give my love to all at home and to Eileen. I'll say goodbye for now honey, so here's all my sincerest and most affectionate love,

Yours ever,

Len xxx

In the meantime, in the weeks I was there, I'd managed to contact some Frenchmen and get some more civilian clothing. I also got a similar bit of help from some Ukrainian girls who were working there. They were doing very heavy work too, especially for women. They were working in Hindenbürghutte just like we were – and they seemed to have the toughest job of all. There were great big cranes carrying huge sheets of red-hot metal across this industrial area. (Exactly where the furnaces were, I couldn't quite work out.) It always seemed to us that the Germans driving these massive cranes were almost aiming for us as they swung about these huge pieces of molten steel. They turned from red to black quickly enough; but even when they weren't molten red any more, they were still so hot that if you walked on those sheets of steel, you suddenly stuck to them.

The Ukrainian girls didn't seem to be intimidated by any of this, because when the Germans swung these huge steel rods down towards the ground, the girls were waiting with big tweezer-like tools. They grabbed hold of the rods to guide them on the final part of their downward journey, taking them all the way down to the ground. I got to know these girls a bit by having a chat to them when there was a spare moment. They were so nice to me that they even used to wash my shirts and we became great friends.

One buxom girl in particular, called Praskivia Patlikova, said, '*Du bist mein Cavalier, aber nichts kind*' – 'You're my boyfriend, but no children!' That's what I think she was trying to say in her broken German. But she wasn't my girlfriend;

I didn't fancy her at all. I didn't even flirt with her, but she seemed to have chosen me in her own head.

They were all heftily built, those Ukrainian girls – they had to be to handle their job – big girls in boiler-suits and berets. They were very helpful, though. They got me one or two more bits of civilian clothing, so I'd look the part when it was time to escape. And that moment wasn't very far away now. They found me this rather saucy Tyrolean-style hat, with a feather on the side. They also got me some dye, so I could make some khaki-coloured army trousers go dark blue. They knew I was going to try to escape but they didn't turn me in.

Pretty soon I had everything I needed to make my move. I was going to go over that wall, down into the street below and take it from there. My final note to Sylvia was on 2 April 1944 – almost two years to the day since I'd been shot down. Details of my precise whereabouts were no longer important. It was my coded message to her: I was off.

> My Dearest Sylvia,
> Just another line honey to let you know I'm still alive and kicking. I do hope you are getting my letters OK. Have mum and dad written to you recently and told you I'm on another party now? The number [of the camp] doesn't matter much so I won't bother about it. I'm still loving you with all my heart Sylvia and longing to have you in my arms again.
> All my fondest love dear,
> Len xxxx

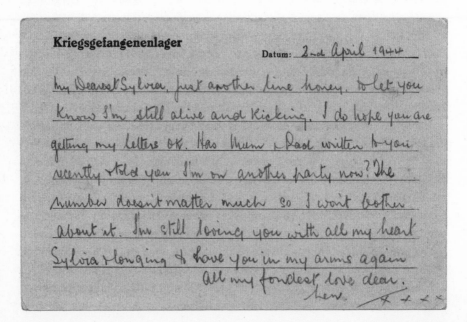

Kriegsgefangenenpost

Postkarte
Geprüft

An

Miss Sylvia West

Gebührenfrei!

Absender:

Vor- und Zuname:

Pte Leonard Murray

Gefangenennummer: _21833_

Lager-Bezeichnung:
M.-Stammlager VIII B

Deutschland (Allemagne)

Empfangsort: *Exeter Road*

Straße: *Braunton*

Land: *North Devon*
Landesteil (Provinz usw.)
England

This was my big bid for lasting freedom.

It was nearly Easter 1944 – and the day before I was due to escape. I had my 'Ausweiss', my identification papers and my money, which the Escape Committee had also given me. It was all tucked away together in my breast pocket. Then, quite suddenly, as we came back from a day's work in Hindenbürghutte, the Germans herded us all into a big area and started to search us. I had my escape papers in my breast pocket and I was thinking, 'What a foolish thing to do, to have them on me when this isn't even the day I'm going to escape.'

'Line up! Two metres apart!' they barked.

There was confusion and a bit of panic as they began searching us. The more they searched us the more they found. In fact, they were turning up some extraordinary things. They searched one bloke and found a spirit level. It was almost as long as he was. Why would anyone want to pinch that? Anyway, the Germans piled all this stolen stuff into a big heap in the middle of us. The pile grew higher with every passing second. And it was only a matter of time before they got to me, to see what I was concealing.

A dapper German officer, beautifully attired in his Gabbadine-style green uniform, had his eye on me for some reason. He came straight over, ready to shatter all my dreams of freedom. Perhaps he could sense I'd been acting a bit agitated, I don't know. A German soldier had seen the officer focusing on me, so he started to frisk me, thinking he would do the work for his superior. But as soon as he touched me, the officer ushered him and the other soldiers away.

Apparently this was a job he wanted to do himself, to show the other soldiers how it should really be done. Had he been tipped off? The elegant officer started searching me and quickly came to my breast pocket. He gently undid it, quite calmly and deliberately, and the first thing he brought out was a piece of paper. It was bound to be incriminating.

'What a fool I've been,' I thought.

He looked me in the eye and demanded, 'What's this?'

I looked more closely at the scrap of paper and the penny dropped.

'Ah, it's the words to Lili Marlene,' I said, trying to hide my relief.

'Why?' he asked. (You could use all kinds of literature to send coded messages.)

'It's a nice song,' I said simply. 'I like it and I've been trying to learn the words.' (This was true.)

He put the piece of paper back in my breast pocket and said, 'Any other German songs or literature you like?'

'Oh yes,' I said. 'As a matter of fact I've just learned a German poem about mermaids in the Rhine, and I like it very much.'

'Aahh! Die Lorelei? Henrich Heine?'

'Yes,' I said.

'We'd better hear it then,' he said. Was he still suspicious of me? Was he going to search me more thoroughly if I couldn't recite the poem and appeared to be lying?

'I can certainly give you the first verse,' I offered.

'I'm waiting for exactly that,' he said, almost like a challenge.

I took a deep breath and off I went. Did the success of my escape depend on this? I tried not to think about it. I just relaxed as best I could, and let the words come back to me:

> *Ich weiss nicht, was soll es bedeuten,*
> *Dass ich so traurig bin,*
> *Ein Marchen (umlaut on a) aus uralten Zeiten,*
> *Das kommt mir nicht aus dem Sinn.*
> *Die Luft ist Kuhl (umlaut on u) und es dunkett,*
> *Und ruhig fliesst der Rhein;*
> *Der Gipfel des Berges funkett,*
> *Im Abendsonnenschein …*

I recited the verse without pause or mistake and even seemed to give this German officer pleasure with my delivery. I couldn't have recited the poem in English, but here's a translation so you can get a sense of the meaning:

> I know not if there is a reason,
> Why I am so sad at heart,
> A legend of bygone ages,
> Haunts me and will not depart,
> The air is cool under nightfall,
> The calm Rhine course its way.
> The peak of the mountain is sparkling,
> With evening's final ray ...

German folklore claimed a 120-metre-high rock in the Rhine Gorge was linked to feminine water spirits, mermaids or Rhine maidens. Nothing could make a German happier than the notion of a British prisoner taking time to enjoy their culture. He didn't know I'd be out of his stinking country within a day or two if only he'd get lost. But I knew the search hadn't even started yet. It could only be a matter of time before he pulled out my escape papers and dashed my hopes.

He tapped me on the shoulder, almost fondly, and gestured gently. What was he up to now?

'Go on. Back to the barracks,' he said.

I could scarcely believe it. He'd been won over by my knowledge of a few poetic German lines.

You'll be wondering why he didn't find my escape papers. The moment I'd seen the Germans coming in, I'd grabbed them. I'd managed to pull the papers out quite easily, because they were all bunched together in a little package. While they were telling us to line up 6 feet apart, there'd been just enough time to drop my escape papers down the back of my battledress. I'd made sure it was tight at the back, so they came to a rest at the back of my waist.

When he'd pulled out the piece of paper, I hadn't even known what it was at first. I thought I'd emptied my breast pocket before putting the escape papers in there. I feared something incriminating had fallen out, or else I'd forgotten that some note had been lurking there, ready to give away my intention to escape.

If the dapper officer had conducted his search properly, he would have found that little bulging package round the back of my waist with no problem at all. If he'd let his soldier carry out the search, I'd have been done for too. But the officer didn't do the job thoroughly at all. In fact, for a nation that was supposed to do everything to such a high standard, there were lots of things the Germans weren't doing properly. And it didn't stop there.

I went back to the barracks a mightily relieved man, until I saw that the German search-squad had turned everything upside down and the place was in a terrible state.

I thought of my 'civilian' trousers, my escape trousers, dyed navy-blue for life on the run. I'd pressed them by putting them under the mattress. To my horror, when

I neared my bunk, I could see them, in plain sight for all to see. The Germans had turned the bed upside down in their search and there they were.

Incredibly, the guards either hadn't noticed the trousers they'd uncovered, or they simply didn't worry about them, assuming it was natural to have them tucked away there. They didn't seem to question why these navy-blue trousers would be in a military barracks occupied by Kiwi soldiers. They didn't stop to think that someone might be planning to use those trousers to pretend to be a civilian. German 'squaddies' were very simple; you could pull the wool over their eyes really easily. But even now I struggle to understand how they could have seen nothing out of the ordinary there. I'd been incredibly lucky twice in the space of a few minutes.

I knew my luck would run out if I dithered a day more than I needed. I was going to go the very next day – before anything else happened.

★   ★   ★

I still had an ordinary uniform on when we reached that factory the next day. Round the back of the warehouses, next to the wall on the site, that pile of earth was still there, almost beckoning me. It had been well-trodden, that route over the wall. It was obvious that some of the workers had recently used it just as I was going to use it – as a quick way out of the factory area.

No time to waste. It was 8 a.m. on Good Friday 1944 – and my moment had come at last. I looked up at the sky. There was still a chill in the air and it looked as though it might rain. A fair-haired New Zealander called Dave had agreed to help me. He had a bucket, ostensibly to make tea for the workers – at least that was going to be his excuse if he was challenged. He came along bang on time, I took my uniform off as quickly as I could, and dropped it into the bucket so that he could hide it or destroy it. For a moment I was standing there in my underpants, which would have aroused immediate suspicion had any German guard passed by. Hurriedly I threw on my civilian clothes, which Dave had brought along in a bag. I had a hold-all too, to support the story that I was travelling as part of my job.

I climbed the mound, just as I'd imagined doing ever since I saw it. The earth was firm and I was at the top in an instant. I threw the briefcase down first and swiftly followed it. It was a wonderful feeling, going over that wall and dropping down to freedom. Suddenly I was in the street below, no longer a prisoner after all those years. It was amazing, the sense of elation, hard to explain. I felt so light-footed, as though I'd been bogged down by years of captivity and now I almost had wings. But it was very quiet out in the real world. There were no German civilians around at that time of day – they were all working by then. I felt I was already on my way back to Sylvia. I had a lot to do before I could make that dream a reality, of course, but for the first time in years, I could be the master of my own actions.

Unfortunately the very first thing I did was make a big mistake. The plan was to take a bus west, so I went to stand by the first bus stop I saw. But I'd never been abroad before, and I'd overlooked something very basic. When the bus finally came round the corner, bright red and making its way west, it arrived on the other side of the road. It had come and gone before the penny dropped. Somehow, despite all the meticulous work that had gone into creating my new identity as a Belgian civilian, I'd forgotten that the Germans drove on the wrong side of the road. Their buses, like everything else, drove on the right.

Why hadn't the Escape Committee told me, when we'd gone through everything? They must have thought I knew. It was so obvious. The bus stop I'd selected was on the left-hand side of the road as far as I was concerned. But it was actually on the right-hand side of the road, which was no good to me at all. It had been placed there for buses heading in the opposite direction.

I felt a momentary feeling of panic, a horror in the pit of my stomach. For all I knew the German guards had already spotted that I was missing from the New Zealanders' work party, or were just about to make the discovery. That bus might have been my last chance to get clear before the alarm went off. And there it was, disappearing into the distance. What a bloody fool I'd been, but despair wasn't going to help me now. I composed myself and walked as calmly and as casually as I could towards a bus stop on the other side of the road. Then I realised that any German civilian who had witnessed this farce would be suspicious right away. Had the locals been told to look out for escaped prisoners, to be vigilant at all times in case anyone acted suspiciously? I walked along a bit on the other side of the road, just to get clear of the scene of my mistake. I came to a halt at a fresh bus stop, joining two people, the first I'd seen, but going in the right direction this time. They must have only just arrived.

Trouble was I knew I'd have to wait a while, because I'd just missed the bus that would have taken me on my way. How long would it be before the next one came by? Would I hear a commotion in the industrial complex above before I could get away?

'Be patient,' I told myself. 'Even if someone raises the alarm, no one down here knows they'll be looking for me.'

Before the silence could be broken, I saw it. Another bus! And the sign said 'Gleiwitz', which was my first destination. The driver stopped and now I faced my first true test, my first words with a German civilian. I'd like to think I was pretty good at speaking German by then. In fact, one of the guards had said I almost sounded like a native. Almost. That wasn't quite good enough to pass off as a German, but it was good enough to pass off as a Belgian electrician doing a bit of work in the country. Would the driver be suspicious?

To keep cool you had to believe that you were irrelevant to everyone around you, which was basically true. As long as there was nothing untoward going on, you were just another bloke going about his daily business like they were.

I was going to be just another passenger, paying the driver for a ticket, just like the rest. When I thought about it like that, I didn't feel nervous. I stepped onto the bus behind the others and did exactly what they did.

'Gleiwitz, *bitte.*' A simple transaction and the driver was on his way. I didn't make eye contact with the other passengers. If there was anyone looking hostile it wouldn't have done me any good to meet their gaze. I just went and sat down as casually as I could and we rumbled out of the area. Somewhere behind me, my New Zealand friends would be trying to get rid of that bucket-full of uniform. Over in my old compound, Len Murray would be trying his best to pass himself off as Moggy Mayne, downed British airman. Could they all keep the secret of my escape for as long as it took? That was out of my control now. That all belonged to another world. The world of prisoners.

14

BERLIN AND THE COAST

The Escape Committee hadn't created a truly convincing cover story for me, despite the technical excellence of my papers. I didn't know if I had a fictional wife or children and I didn't know anything about Belgium either. I certainly didn't know anything about how to be an electrician. I couldn't have talked about the trade for more than five seconds. All in all, if I was questioned in any detail at all about my adopted identity, I'd be in terrible trouble.

I was heading west to Gleiwitz, towards another job, that's what I told myself I'd say. And if no one had reason to doubt me, I'd be just fine. As we rumbled along, I knew deep down that I was trapped on the bus for now. I couldn't just jump off if there was any trouble. But what could I do, except try to relax and enjoy the view for an hour? Before I knew it, the bus had pulled up at Gleiwitz railway station and I was getting off. It already felt like I'd achieved something. I was away from the immediate scene of my escape, well clear of the zone where there might be maximum suspicion. At least I thought so, until I began to walk up a lane from the bus stop towards the ticket office. That's when I saw two men who set off all kinds of alarm bells inside me.

They were smart in their trench coats and hats, but still seedy-looking somehow. They didn't seem to be doing anything; they certainly weren't buying tickets to get on a train. They were just loitering by the ticket office, as though they were waiting for someone. Gestapo! I was convinced of it. It looked like they'd received a phone call from the camp. Someone had escaped, just watch the station for a while. I didn't know for sure that they were waiting for me in particular, but they seemed ready to confront anyone who didn't look quite right. I didn't even know if they'd seen me. I was still about a hundred yards away, right at the bottom of the pathway leading to the ticket office, so I hoped they hadn't spotted me yet. As inconspicuously as I could, I slowly turned. That's the first thing an escaped POW would do, I knew it. But there was nothing else to do, because to walk straight towards them was a risk I didn't fancy taking at that stage.

'I'm going to have to walk around town for bit until they go away,' I told myself. I began to move away from the station. Had they seen me? Would they follow?

'Don't look back! Whatever you do, don't look back! You'll know soon enough if they mean business. You'll hear a demand to "Halt!" if you've been rumbled. Keep walking. Slowly. That's it. Nothing yet. It'll take them a while to catch up with me. Keep walking. Still nothing!'

I turned into another street and lost myself in the crowd. Relief swept over me. It felt good to be anonymous. It felt wonderful to be free. Still free! But soon I knew it would be time to try again. I went back to the path leading towards the railway station and looked towards it from a distance. They were still there. Damn! This happened a few times; and at one stage I thought I'd have to gamble and try for the ticket office, whether the Gestapo men were there or not. It was vital to get clear of the entire area before the Germans mounted a methodical search for me. This was the nearest railway station to the POW camp; it was an obvious point to set up watch for an escaped man. Was I trapped already?

Finally I returned to the bottom of that lane one more time and looked up casually.

'They've gone! Thank God! Unless of course they've seen me first this time and they're waiting in the shadows somewhere. Is that what's happening? Are they out of sight but ready to pounce the moment I come closer?'

I went up to the ticket office anyway. I had to buy my ticket. No one pounced on me.

'Goerlitz, *bitte.*' Before I knew it, I had a ticket in my hand.

One more town in the right direction. Step by step, little by little, I was getting away. I had to take slow trains to small places and stations. The fast trains were used by the military and they'd be too risky. If I was patient, I'd find my way home.

The train chugged away from Gleiwitz station and within an hour I was in Goerlitz. A little further clear … but there was something I didn't know about Goerlitz. It was the regional centre of the Gestapo in the east. As far as I was concerned, places like Gleiwitz and Goerlitz were only stepping stones on the way to the biggest place of all, and perhaps the biggest gamble.

'Berlin, *bitte.*' There. I'd said it. Berlin. Heart of Nazi Germany. I was going straight into Hitler's backyard, exactly where I wouldn't be expected. I had no idea what I'd find, but the big city might well provide me with cover and a means to continue my journey north-west.

The sense of anticipation, as we neared Berlin was difficult to describe. Had the British and Americans managed to bomb the place into a state of ruin? Not from what I was seeing so far, as the railway tracks led into the south-east of the city. In fact, I was amazed by what I saw; and once the train came to a halt and I walked out of the station, the happy atmosphere almost carried me away.

The sun had come out, the sky was bright blue, the air was clean, and there wasn't a hint of rubble; the place was positively vibrant. Perhaps the Berliners didn't feel as joyful as I did. Perhaps they didn't look at the spring trees coming into leaf, or the vivid beauty of the blossom, and reflect quietly on how wonderful it was to be alive, to be free. Perhaps they didn't appreciate just how beautiful their streets seemed to me, with trees on either side of the road. But the locals looked happy enough as they went about their business. There were no ruins. There was no evidence of hardship. Everybody was well-dressed; there was no obvious sign of suffering. In fact, some of the middle-aged women looked very elegant indeed in their fur coats. Later I heard suggestions that all the German women had sent their coats to the Russian front to warm their soldiers there. Not the women in south Berlin; not from what I could see. Elegant, beautiful women, classy, clean Berlin in this glorious Easter sunshine of 1944. This wasn't what I'd expected. It didn't seem like Berlin at all, but it was.

Perhaps I should have felt disappointed that Berlin wasn't on its knees, begging for relief from the Allied bombs. Perhaps I should have felt angry that they seemed oblivious to the dreadful suffering their country had caused, the death of my friend Stan Clarke and a million like him. I'd had years to think about poor Stan and I'd never forget him. But did I feel like screaming at the Berliners, or doing something to give expression to my outrage? No. I just thought it was lovely. And it felt lovely to be part of this happy throng. That's how it was. And if you think that's strange, then try spending two years in a POW camp, chained or restricted some of the time, all privacy and most rights denied you for years, and then suddenly experience freedom in all its glory. Even if you're in an enemy city, you'll feel exactly the same as I did. Elated, excited, alive!

'Don't walk like a military man,' I told myself as I struck up a brisk pace. We'd been warned about this by the Escape Committee. A military man develops such a purposeful walk, even a sort of march, that he is easily recognisable if someone is looking out for it – the Gestapo, for example. For all I knew, I might come to check-points in the road. So I made it my first objective to force myself to walk more slowly and casually.

Before long, I saw a little shop where they were selling soup. I went in to take a closer look. It was carrot soup. I didn't even like carrots, but I paid three marks, sat down and had some of that soup anyway. It gave me a moment to collect my thoughts and think about what I had to do next. I didn't know where I was exactly; I just knew I was somewhere in the south of Berlin. So the plan was to head north – as simple as that. Get across Berlin to a place just north of the city centre, where I assumed there'd be a railway station offering me a way out towards the coast.

I walked for what felt like hours, heading north towards the city centre. The spring in my step was probably there for all to see, even if I was trying to walk slowly and casually. Suddenly I saw some soldiers walking towards me. I felt nervous. Up to that point, I'd been surprised by how few soldiers I'd seen coming in the opposite direction. So what did this lot want? Were they on to me? But they didn't even seem to see me, they didn't notice me, they just walked on by.

I didn't want to talk to anyone and I didn't have to; but the further I walked, the more a nagging worry began to enter my head. Try as I might, I simply couldn't find another railway station. I needed one desperately, to help me continue my escape north-west. Gradually it dawned on me that I was going to have to ask someone. It would have to be someone who would definitely know, who would perhaps be used to telling strangers where to go if they were in need.

That's when I saw him: a traffic policeman in the middle of the road, directing the cars with a confident wave of his arm or an emphatic gesture to stop. I suppressed all fear as I approached him. I didn't let negative thoughts enter my head, I couldn't. I strolled straight up to him and asked him the all-important question with a smile.

'*Bitte, Herr Offizier, wo ist der Bahnhof zum Norden?*' ('Could you tell me where I can find a railway station to take me north out of Berlin please sir?')

It was a gamble alright. Would he find it strange and suspicious that someone could be so hopelessly lost in this city? I didn't see why. I was fair-haired, I was quite smartly-dressed. I spoke good German. Even if he didn't think I was German, he would think I was a friend of the Germans from a neighbouring country in northern Europe.

That's what I thought. But the traffic policeman put a heavy hand on my shoulder.

'Is he grabbing me? Is the game up? Shall I run?'

He turned me around, physically. 'There.' That was all he said.

He pointed north, or at least in the general direction where he knew I'd find the railway station I was looking for. And that was it. He let me go and went back to directing the traffic. And I went back to being an escaped POW walking through Berlin, relieved that I was no longer doing so aimlessly.

Sure enough, it wasn't long before I stumbled across another railway station. Trains were heading north-west and I bought a ticket for a place called Prezlau. As before, no one cared about me. The train pulled away from Berlin and I felt fresh excitement. One more train after this and I'd be at the coast. All in a single day! Everything was going to plan. To have come through Berlin safely and without detection was an achievement in itself. My confidence was high.

'Not long now, Sylvia. I'll be back to you before you know it, my darling.'

Step by step. Bernau bei Berlin, Melchow, Eberswalde, Angermünde, Flieth-Stegelitz … and we came into Prezlau. I bought a new ticket and this time there was no hiding my destination. Stralsund, here I come! One Swedish-bound boat was all I needed. Then it was going to be goodbye Germany. Forever.

That final journey was uneventful, except for the keen feeling of anticipation, which was made more acute by the number of times the train stopped. Anklam, Klein Bünzow, Züssow, Gross Kiesow, Greifswald … We weren't even halfway there, and the stations kept coming and going. I'd just have to stay patient. After two years, I could cope with a few more stops. Wackrow, Klein Kieshof, Miltzow, Wusten Felde, Teschenhagen … and finally, at long last that same evening, Stralsund.

I'd made it. In some ways this was going to be the trickiest part of the escape, but the neutral Swedes would surely help me if I found them. This was what the long journey had been all about. I was tired but felt fresh adrenalin surge through my body as the train rolled into the little seaside town.

Once clear of the station I found myself walking down charming cobbled streets, with pubs beckoning me. Did I fancy them? Oh, not half! It was so tempting to go in and have a pint. It had been so long! I could hear people singing German songs in one pub, it sounded like they were having such a great time. I wanted to join them. I wanted to enjoy myself, feel normal again. But I didn't dare enter – it was just too risky. If I was going to get into a conversation, it had to be on my terms. I was looking for a Swede to talk to. Someone I felt I could trust; someone to reveal my plan to, then ask for help. But I just couldn't see anyone who looked like a Swede. Maybe they were all in the pubs with the Germans; but if they were, then it was no good to me.

Finally I heard two men speaking French and decided to take a chance.

'Can you help me?' I asked. 'I'm looking for some Swedes to take me out of here on a boat.'

The Frenchmen looked horrified and in that instant I realised I'd made a big mistake. 'Don't worry,' I added, trying to calm them down with my relaxed attitude. 'Just tell me where the dockyard is then, please?'

But they just shook their heads and hurried away, as though I could give them the plague just by looking at them.

I decided I'd have to go and find the dockyard by myself – but not that evening, in case the French had raised the alarm there. Trying not to feel downhearted, I returned to the railway station, where I thought a stranger would look less suspicious on his own. That's when I saw it – a map on the station wall, showing quite clearly where the dockyard was. Why the hell hadn't I spotted it on my way out of the station in the first place?

There was an all-night café at the station, quite a nice place where the waiters wore smart uniforms, almost like dinner dress. I went in to have a drink. I was still in there after midnight when I looked towards the door. Military police were coming into the station to check the identities of any drifters. I saw two soldiers, but they weren't in ordinary uniform. They had great big metal plates across their chest and big boots on. I was obviously going to be their number one target. It was too late to make a run for it so I had to think very quickly. I lifted my 'Ausweiss' gently out of my jacket, so the travel papers would be in my hand as the police came closer. Then straight away I slumped down on the table and made out I was asleep, hoping the sight of the Ausweiss would be enough to stop the police from waking me. It was a long shot, because there was no reason why military police should take pity on a suspicious character and decide not to wake and question him. But somehow it worked! I felt the Ausweiss being taken quietly from my limp hand and then returned to it, without so much as a word. After some brief refreshment, the military police went on their way.

It was a wonderful feeling. I was still a free man, and in a few hours I could go to the docks. Perhaps the Swedes were all there. That's it! Maybe they were all on their boat, ready to leave Germany for their homeland that very next morning. It wouldn't hurt them to take one more. Or perhaps I'd be able to make myself almost invisible in the anonymous, early-morning rush to work, then stow away when no one was looking.

It would be getting light soon; the time was right to make my move. But still I couldn't find the dockyard. I'd imagined it would have been obvious after looking at the map in the station. But it wasn't as I'd expected at all. I came to a crossroads in the town. One way seemed to lead further into the city centre. The other way, I hoped, led to the dockyard. I chose that path, walked a few hundred yards, and there it was! I'd chosen right.

My heart sank a little when I couldn't see a boat in dock – Swedish or otherwise. But if I could gain entry to the dockyard, I could find a place with a view of the whole port, somewhere I could see what vessels were coming in and out. I couldn't just walk through the main entrance and into the dockyard. They'd start asking too many questions. I'd have to go over the fence when no one was watching. I walked around the perimeter until I found a suitable place, threw my briefcase over and followed it. I was up that fence in an instant and coming down the other side, when I heard the sound of a door opening. There was a hut about 50 yards away. Everything had been so quiet that I hadn't seen the hut as a problem.

A little, middle-aged German came out. He'd seen me, he already had a revolver in his hand and he was coming towards me. What now? Part of me wanted to run for it, but that would make him shoot. If I wanted to get back to Sylvia and England, I was going to have to get the better of this man. Maybe I could just give him one of my best right hooks and make off before he came round. I knew a few tricks, I could look after myself. It wouldn't be hard to trip him up. But as he came closer, pointing his revolver at me, I noticed the German's hands were shaking violently. That threw me a bit. If he'd been calmer and steadier, it would have been easier to take him by surprise.

'Morning, I've got a shift of work to do in the docks but I'm lost,' I said with a smile.

But that desperate ploy just seemed to make the German purple in the face, and he was shaking so much that I thought he might pull the trigger by accident. The slightest sudden movement and he looked ready to shoot, because he seemed more scared than I was. And somewhere in those frantic seconds my dream of lasting freedom died, my chances of escape just disintegrated. My hopes of seeing Sylvia, of marrying her that summer, were dashed. How could I let it all go so easily? Why wasn't I doing something desperate to stay at liberty? I still felt tempted to take him on, but it wasn't happening. I wasn't even running. Instead I was putting my hands up, letting him arrest me.

You're constantly weighing things up, consciously and subconsciously. What if I got him down before he shot me? What then? The authorities would soon know there was a dangerous man on the loose. Even if I knocked him out, the German would come to his senses eventually and then he would tell the authorities all about me. And if he didn't come round, then in the Gestapo's eyes they would be looking for a murderer, a deadly enemy spy, someone to be tortured when found, then shot. By the time they finished with me, being shot would probably feel like a mercy.

My plan had depended entirely on not being rumbled. But I had been; there was no getting round it. There was nowhere to run, not really. No ship about to set sail, no obvious reward for trying to destroy this man – quite the opposite.

Above all I had to survive. And in order to survive, I knew what was necessary. It didn't matter now that I'd successfully crossed Germany all alone, covered hundreds and hundreds of miles and come within a whisker of escaping to a neutral country, from where I could get back to Britain. It had all been for nothing. In that terrible moment, I had to admit it.

'I am an escaped prisoner of war,' I told the shaking German reluctantly. 'You must hand me over to the military. You must give me to the German Army.'

That was the most important thing, now. I'd been told this by the Escape Committee people. 'If you are caught, make sure you become the property of the German Army again as quickly as possible. They won't hand you over to the Gestapo because they don't like the Gestapo any more than we do.'

The night watchman made me take my shoe laces off and he undid my braces. Then he took me straight to Stralsund police station – or at least it looked like a police station. I was starting to feel quite miserable by then. All that effort, just to be captured at the final hurdle. Why did he have to come out of the hut just when I was climbing over? Why hadn't I been more careful? But there wasn't much time to feel sorry for myself, because I suddenly had something else to worry about. The men in the police station called for a couple of marines, and they were all angry about something. Whatever it was, they were looking to take it out on me. Then it became clear.

'Why do you bomb German women and children? Why?' they demanded.

'I don't!' I protested quite truthfully. 'Not me! I'm Coastal Command. I'm not Bomber Command!'

This seemed to pacify them a bit. Then something bizarre began to happen. A bloke kept popping his head round the door.

'Plenty manger, plenty work!' he said. Turned out he'd been a POW in the First World War. His motto was that if you do a lot of work you'll be fed a lot of food.

'Plenty manger, plenty work!' he kept saying it.

I didn't know if I agreed with him. I didn't need a lot of food and I didn't like doing a lot of work – not for the Germans anyway. We were just different people, this strange man and I.

The marines who'd come to pick me up said it was time to go. They took me to a special glass house for bad-boy German marines. It seemed to be a place where they were punished for their misdemeanors. There were some really rough types in there. If my captors chucked me in with that lot, I wouldn't stand a chance. Luckily they didn't. And it turned out these two young marines who had taken charge of me were really nice types. They even offered me chocolate. They had to throw me in a cell, of course, but I had it to myself. And they gave me fruit! Can you imagine? Apples! I hadn't tasted fresh fruit for years!

Well, if they were hoping to make me compliant with these little gifts, they succeeded! I obeyed the rules and stood to attention whenever anyone came in. It wasn't in my interests to upset these people and frankly I saw no reason to do so. They had to keep me away from the Gestapo, I was depending on them.

They let me into a little square to stretch my legs. I felt a lot of German eyes focused on me, looking down from the cells which surrounded the square. So I did a bit of shadow boxing to show them I wasn't to be messed with. I was showing off really, trying to restore my pride after my capture. It did the trick.

I wasn't hiding my identity. When they caught me I said I was an escaped prisoner of war and I gave my real name and POW camp number – Maurice Mayne, 24846. I told them to contact the camp, because by now they'd know I was missing. This caused a good deal of confusion with the Germans in Stalag VIIIB, when they were called and asked to verify my story. As far as they were concerned, Maurice Mayne wasn't missing. He hadn't escaped at all. In fact, no one had escaped. They still hadn't realised that Len Murray had taken my identity. And even though I'd taken Len Murray's identity, Len Murray hadn't been noticed missing either.

Eventually they all began to accept that I was indeed an escaped POW from Lamsdorf, because a couple of soldiers from Stalag VIIIB were sent to collect me and take me all the way back across Germany. It was a journey I'd never forget.

15

THE EXECUTION THREAT

Going back through Berlin was a whole new experience – and not just because the thrill of freedom had been taken away from me for the return journey. This time I had the chance to take a proper look at north Berlin. I was staggered by what I saw. It was in a terrible state, rubble everywhere. Big roads had been reduced to little lanes with the rubble piled high on either side. There didn't seem to be any proper roads any more, just these rubble-strewn paths. The bombs had certainly hit home on this side of the city. It was a far cry from the beautiful spring day on the south side, with the trees and the blossom and the clean air. And I was about to be confronted with a different reality of war.

My guards were exhausted, having travelled all the way from Lamsdorf to pick me up and then back to Berlin. They wanted to put me somewhere secure for the night so they could get some sleep. They took me to what looked like a big hotel from the outside, with a German guard posted on the entrance, sitting on a stool. When the guard told them I couldn't stay in there, it was no surprise to me. I wondered why they'd thought I'd be allowed to stay in a big fancy hotel in the first place.

But then one of my guards told me, 'Come on, come with me, I want to show you this.' The guard relented and decided to give us a little tour of what was really inside. And that's when I felt relieved that he'd told my two guards that I couldn't stay there. The place had been stripped down inside, so that it was now a vast hall. And filling that hall was nothing but huge cages, with bars as thick as young pine trees. These cages each had about twenty or thirty men inside, some peering through these bars, most pacing up and down anxiously. We were told they were all deserters, mostly from the Russian front.

'You're better than them! Rubbish, these men are,' the guard said. 'You're better than them.'

'Yes,' I agreed hastily.

Army, Luftwaffe, you name it, all kinds of German forces were represented in that place. The reason they looked so restless was because they'd been told they were going to be sent back to the Russian front. Sometime soon their units were coming to pick them up. God knows what was going to happen to them then. They already knew how bad it was at the Russian front, which was why they'd deserted in the first place. To be sent back was almost like a death sentence. These doomed men were probably destined to be executed, or to die in battle, or else be captured, frozen and starved to death in the hands of the Russians.

One of my guards told me, 'You can't be in amongst that lot.'

I couldn't have agreed with him more quickly. I was taken off to another place, which looked more like a regular prison, in the south of Berlin. My guards knocked on the door but were soon told the place was closed. Just as we were turning away, though, the prison officer called us back and told my guards that there was still a cell I could be put into for the night. I wasn't too keen, but these blokes had to have a sleep and the decision was made. I was taken upstairs and put into a cell which was every bit as horrible as I'd imagined. There was nothing in there, except a dirty old blanket in the corner. I was given no food, nothing at all, just put in there for the night. It was a relief when I heard footsteps nearing the cell early in the morning. My guards had come back to pick me up and take me away.

Before I knew it, we were going through the last of Berlin, back in the wrong direction from my point of view, and I couldn't have been more down in the dumps. I thought of that fantastic set of escape papers, which had of course been removed the moment I was recaptured. All the superb work that had gone into them; all for nothing. Then I thought of Sylvia and my family. I'd given them hope, through the letters of 'Len Murray'. Those hopes were going to be dashed as soon as they realised I was back in the Stalag.

But then something happened to put such thoughts out of my mind. Suddenly it wasn't about the crushing disappointment of moving from blissful freedom to recapture and imprisonment. Before I knew it, my struggle was redefined – a simple matter of life or death.

I was sitting on the edge of a seat at one of the smaller stations on the way back; a countrified place, I forget the name. But it was somewhere on the Berlin side of Gleiwitz and Goerlitz. There was nothing but Germans around me. My guard, who was a marine, met several old friends who used to be in his regiment. They got talking.

One soldier looked at me and asked my guard, 'Who is he?'

'Oh, he escaped.'

And the other man said, 'Well he was lucky, because those others escaped and fifty of them have just been shot.'

The chilling thing was that he was very friendly and his tone was all very nice, in keeping with the serene village atmosphere where we were. Then he glanced in my direction and made a sound.

'Bang!'

He was even smiling, but he didn't quite say it like a joke. He turned to me again.

'They might shoot you when you get back.'

He wasn't malicious about it, simply factual as far as he could tell. He wanted to give me this information as cordially as possible. But he couldn't feel for me, not properly. He couldn't put himself in my situation or fathom what this news might mean to me.

But what was he talking about? How could fifty escaped prisoners be shot? Had there been a break-out from my camp? Did they decide to make a run for it rather than be recaptured? Had my friends all been shot? What had led to this extreme action?

I soon found out. On the night of 24–25 March at Stalag Luft III, not all that far from Stalag VIIIB, there had been a mass break-out. It became known as 'the Great Escape', and later they even made a big film out of it.

The boys there had dug tunnels and planned for about 200 people to get out. But the alarm went up after seventy-six had escaped into the woods. It was still an incredible achievement – and our brave blokes had caused chaos across Germany. All that had happened just as I was preparing to escape myself. Unfortunately, seventy-three of the seventy-six escapees had been caught and rounded up. That should have been it, according to the Geneva Convention. Back to their POW camp, or perhaps on to an even more secure place of incarceration.

Disgustingly, Hitler ordered Himmler's SS to execute fifty of them instead – including twenty-one British lads. The atrocity had taken place not far from Goerlitz, quite close to where I was standing on that platform, listening to Germans debate my immediate chances of survival or execution. Unbelievable! If I'd been picked up by the wrong people on the way towards Berlin as a free man, there's little doubt I'd have been shot already. As the German soldiers had pointed out so callously, the danger hadn't passed. If we went back the wrong way and the SS or Gestapo learned that I was an escaped prisoner, I'd meet the same fate. We still had to get past Goerlitz.

So I kept asking my guards, 'Which way are we going back?'

Another time I asked them straight, 'Can we go round Goerlitz?' I tried to break the tension by adding, 'I've never seen that part of the country before, can we go that way?'

My guards were quite laid back, they understood my concerns. I didn't want to go through that area of Goerlitz where I might be picked up and shot. Luckily, I don't think my guards wanted that to happen to me either by then. They seemed to have warmed to me and may even have felt responsible for me.

Later I heard that there had been three successful 'home runs' from the Great Escape. One, a Dutch pilot called Bram van der Stok, had reached freedom by going through France and Spain. But the other two, Norwegian pilots called Per Bergsland and Jens Müller, had done something similar to me. The only difference was, they'd succeeded where I later failed. They had managed to take a boat to neutral Sweden and on to freedom.

Had all this contributed to my capture? Had the guards and night-watchmen around the dock areas of German ports with routes to Sweden been ordered to exercise extra vigilance in the aftermath of the Great Escape? Had Swedish boats normally to be found in Stralsund been affected somehow? I'll never know and I'll certainly never blame the Great Escapers for what happened to me.

Later it was rumoured that one of the men who had helped to plan the Great Escape was none other than Wing Commander Mervyn 'Willy' Williams, the man who had tried to send us against the *Tirpitz* back in March 1942. If true then, indirectly at least, Williams had put my life in grave danger for a second time – though I wouldn't have held it against him for a moment. This was still war. Many men were trying to undermine the Nazis in any way they could. Perhaps I'd managed to undermine them too, in my own little way. But what price was I going to have to pay for that?

Until I'd heard about the executions, I'd thought my probable punishment for going on the run across Germany would be a spell in the cells. To be thrown straight in there for a fortnight was about average. Now, as I was marched through the main gate, a couple of weeks in the cells were something to pray for. A fortnight there might mean hope for the future. If I lasted that long, perhaps they weren't so impatient to execute me.

Of all the people who might be passing as I came back into the camp, I never expected to see John Sinclair – but I did. We had drifted apart completely. There'd been a lot of men in the RAF compound and our paths didn't cross. But there he was, with a friend of his, and it was the first time I'd seen him for ages. He couldn't speak to me, because I had an escort on both sides, but I heard Sinclair say to his mate, 'Oh dear. That guy used to be my "oppo".'

That was an expression some men used to describe a fellow crew member, when you'd been on operations together. Sinclair had been on the same Beaufort crew, we'd spent years in the same camp, but our situations in that instant could hardly have been more different. He was relatively safe. I wasn't.

Fears leapt about at the back of my mind: I might suddenly be rushed out and driven away in a Gestapo truck, taken to a quiet spot where they could execute me without a fuss. Over the first two days alone in the cells, these fears grew and tormented me. Then someone threw an already-lit cigarette into my cell – not to try to set it alight, but as a gesture of kindness. One of the Germans must have done it, and in that moment I just thought I must be over the worst, and they weren't going to shoot me after all – however bad the general climate had become with regard to escapees. If there was a moment when I knew I wasn't going to be treated like those poor fifty executed men, this was it.

Luckily I'd never heard about the widespread custom for a condemned man to be handed a final cigarette to enjoy, just before he is dispatched to the next world. I just took it to be a sign that I was back amongst friends, in so far as your captors could ever be your friends.

I was supposed to do a fortnight in those cells but after a week they put me in the standard punishment barracks instead. There were all kinds of characters in there. One bloke, a fair-haired RAF pilot, had tried to nick a Messerschmitt to fly home in. He was going to be moved off somewhere else for that – probably Colditz, the castle where there was said to be no chance of escape.

I hadn't tried to steal a German plane, but what sort of backlash was I going to get? I'd heard no talk among the German guards of moving me on. In fact they didn't treat me too badly at all. The impression I got was that they thought I'd made a good escape and they treated me with a kind of respect for it. They still didn't know who it was they were respecting, though. When I was caught in Stralsund and was so keen to avoid the Gestapo, I'd given my captors my real name – Maurice Mayne. But when it emerged that no Maurice Mayne had been missing from Stalag VIIIB, I realised I'd have to carry on being Len Murray back at the camp. The boys would need me to be Len for a while longer, at least until they could spirit the real Murray back from the British RAF compound to the New Zealand army compound. It was all quite comical really, but it wouldn't have been for old Len if he'd been rumbled all of a sudden.

In time, the Escape Committee would manage to do the switch again and save Len from bother. They were up to all sorts of tricks, the Escape Committee – they were very good. I couldn't blame them for my capture, or for the fact that there'd been no Swedish boat in port when I reached Stralsund. I didn't doubt it was a place where Swedish boats regularly docked. I must have just arrived there at the wrong time. I'd got all the way across Germany and then my luck had run out. That's the way things could go, I had to take it on the chin now and get on with it. To keep looking back at those 'if only' scenarios would have been dangerous, because my spirits would really have taken a nosedive. You couldn't change the past, you had to stay in the present to deal with daily challenges, and retain your hopes for the future.

There was plenty going on to stop me moping. When I went into the punishment barracks as Len Murray, there were some real rogues in there. The Germans shoved me in with no kit at all, which might have left me vulnerable. Luckily a weird and wonderful character saw the fix I was in. The blokes in there may have been rogues, but very quickly they took me under their wing – especially a Scottish chap called 'Molky'.

He was an unusual man for many reasons. For a start, he didn't just call himself 'Molky' – he called everyone else 'Molky' as well.

He put his arm round me and said, 'What do you want, Molky? A cup of tea?'

I thought he must be joking but I played along and said, 'Yes, alright. Thanks.'

I suppose I was looking a bit bedraggled because I'd just come out of the cells.

'OK, I'll get you a cup of tea,' he said.

'How's he going to get me a cup of tea in here?' I thought to myself. There was nowhere to brew up as far as I could see.

But he went off to the end of the barracks, and sure enough some blokes were huddled round their little stoves. Blowers! Even in there!

Molky brought me back a cup of tea and quickly got everything organised for me. He found me a bed. He found me blankets. He looked capable of nicking anything. He was only about 25 but a proper rogue, because his ambition when he got back to Britain was to become a smuggler and a cattle-rustler. His brother was a butcher, so he planned to be a rustler to supply his brother's business.

I fought Molky bare-fisted. Not because there was any animosity between us, but because he wanted to. Instead of making a ring to box in, we just stood in between the beds, so you couldn't get away. We fought more than once and poor Molky's nose was in a terrible state. I can see it now. He would fight bravely but with no technique, so he always came off second best. Even then he wouldn't let me stop.

'Try that again,' he'd say.

So I'd come through his guard with an upper-cut and smash his nose again. It would be covered in blood. And I mean covered!

There were one or two other blokes who wanted to fight and it suited me as a small man in a small space like that. But Molky got the worst of it because he wouldn't give in. And the day after I split his nose, it was still bleeding. We called the guards and told them a man had fallen and broken open his face.

It so happened that all this coincided with the day the Germans were allowing 'England' to play 'Scotland' in a football match. There was tremendous excitement about the match, even in the punishment barracks. In the main part of the camp, there was a football pitch drawn up between two barracks. It was all soil, no grass, but no one cared about that. The crowd was already gathering around the borders of the pitch, ready to watch the big match. You could bring stools out of the buildings and put them down on the touchlines. Even the Germans came down and sat on stools like well-behaved spectators.

I couldn't be in this game for obvious reasons; but there were going to be some professional footballers in it, much better players than me. A bloke called Lovery, who used to play for England and Coventry, was one. And there were brothers – twins called Stephens, I think – who used to play for West Ham. They played for the Hammers for a season after the war if I'm not mistaken.

Anyway, we told the guards there was a man badly injured and they brought in a stretcher to take Molky to hospital. They put Molky on the stretcher, and as they carried him past the football crowd, he just jumped off and disappeared into the mass of spectators. Had he let me beat him up that badly, just so he could get out of the punishment barracks to watch the football? I'll never know, but if he sacrificed his nose to watch the soccer, it sort of backfired on him, because England won that match 1-0. It had taken us two years to avenge the defeat of 1942, and now at last it was our turn to enjoy the bragging rights.

Molky was just one of many extraordinary characters I came across. I remember a couple of Irishmen, one of whom made a habit of breaking out of the camp – and then breaking back in again when he felt like it! All kinds of eccentric and resourceful people were in Stalag VIIIB. Some of them wanted to help me escape again.

I was now perceived as someone capable of a 'home run,' someone to whom the Escape Committee should give more of their precious resources. To my astonishment, I was still in the punishment block when they managed to smuggle in a fresh set of papers for me. It was a tremendous boost to morale; and I was all set to have a second go. Maybe I'd be able to learn from my mistake last time. Maybe I'd be able to get all the way home and have Sylvia in my arms inside a month or two after all! But it wasn't long after I got out of the punishment block when we all heard the announcement. It came from Hitler himself: from now on, all escaping prisoners were to be shot on sight.

It was a sobering thought and time to weigh things up again. We knew the Allies were winning the war by now. Soon they'd be back on the European mainland and ready to finish Hitler once and for all. We didn't know about D-Day yet, but we had a sense the war might be entering its final phase. It couldn't last forever, could it? Germany was weakened, becoming desperate. I'd seen with my own eyes some of the German servicemen who had deserted from the Russian front. It looked like an army in chaos to me.

I soon realised that my best chance of getting back to Sylvia and my family was to stay put for now. Even the Escape Committee wasn't encouraging escape any more. Everyone was a bit shocked by the change in the climate. We just needed to stay where we were and bide our time.

By 14 May 1944 I was ready to break the sad news to Sylvia that I wouldn't be seeing her any time soon after all. I tried to hide my disappointment and remain upbeat.

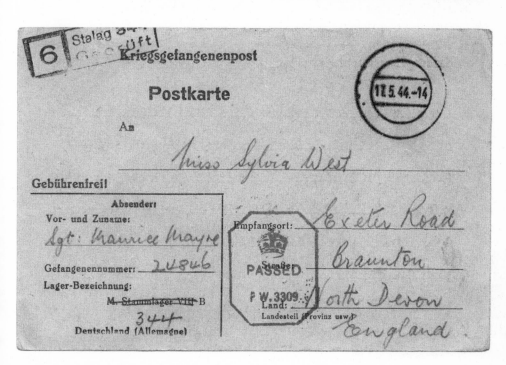

Kriegsgefangenenlager Datum: 14th May 1944

My Dearest Sylvia - Here I am once again in 344 after having escaped on my own & been recaptured. Everything is fine now so don't worry. There was quite a big stack of mail on my return, including many from you. Was thrilled to read about your visit home. I will answer your letters in my letter card next week. Am thinking of you all the time dearest. Heres all my fondest & sincerest love Sylvia yours ever Maurice

Stalag 344
6 Geprüft
Kriegsgefangenenpost

Postkarte

An

Miss Sylvia West

Gebührenfrei

Absender:
Vor- und Zuname:
Sgt: Maurice Mayne

Gefangenennummer: 248446

Lager-Bezeichnung:
M. Stammlager VIII B
344
Deutschland (Allemagne)

Empfangsort: Exeter Road

PASSED
P.W.3309

Braunton
Straße: North Devon
Land:
Landesteil (Provinz usw.) England

11.5.44.-14

My Dearest Sylvia,

Here I am once again in 344 [Stalag VIIIB] after having escaped on my own and been recaptured.

Everything is fine now so don't worry.

There was quite a big stack of mail on my return, including many from you. Was thrilled to read about your visit home. I will answer your letters in my letter card next week.

Am thinking of you all the time dearest. Here's all my fondest and sincerest love Sylvia.

Yours ever,

Maurice.

It felt good to be able to use my own name again, but terrible to remain a prisoner.

When we heard about D-Day, we felt we'd made the right decision to forget about escape. The Allies had just started to sweep east; the Russians were sweeping west. Sooner or later, Berlin was going to cop it. Those happy scenes I'd witnessed in south and central Berlin weren't going to last. Perhaps they were already a thing of the past, and the rest of the capital had become rubble like so much of the north.

Back in Lamsdorf, I had extra responsibilities now. I was Barrack Commander towards the end, democratically elected, which was nice. Then a bloke called Mickey Orr, a New Zealander, challenged my authority. He was an actor, and later he went back to acting in New Zealand. He'd managed to get himself in with the army acting people at the camp. They used to be allowed to use one empty hut for a bit of acting. They wrote plays and he could put on a right voice when he was acting too. Because of that, he used to get privileges. He used to

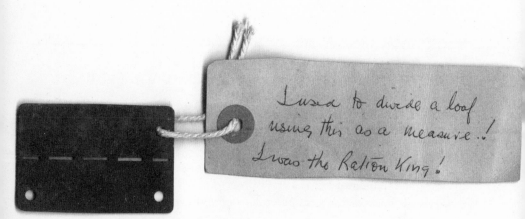

I used to divide a loaf using this as a measure..! I was the Ration King!

'Ration King Ruler!'

McMAYNE W/O 1253284 RAF
PRISONER of WAR No 24846
Lamsdorf, Germany 1942 – 1945

'I'm just a set of numbers ... for now.'

come back to the barracks late, because the Germans used to bring him back personally. One night he brought back a big cardboard box, a prop he must have used in a scene. And a cardboard box like that was gold dust in a prison camp. You could do all sorts of things with it.

As Barrack Commander I was making a cozy little office area at the back of the barracks using cardboard. Everything that came into the barracks was to be handed over to me, usually for sharing; but in this case the box was going to go towards my office project. If I had an office then there was somewhere for people to come, so that they could air their grievances in privacy. It was for the good of the barracks community, but Mickey Orr thought he was going to keep that cardboard box for himself.

I said, 'No Mickey, we'll have that box.'

He said, 'You can't have it.'

I said, 'These are the rules we've made, and we're having the cardboard box.'

He wasn't having it, and said, 'You Pommy bastard!'

That's when I hit him. Mickey went flying across the room.

I said to Orr, 'Don't you ever say that again. Do not call any Englishman that again.'

But Mickey had a bit of misplaced confidence in his own fighting abilities, or else he was desperate to restore his wounded pride. He got to his feet and tried to put his hands up in true actor's fashion, ready for a fresh scrap. Maybe he thought he was in some sort of movie, but real fights could end really badly for the loser.

I told him, 'Put 'em down Mickey, else I'll kill ya!'

Finally he saw some sense and did as he was told. He didn't call me a Pommy bastard again and he didn't call any other Englishman that within my earshot. We got the cardboard box too, so my authority had been restored.

They had made me 'Ration King' too. This was probably because I was a fussy eater, who could be trusted not to get greedy with whatever food we were being given. For example there were certain soups I just couldn't eat. Ghastly soups! Try eating the sort of swede soup we were given and you might not fancy it either. It was just swedes in water, brought to us in a dirty great dustbin. I couldn't stomach it, any more than I could eat much of the cabbage soup. There were some blokes who liked it so much they would literally scrape the bottom of the barrel. 'Tex' Hyde took a photo of someone doing just that, and you could understand it, because there was plenty of hunger around. But I knew where these latest cabbages had come from – near the toilets – and that probably didn't help my appetite for them. Also, I didn't like the way cabbage soup on its own stank just like a toilet – it was disgusting. So I'd let anyone have mine, rather than down it myself. That made me the best candidate to be Ration King, along with the fact that I was fast with those fists if there were any disputes. Obviously I was guaranteed a really nice portion of anything more appetising than swede or cabbage soup, if ever it did come our way. So were all my pals, I don't mind admitting it. If I liked someone, I'd use the ladle to give them the thicker stuff from the bottom of the soup. If I didn't like someone, I'd run the ladle through the top of the soup, where it was thinnest.

I had a piece of metal which helped me to measure the precise thickness of bread each man should have as his portion. I still have that piece of metal.

The heat of the summer was upon us again. It always reminded me of Sylvia and Braunton back in 1941. I could sit in the sun in the Stalag, close my eyes, feel the warmth and try to imagine I was back with Sylvia. On 1 July 1944, I put my thoughts and feelings down on paper for her:

My Dearest Sylvia,
The weekend is here again, with quite nice warm weather and so I'm feeling a little blue at having to be away from you. Time seems to be travelling so quickly, that it's difficult to believe that I first met you dear about three years ago. It hardly seems that to me. Ever since I've been away from you darling the summers don't seem to have been half so glorious as the one I spent with you. But this one, I'm sure will be the last during which my heart is and will be aching for you Sylvia. I haven't heard from Mum and Dad for some time but of course the mail is slowed down considerably now, so I mustn't grumble … Well darling the time is not so very far away now, when I shall carry you home as my 'blushing' bride and then – well everything will be wonderful. Goodbye for now sweetheart. All my most affectionate love, yours always, Maurice xxxx.

It was late summer and three years since I'd seen Sylvia. My escape had failed, letters from her had dried up – I hoped only temporarily. I knew the Allies were winning the war and it was only a matter of time before I'd get back to Sylvia, unless something terrible happened in the chaos of the end of the war. I had to have faith that Sylvia could see an end to our separation too. The alternative didn't bear thinking about.

16

DEATH MARCH

When you've built your hopes for a happy future around one young woman, her letters become as important as the air you breathe. Cut off the mail and it feels like your oxygen supply has been cut off too. You start to suffocate in the silence, you wonder what has happened, you pray for the endless separation to be over.

When I wrote to Sylvia on 8 August 1944, I was determined to push all negative thoughts out of my head:

> I've had so little mail lately that I hardly know what I can write about. But don't think I'm blaming you honey, because I know how the mail is nowadays. Still I don't think we'll have to worry about letters much more now Sylvia. I feel very optimistic about getting home this year and putting an end to this dreadful period of waiting that you have had to endure. My heart always pounds with excitement every time I think of the occasion when I'm going to see you again for the first time, throw my arms around you and smother you with kisses …

But the lack of contact threw me into temporary despair. Each man had his limit and sometimes it felt like I was reaching mine. The lingering disappointment of my failure to reach Sweden and home was still nagging away at me. The weather was gorgeous, but what use was that when I had no freedom? Just three days later I penned some more lines to her:

> My Dearest Sylvia,
> Just a line to let you know I'm still doing my best to keep smiling etc, but sometimes I feel as though this monotonous life will get me down. If it wasn't for the thought of coming back to you, I'd have done something reckless long ago …

Just when dark moods were taking over, a letter from Sylvia came through and my sense of humour returned. I depended on Sylvia emotionally; it was as though my survival rested on any old line she could send me. She understood this and so wrote as often as she could. When she was stuck for something to say, she'd write about the fruit and vegetables she was picking. She couldn't fully appreciate what torture this was for starving prisoners of war – to her she was simply telling me what she'd been doing. Even this innocent form of torture was preferable to silence but on 9 September I dropped a gentle hint:

> ... Your letter telling me about the greenhouses etc, really make my mouth water dear. You've no idea how much we yearn for fresh fruit etc here ...

The slow starvation couldn't last much longer, because Germany was obviously losing the war by now. Why didn't they just give in and have done? Then I could be home in no time. Hitler, of course, wasn't like that but I was convinced this had been the last summer I'd spend here.

Before we knew it we were in autumn. The Germans let us use the huge parade ground for a rugby match. I played for 'England' when we took on 'New Zealand'. I hadn't played much rugby before that, but they wanted me to play on the wing after they discovered I could run fast. Half of the New Zealanders were Maoris and some of their players had even lost hands when they were shot down or captured. They still beat us! They wore leather caps on their heads to show they meant business and they had too much skill in whatever hands they still had. They certainly had our respect for that victory, even if it hurt to lose.

We heard rumours that the Germans wanted to play us at football and that caused a bit of excitement. We'd have done anything to beat them, but the match never materialised. Perhaps the guards were banned from making it a reality by their superiors. Besides, the German guards had more important things to worry about towards the end of 1944 – like how they were going to survive in the long run. The Russians were coming. And if the survival of the Germans was in doubt, so was our survival, since they controlled our destiny.

This fact hadn't been lost on relatives back home, who were only too well aware of the general strategic picture. Indeed by September 1944, the matter was serious enough to warrant a mention on the front of *The Prisoner of War*, which described itself as 'The official journal of the Prisoners of War Department of the Red Cross and St John War Organisation, St James's Palace, London SW1.' Its editor wrote:

> Relatives of men in camps in Eastern Europe are anxious, as I well know, for news of what is happening to them as the Russian advance continues. It is likely that the Germans will have taken all possible precautions for the safe internment of these men; but rumours about movements of prisoners, as one might expect, are difficult to confirm. All that we know definitely is that prisoners at Stalag

XXID at Posen, Poland, and Stalag Luft VI at Heydekrug have been moved to
other camps. Letters have come from them from Stalag 344 VIIIB, Stalag 357
(Thorn), and Stalag Luft IV (Tychow) ...

So we had people moving west to us from POW camps further east. And it didn't
take a genius to work out that the further west the Russians came, the sooner we
too would all have to move in that direction to stay ahead of them. That, of course,
assumed that Hitler's policy would be to preserve us rather than exterminate us.

We sent our Christmas greetings early as usual, and I hoped they'd reach home
in time for the festive season. You tried to keep things upbeat in these letters, you
didn't want to bring your family down. It was all about the future. Sylvia had
never stopped writing and I had her letters all neatly stacked up in chronological
order by my bunk. But the closer the Russians came that Christmas, the more
uncertain the atmosphere grew in the camp. It was bordering on unstable, because
the guards were becoming uneasy about what might happen to them. Snow had
fallen, it was freezing cold, but there was a hot excitement in the air. It was very
strange and difficult to describe.

In my final letter to Sylvia from the camp I tried to sound as reassuring as
possible about what lay ahead for us:

> ... I must tell you that I still love you more than ever and am missing you pretty
> badly these days. Gosh aren't we having a long wait Sylvia? Still if we exercise
> that virtue of patience everything will come right in the end. At the moment, in
> camp, snow lies all around and it's very cold. Our Red Cross parcels still haven't
> arrived, so we are all anxiously awaiting their arrival, praying they will be here
> in time for Christmas ... You know dearest I often wish I could go to sleep here
> until the war was over and then wake up to find you in my arms. That would do
> away with all the misery of waiting. Well sweetheart, here's the end once again.
> So for the time being Cheerio darling and here's all my sincerest fondest love,
> Maurice xxx

And that was it. Events took over after that. Terrible events. By January, the
advancing Russians were said to be no more than about 12 miles to the east.

On 29 December, it happened. An officer came in and barked, 'Everybody
outside! Now! Bring a bit of food with you!' So that's what we did, and in that
instant I lost all Sylvia's beautiful letters forever. There wasn't time to gather them
up; and anyway, I reckoned I'd be seeing Sylvia very soon in the flesh, living my
life with her, so I wouldn't be needing to read her letters to remind me of her
any more. The food was the priority, though we didn't know immediately that
we were never going to return to the camp again. What I also grabbed were the
chains that had bound me in reprisal for Dieppe back in 1942. I'd hidden them

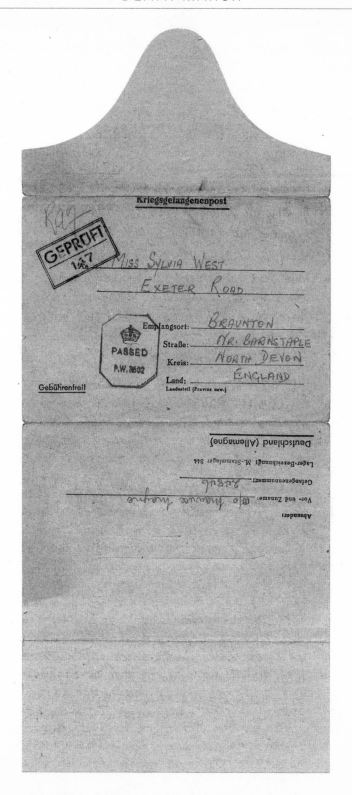

Kriegsgefangenenpost

Ra7

GEPRÜFT
1.17

Miss Sylvia West

Exeter Road

Empfangsort: BRAUNTON

PASSED
P.W. 3502

Straße: NR. BARNSTAPLE

Kreis: NORTH DEVON

Land: ENGLAND

Landesteil (Provinz usw.)

Gebührenfrei

Deutschland (Allemagne)

Lager-Bezeichnung: M.-Stammlager 344

Gefangenennummer: 24846

Vor- und Zuname: c/o Thomas Hoping

Absender:

'I promise to provide for Sylvia.
But first I must survive.'

17th Dec. 1944

Dearest Sylvia, Once again I'm here to tell you
the same old things, though I know you'll always
excusing me repeating myself. First of all
honey, I must tell you I still love you dearer
than ever & am missing you pretty badly
these days. Gosh aren't we having a long
wait Sylvia? Still if we exercise that virtue
of patience everything will come right in
the end. At the moment, in camp, snow
lies all around and it very cold. Our Red
Cross parcels still haven't arrived, so we
are all anxiously awaiting their arrival,
praying they will be in time for Christmas
Meanwhile I'm spending most of my
time studying various subjects that may
be of help to me when I get back. You see
Sylvia dear, I really aim to do well
when I get back, so that you & I
can really live happily. You know
dearest I often wish I could go to sleep
here until the war was over & then wake
up to find you in my arms. That would
do away with all the misery of waiting.
Well, sweetheart, heres the end once again,
So for the time being Cheerio darling theres
all my sincerest fondest
love
Maurice
x x x

away inside my bed mattress and I thought I might need them if I was going to have to fight for my life in some way. They were also a grim souvenir of the worst of the captivity, something I could keep and show people if ever I got home.

As the RAF contingent lined up on the parade ground, a German officer called Captain Mause announced that he was in charge of us now. There were about 800–900 of us by then and we were closely flanked by German guards. Mause marched us out of the camp and we headed west. By then, we probably knew deep down what was happening. The Germans were trying to stay one step ahead of the Russians. The camp that had been home for two years, apart from an exciting excursion to Berlin and Stralsund, was disappearing from view behind us. And we were never going to see it again.

At first spirits among the lads were high. We were lively, with people cracking jokes down the line. The tedious monotony of life in the camp had been broken forever. What's more, we were heading west, towards home. Granted, we had thousands of miles to walk if ever we were going to make it. But it felt so good to be moving in the right direction.

The snow still lay thick on the ground though, and after one night out beside the road in bitterly cold weather, and then another night, the mood began to change. We realised this was getting serious. We were marching through one of the worst winters on the Silesian plains in living memory. Was this a death march? Whereas the boys had been cheerful before, now everybody went quiet. And when that silence was broken, it was usually because somebody was irritable about something and wanted to sound off. I didn't feel like that, I wanted to keep people's spirits up and saw an opportunity to make people smile. We'd had a particularly long march one day without a rest, everyone was absolutely worn out; so I shouted up to the front:

'How about a "pause", Mause?!'

I thought this was pretty witty because the words rhymed. 'Pause' was pronounced 'powser' in German and Mause was pronounced 'Mowser'. I waited for a general chuckle but what I got was something quite different. Immediately all the blokes around me turned on me. They thought I might get us all shot for poking fun at our German leader. They told me to belt up in no uncertain terms. No one took a swing at me because most of them had seen me in action. But they put me in my place alright. As for Mause, he didn't give us a pause. He ignored me completely.

It was another hour or two before we were finally allowed to stop, though we were learning by now what an unpleasant experience that could be too. We sank into the snow, which then melted all around us, leaving us soaking and freezing. We tried to drink some of the snow after melting it by cupping it in our hands. We did quite a lot of that during the march but we were always thirsty.

Ken 'Tex' Hyde was on the march and had a camera hidden away as ever. He took some photographs which reflect the increasingly desperate situation we were in, suffering in the bitter cold and scavenging for food if the chance arose. Hyde found a way to escape from the column after eight days. He'd have been shot on the spot had he been spotted slipping away. He was eventually rearrested far enough away to be sent to Berlin to end his captivity there. The Russians freed him on 22 April 1945.

John Sinclair was on the march too, but in a different column, behind me. He tried to hide away in a barn with some other men apparently, but they were caught. Despite being threatened with the firing squad, John survived and was eventually forced to march on. He was rescued just before he would have faded away completely. John, my old Beaufort navigator, was destined to survive the war.

As for me, I decided my best chance of survival was to stay with the main group, at least for as long as it looked as though the fittest would be allowed to live. After several days we stopped briefly at some German Army barracks. We were allowed to go into a barn there and they gave us soup. As you'll know by now, I wasn't a fan of German soup, but this was to stay alive. Someone shouted, 'Soup up!' They

were serving it into the little 'dixies' we had to eat it from, metal pots you could use for cooking and drinking. I got up to rush down towards where the Germans were serving the soup, because it smelt pretty good after what we'd been through. But as I went down, I put my hand on something all wet and sticky. I realised I'd touched a jar filled with some kind of food, and instinctively I licked my fingers. It was a lovely taste – horse meat! This was very popular in Germany in those days. Some prisoners must have got hold of some when they came through here before us. I tipped the horse meat into my 'dixie', and then I was served a ladle of the soup, which filled right up to the top as it poured over the meat. That combination tasted beautiful after what we'd been through.

'That bloody swine,' I heard one prisoner say. 'I've only got carrot soup!'

But then again everybody did – except lucky old me! The meal gave me a terrific energy boost and also made me feel like smoking a cigarette, but you weren't allowed. It was foolish to smoke in a barn at any time, because it could go up in flames. One Canadian lit up anyway and almost paid with his life. The Germans piled in and one of them shot at him. The bullet passed right through the top of the Canadian's hair. That frightened us all to death and we realised that if we stepped out of line on this march, we'd be killed straight away.

The suffering on the march became more extreme. In the early weeks, when the snow was on the ground and it was perishing cold, there seemed to be no let-up. Day after day, plodding through the snow without rest; it was a terrible time. I think we lost a lot of our blokes in that period. As January turned to February we were still marching, and I ditched the chains I'd brought with me, because anything that wasn't essential just became a burden. I was so exhausted, I flung them away.

People were disappearing – but this time not because they'd escaped. If you couldn't keep up, you'd had it. Good men who had spent years writing to their loved ones just as I had; now they could take no more. They didn't have the strength to go on. Their spirits were willing but their bodies were spent. I can't imagine what that must have felt like, the hopeless, helpless realisation that the years in captivity had been endured in vain; that the chance to see their wife or girlfriend was slipping away in the freezing snow; that it was all over as they fell away.

'Keep together!'

That's what kept going through my head. I had to get back to Sylvia, I just had to. Keep together! It was the unwritten rule. I don't remember any of us actually saying it out loud, but we didn't have to. Fail to stick to this rule and it was the end of you. Keep together! If you drop out for a moment, for whatever reason, you are in danger. Don't stay away from the central column for too long! Get back in the middle. Keep together!

The Germans were capable of anything at this point. Most of them had run out of all sympathy and compassion by now. Germany was collapsing – and the soldiers were fed up with being asked to do anything any more. They looked ready to turn on anyone, friend or foe.

At one place I saw something terrible, which has always stayed in my mind. We were going through a pleasant-looking village, but out in the field, tied to a post, was a British serviceman. He didn't have a hat on and it was freezing cold. He must have seen some carrots or something in that field, gone over and started trying to pull one out. The Germans had spotted him and punished him by tying him to that stake and then they just left him there. I heard he'd already been there since six in the morning and it was about three in the afternoon when I saw him. His head was hanging down. God, I often wonder what happened to that bloke. I didn't know his name so I couldn't ever check, but I don't suppose he could have survived that. Either he froze or starved to death.

To my astonishment, some groups were being marched in the opposite direction to us – but surely not for long. One day, while there was still snow on the ground, another terrible sight appeared before us. Young women, hollow-cheeked, eyes sunken deep into their skulls; their bony heads long since shaven of all hair. What vision from hell was this? There were at least thirty of them, under guard. There may have been more because they were all stretched out in a long line. It was so cold and they had nothing over their heads to protect them from the freezing temperatures. Why were they marching east? Everyone was trying to get away from the east, to maintain some hope, but for them all hope was denied.

These girls must have been Jewish. It was bitterly cold and yet they had hardly any clothes on. They had made themselves dresses out of sacking. They weren't even dresses really, just crude covers for what remained of their bodies. It crossed my mind that they might have had no clothes at all for some time before that. Their previous dresses were probably destroyed during multiple rapes or long spells of enforced prostitution. What flesh was still visible had turned a raw pink due to the biting cold. This was a dreadful sight. They had nothing more than cloth wrapped around their feet in the freezing snow and it was a wonder they walked at all; except that their guards were so sadistic-looking that you just knew to stop walking would mean certain death for them. They were dragging themselves along, exhausted. The tragedy was this: to keep walking sealed the same fate for them.

'Where are you going?' we asked.

'Are you Jewish?'

'Where are you from?'

They gave us no reply. They were already half-dead. In fact the ones that passed close by me looked more than half dead, from all their suffering. It was as though their minds had already perished after all they'd been through. It wasn't hard to work out that they were Jewesses. We'd known for a while what was happening to the Jews, though not quite the scale of it. We didn't hear about the camps on the radio, we had other ways. There were blokes being shot down every day, don't forget. We'd had fresh news coming in every week from Bomber Command up until the end of 1944, especially after they'd started their offensive and more and more prisoners came in. The concentration camps were no longer a secret; it was well known what was happening.

Even with Germany breaking down, it seemed that the Nazis wanted one last orgy of murder before they were finally stopped. They must have been leading these poor girls to a concentration camp somewhere nearby. Perhaps the extermination camp lurked in the woods we were passing. It was all too terrible to contemplate. We were powerless to help them, knowing that death wouldn't be far away for us either, if we stepped out of line. They faded from sight and were never heard of again.

Another group was marched 'the wrong way' a bit later. They couldn't have been more different to the poor Jewish girls. I saw giant men, fierce-looking and heavily built. They had a German guard at each end of every group of four. Half as many guards as men! That told you these blokes were considered dangerous. They looked like Mongol or Tartar fighters, being moved east by their German guards. But they didn't look ready to try anything – they looked pretty fed up. Either they were being led to a nearby place of execution, before the approaching Russians, who were only days away, could save them; or more likely in my opinion they were going to be put in prison camps near the front line to stop the Russians from shelling their own men, to buy the Germans a bit of time.

Anyone who had heard of Russian ruthlessness would not have rated the chances of these German guards if they stayed around long enough to surrender to the advancing Red Army. But in the chaos of this widespread German disintegration, Russian prisoners may have seemed like an asset; a human shield might have seemed worth setting up.

All I knew after seeing these sights was that it must surely be better to be on a death march heading west than one heading east. At least moving in that direction we might have some control over our destiny. Our guards were not going to put any extra effort into keeping us alive, that was for sure. If we didn't do that for ourselves, we'd had it.

'For God's sake, keep together at all costs!'

But you do ridiculous things, just to keep alive. We were starving. If you were lucky, the Germans gave you a loaf of bread and said, 'Between two – five days.'

That was it. You were supposed to survive the best part of a week on half a loaf of bread, while marching all day, every day.

One night we reached a barn and I was mucking in with a New Zealander at the time. He was a bit of a weakling but he wanted to look after our bread so I let him. We went to sleep, woke up in the morning and of course the bread had gone. Some other RAF bloke had pinched it to try and stay alive, but in doing so he had put our lives in danger, and that really got to me. Our situation was now critical. We didn't have any bread for the week, because it had only just been issued that day. I thought that if I didn't have some bread I wouldn't be able to march and I would die. So it was worth risking my life to get some more bread for us.

One day we passed a column of army blokes. There were carts on the side of the road and the Germans were handing out their bread. Each group of four men was getting a loaf. I could see them doing that, so I left the RAF column, ran right down the middle of the army column to the front, got level with the Germans throwing the bread, caught a loaf, and rushed back into the middle of the army column. I waited for the shout from the Germans, for the army blokes to step aside so I could be shot and not them. But nothing happened and I managed to run back up through the army column and caught up with my own RAF column before anyone noticed. If I'd have been seen by the Germans guards at any stage of this little effort, I could have been shot in the back as I ran. But I got away with it, perhaps because I was a nippy little type. God, when you think of it! The risk I had taken! It was one of the most dangerous moments of my war. But I got us the bread and that was all that mattered.

I was naturally tough and resourceful, I don't know why. I'm not sure it was down to my upbringing, because it hadn't been such a hard, hungry childhood. Nothing terrible had happened to me as a kid which might have forced me to become this resourceful character. I just was. And consequently blokes used to come up to me and ask me how to do this or that.

'How can we get something to eat, Mayne?' I'd help them if I possibly could, but I wasn't going to risk my life for people I wasn't teamed up with.

On another occasion we woke up in the morning and this weak New Zealander had lost his overcoat – someone had pinched that too. I felt concerned for him; it was perishing cold that month and he might not survive without a coat. I knew he was a bit soft but he was with me, so I almost took it personally.

I said, 'I know who was sleeping next to you, it was a sailor and two other chaps from another column. We'll press on in our column until we see theirs and then we'll keep a look out for this sailor bloke and sort this out.'

We hadn't gone all that far when there in front of us we saw three men – two army blokes and the sailor. The sailor had this dark grey coat on. Bloody marvellous! I should have let the Kiwi go forward to administer his own justice, but I went forward instead. I went up behind the sailor and pulled most of the coat off him. He struggled a bit, but I managed to get the whole coat away in no time, and he didn't fight for it. I went back to the Kiwi and we looked at this coat.

'Cor blimey!' I said. 'There's a different name in this coat altogether!' Anyway I gave it to the New Zealander, and he made do with it.

I don't know what happened to the sailor whose coat I'd taken. Maybe he stole someone else's. It sounds terrible in peacetime, all this. But I was looking after my own. It was becoming a case of 'each man for himself', as the theft of our bread had shown. I approached this crisis in a simple manner: I was ready to have a fist-fight with anyone who wanted to get in my way. I was going to survive and so was anyone I was with – if I could help them to do so.

But for some poor blokes, survival became physically impossible. One by one, I lost sight of mates who'd teamed up with other people, and many of them I never saw again. I don't think stragglers were shot because I think we'd have heard the shootings – but they might have been. I think they just collapsed and froze to death, and then they were just left by the side of the road. It was up to the Russians if they were buried or not later. They probably weren't, because at that stage the ground was so hard. Besides, the Russians had other things to focus on – like catching up with the Germans and destroying them.

In some ways you could understand why our march was so relentless, as the Germans were desperate to stay ahead of the Russians at all costs. They were under no illusions about what would happen to them if they fell into Russian hands. After all the atrocities the Germans had committed on their own advance east, revenge was going to get ugly.

We were dragged along mercilessly in the wake of that German fear, often scavenging for food to supplement the completely inadequate rations given to us by the Germans. The further we went in these sub-zero temperatures, the more the 'Long March' west became the 'Death March'. Much depended on your fighting spirit, your core fitness and general health after all those years of deprivation. I suppose the fact that I was a sportsman helped me. I wasn't short of fight and I wasn't afraid to put myself first when I had to either. I wanted to see Sylvia again, I wanted to see my family again. I had the basic fitness to keep me going when others couldn't carry on.

But everyone has their limits and I was nearing mine. Sometimes we'd reach somewhere and rest up for two or three days, but not very often. Mostly there was just an incessant assault on your reserves of energy and physical well-being. By the end of March, covering all those miles on foot had taken its toll. The sole of one of my feet just fell off. You weren't supposed to take your boots off when you got to a barn for the night. The Germans could call you out for shouting or any minor offence, and if you weren't booted and ready to go running to them, you could be shot for disobeying an order.

But at this point I just said, 'I must take my boots off.'

And when I took one boot off, I took the sole of my foot off as well, because it had stuck to inside of the boot along with the sock. It didn't hurt me, but when I looked in the sock there it was, the sole of my foot, padded and hard. And when I looked at the rest of my foot it was all fleshy. It wasn't raw flesh, but it was soft and tender flesh, so this detachment must have happened at some point earlier, while I'd been marching. I hadn't even noticed.

I didn't try to put the sole of my foot back on; I decided there was no hope that it would all knit back together in time. It was past that stage, I had to admit it, so I just chucked the sole of my foot away. I put a bit of blanket in the bottom of the boot to cushion what was left of my foot a bit. And then I put the boot back on again, as though nothing had happened. You didn't dare keep them off to go to sleep anyway, and not just because of the Germans. Someone on your own side might steal them in the night, and then you really would have had it.

I enjoyed one surreal experience late in this terrible march, as we all struggled to keep trudging west. A group of French women passed us on a horse and cart, moving in the same direction, yet apparently in better shape physically and in much higher spirits too. There wasn't even a guard with them! Whether they were prostitutes or workers who'd been given a degree of freedom, I don't know. When we shouted out to them, they began singing 'It's a long way to Tipperary' to cheer us up! To the west lay France, ultimately, so I suppose you could just about understand their optimism. Yet it was a mystery to me how they had remained so buoyant through their own misery. I hope they found a way to stay alive and gain the sympathy of those who stood in their way, whatever it took. For those of us who had survived this far on our long march, the situation was becoming critical.

We were all so hungry and thirsty. Eventually in early April, my constant nagging hunger and thirst cost me dear. I found some sort of root vegetable and ate it. The moment I got it down my throat I felt this terrible burning sensation – it was unbelievable. It was scorching me, there was something in it or on it that was reacting with the skin in my throat and it was agony. I felt I had to drink something to counteract the heat in my throat.

We'd been given a quick break by a ditch, which was filled with water. Some basic instinct took over within me, and I drank from that ditch. Before long I went down with dysentery – and I had it very bad, with terrible pains in my stomach.

'Keep together! I've got to stay in with the others!'

I knew it but I couldn't march any more, hard as I tried. I put everything into it, knowing I might be shot or simply left to die if I couldn't keep up. That was a very real fear after what had happened to so many others. I saw death as the inevitable consequence of my weakness now, if I gave into it. I tried so hard to drive myself on. But it was hopeless. All my strength had gone out of me, I couldn't control my bowels. I was filthy and exhausted. This must have been the sort of thing that had happened to all the others. I was no different, after all. My love for Sylvia could not keep me on my feet.

They took me off the march. Every man has his limit and after more than three months of marching and suffering, I'd reached mine. Was this it? After being shot down, after years of survival, after my escape and recapture, were these to be my last moments? Shot or just left to die on the side of a snowy road, covered in my own shit?

17

CHAOS AND SALVATION

They didn't put me out of my misery. I was barely conscious by then, so I didn't fully realise what was going on. But then I had this sensation of caring hands putting me on a cart. I wasn't sure if some of my fellow prisoners were doing it, or the Germans. Where these people came from didn't matter. I wasn't being killed; I was being put on this cart instead, along with a few other men who were also too ill to walk by now. A slight sense of relief rose within me, even though my body was failing me. I was beyond thought or powers of analysis; it just felt better to be on that cart than crawling towards a lonely death on the side of the road.

If we'd been on another part of the march, I'm convinced the Germans wouldn't have allowed or displayed this mercy. But it turned out we were only a few miles from a place called Bad Sulza, near Leipzig, in an area of Germany called Thuringen. This was where Mause had planned for us to rest up for a while. Stalag 9C was to be the temporary home of the marchers. Whether or not the same went for those who were too ill to be looked after easily wasn't clear. If the Russians closed in again and we hadn't recovered, it would probably be a bullet in the back of the head.

One thousand four hundred of us had left Stalag VIIIB on the long march to Bad Sulza. By the time we got there, we numbered 400. I lost all my friends on that march, there were hardly any of us left when we got to Bad Sulza. It was very confusing for me, because the only blokes who were left were men I didn't know. A thousand of us had died on the way to this place, and the dying hadn't finished yet.

I was dumped in a side-room in a building at the camp. The room had a cold stone floor, which was covered in straw. I was being treated like an animal but I wasn't alone. Quite a few of the blokes had dysentery by now, and some of the worst-affected were put in there with me. We must have smelt lovely together.

Perhaps the German guards had decided none of us were going to make it, because we were all so weak. No food was wasted on us; that's for sure. I slipped in and out of consciousness; I don't know how long I was in that place.

Then in the middle of the night I was awoken, and suddenly I saw a German uniform by the side of me, an officer's uniform.

The officer stood over me and he said, 'How many times?'

I took that to mean how many times was I 'going to the toilet' each day. 'Eighteen,' I answered.

He told me, 'You won't have to go any more.'

I found those words quite chilling. They must have had enough of us. They'd given us a quick chance to get our strength back but it hadn't happened in time. So those of us who weren't showing any signs of recovering were going to be shot. And yet his words were almost delivered like a consolation.

'We're going to kill you now, but at least you won't be shitting yourself any more.' That's the way I read it; a moment I'll never forget.

Then he added, 'I'll give you some medicine.'

It had only been a second or two between his previous remark and this one, but for me it was the difference between life and death. Now I thought I could pick up a hint of compassion in his voice.

'Take these pills; go to sleep and when you wake up, all this will be gone.'

Again, it was possible to read into this some sinister meaning. But I was in so much discomfort that I just wanted to take him at his word and follow his advice. I wanted my suffering to be over and so, thank God, did he.

It turned out that he was back from the Russian front on leave. And he had used some of his precious time away from that hell to show some humanity; to come to see us in all our degradation, accompanied by his batman. He had walked among us in all our filth, to try to make us better. It might be going a bit far for a Cockney gunner to call any German from that terrible time an angel. But if one was, it was him.

He gave me some pills in a sort of cocktail: 'Bella Donna', Opium and Luminol. Almost immediately I drifted off into a peculiar sleep. When I woke up, the terrible pain and the worst of the dysentery had gone, as if through a miracle. My bowels were still not right, it doesn't just disappear completely, and I was still very weak but I was so grateful to that nice man. It is no exaggeration to say this German officer had saved my life. I hope he didn't die back on the Russian front when it was time for him to return there. He'd already gone by the time I woke up, and so I never saw him again.

When I looked around me, I discovered that an American had lain next to me while I was asleep – or else been dumped there. It seemed probable that he'd managed to lose his unit during the fighting between Americans and Germans in this area three or four weeks earlier. What had happened to him since was a mystery. By now people could come and go at this camp almost as they liked, because the Germans were in such a state. So this American had either crawled into my little room of his own accord, or else the few Germans who still cared

about such things had seen him arrive, taken one look at him and decided that
they hadn't liked what they'd seen. That would have explained why they might
have stuck him away with me, where he couldn't infect the main camp population
with whatever problem he had.

Personally I didn't realise just how bad this American's condition was; how could
I? There wasn't any obvious wound on him; and though he wasn't talking, I just
hoped he needed a good rest before he could tell me what his name was. But in the
middle of the next night, he made this terrible noise, like a death rattle. And all of a
sudden he was dead. I never did find out what was wrong with him, who he was or
why he had died. Was my side-room still the place they put people to die?

In the morning I managed to attract the attention of the few German guards
who were still around, and told one of them what had happened. An English
orderly was detailed to deal with the body.

The Englishman took one look at this American and said, 'He'll have to be
buried straight away.'

So they found this big long paper bag and slid him into it, tied the ends and
took him away. It was very, very crude. Where he was buried, poor devil, I don't
know. The only bright spot was that he left his cigarettes behind. And for me that
was another life-saver. The cigarettes were Canadian, called Sweet Caprol, and
he left about 200 of them. He couldn't smoke them and I couldn't smoke many
either in my condition; but they soon came in useful.

There was barely any food, but a couple of Belgians came round selling icing
sugar. I didn't know where they had got it from and I didn't have any money,
either. But I knew that icing sugar would be just what I needed to get some
much-needed energy into my body.

'Cigarettes for icing sugar!' I demanded, praying they were either smokers
themselves, or saw what a profit they could make from the few Sweet Caprol
packets I was offering them.

'It's a deal,' they replied, to my relief.

That icing sugar tasted like heaven. It helped to revive me, and what's more it
turned out that I didn't have to march any more. A fresh load of prisoners came
into the camp, but the German guards were slipping away all the time. I managed
to scrounge a little bit of food in return for some more of the dead American's
cigarettes. Crucially I kept this bread and soup down. It wasn't much but it was
something; and I could feel my strength slowly starting to return.

Suddenly there was a terrific commotion outside. The German guards who
had remained were running down the road as fast as they could. We could hear
shots. Apparently the Americans were approaching very fast, and shot one of the
Germans in the arm.

The next thing that happened was that a couple of American vehicles went
by the camp, creating uproar. Some of our boys tried to climb the barbed-wire

fences to jump onto the trucks. They were worried we'd just get by-passed by the Allies during their advance.

The Americans stopped long enough to ask, 'What do you want?'

'We want food!' came the reply. 'We've got no food at the moment.'

'OK,' the Americans replied, 'leave it to us.'

They drove off and there was nothing left but to trust them. Sure enough, some American soldiers came back later with four live pigs and drove them into our camp. Then an American said, 'Is there anyone here who is a butcher?'

A nineteen-year-old British lad piped up and said, 'Yeah, I used to help at a butcher's shop!'

So he was put in charge of killing these pigs and must have made a decent job of it, because they were roasted by midnight.

That's when the cry came, 'Pork up!'

I was still pretty weak at that stage and I was almost crawling in the general rush to get to the meat. It had been cooked in old tin cans that had been left by previous prisoners. Even those who couldn't run still got some pork – including me. It tasted marvellous, but of course it was too much for our fragile digestive systems, and the next day we all had what felt like a touch of dysentery again.

It wasn't serious, the Germans had all been cleared away, and it dawned on me that at last I was free – really free, for the first time in two years. I was so happy and my sense of humour had returned.

It was 15 April 1945, three years and two weeks since my ordeal had begun. The first thing I wanted to do was to let my family know I was safe, because I knew they'd tell Sylvia immediately. So I wrote them a letter, and pointed out at the bottom, in capital letters, that it had been 'TYPED ON A LIBERATED GERMAN TYPEWRITER'.

That letter survives to this day:

Dear Mum, Dad and Ken,

Today I have been liberated by the goddam Yanks and so you can expect to see me home soon. You can imagine how excited we are at the thought of meeting everyone again. It hardly seems true that we are free men at last and that our days of confinement behind barbed wire are at an end. During the past month or two the Hun has caused us and thousands of other prisoners quite a lot of suffering and it does us the world of good to see the Yanks handing it out to them. Well my mind is in such a whirl that I find it difficult to concentrate on anything for more than five minutes at a time, so do forgive me if this letter is only a brief one. Give the news to Sylvia and of course my love to her as well. Here's all my fondest affection till I see you all again,

Cheerio,

Maurice xxxx.

April 15th 1945.   To
Stalag 9c,   Mr. and Mrs. Mayne,
Bad Sulza,   44 Mundania Road,
  Thuringen,Germany.   East Dulwich,
                                            LONDON S.E.22.

Dear Mum, Dad, and Ken,
            Today I have been liberated by the goddam Yanks and so you
can expect to see me home soon.You can imagine how excited we all are at
the thought of meeting everyone again. It hardly seems true that we are
free men at last and that our days of confinement behind barbed wire are
at an end.During the past month or two the Hun has caused us and thousands
of other prisoners quite a lot of suffering and it does us the world of
good to see the Yanks handing it out to them. Well my mind is in such a
whirl that I find it difficult to concentrate on any one thing for more
than five minutes at a time, so do forgive me if this letter is only

   a brief one. Give the news to Sylvia and of course my löve to her as
well.Heres all my fondest affection till I see you all again,

                              Cheerio,
                                 Maurice   xxxx
                                 _____

Typed on a "liberated"
German Typewriter

'I'm free! Tell Sylvia I love her! At last I know my nightmare is nearly over.'

There was a kiss for each one of them: three family members and one young woman I fully intended to make a family member as soon as I could!

The next day there was an announcement. The Swiss Red Cross was going to come into the camp with a load of vans and take men from there all the way to Switzerland, to freedom and recuperation. Sure enough they came in with these Swiss doctors, speaking French and Italian, and they started examining the men most in need. The chests of some of the army blokes were in a terrible state – all bones. I was thin, but by comparison I still had flesh on me. Some of these men had been wounded and left behind after the battle around Bad Sulza, in that fighting before we arrived. These poor men had begun to starve before they'd managed to wander into the camp.

Anyway, the Red Cross blokes were telling those chosen, 'Go and get into the white van and we'll take you all the way to Switzerland.'

What a relief that was for them. The war was almost over, Germany was in a terrible state, and these men didn't have to be in Germany any more. I wanted to be with them. The doctors examined men one by one and eventually they came to me. They examined my chest and said it was OK. I looked at the vans filling up with men and said hopefully, 'But one of the white vans will take me up to Switzerland?'

The doctor looked at the vans too, and said, 'No, no, no. Not you. Those men, they're really not very well.'

'What about me?' I asked. 'I've been ill too.'

'Sorry, compared to them, you're fit,' came the reply.

I was almost pleading with them. Take me to bloody Switzerland! But they had made their mind up. If your condition was no longer life-threatening, you stayed.

So I went out and did a bit of looting instead. It wasn't just me. There was a lot of looting going on around the camp. And what better way to enjoy my newfound freedom than to go on a nice little looting spree of my own? I went out of the camp with a Frenchman and two South Africans to have our bit of fun. In some ways we'd been beaten to it, because there were a large number of prisoners already out there, looting anything that looked worth the trouble.

After a while, we found ourselves in this big factory. An English officer was already in there and he had a question for us, 'Anyone want a length of cloth for a suit?' He was holding up a roll of material and it looked pretty good.

Well this was right up my street, considering the job I'd done with my father before the war.

'Yes, I'll take a look!' I said. Since I was in the textile trade, I thought I could appreciate the value of what was on offer. The material looked just fine. Perhaps the English officer knew a thing or two about the business too, because he very skilfully tore off a length of suit material from this big roll. I knew exactly what I

was going to do with it. I was going to take that material home to my father and
have a suit made out of it, just for him.

I suppose I shouldn't say it, but I quite enjoyed the looting. You've not been
able to do anything you want to do for so long, and then suddenly you're let loose
like a kid in a sweetshop. Right or wrong, it was fun.

We'd knock on the doors of houses and cottages and the Germans were scared
stiff, so they'd give you cakes or whatever. We didn't feel too guilty, we'd had our
share of feeling scared, but we weren't abusive. And you can imagine how good
those cakes tasted after POW delights such as swedes and water in a dustbin! One
time, four of us went to a farm and looked to see what animals might be in one of
the buildings at the back. I spotted something and said to the other lads, 'There's a
chicken up on this ledge but I can't quite reach it.'

Just at that moment, two Russians came in – quick as a flash. They'd probably
just been released from a POW camp too. I pointed to the chicken and one of
them, who was much taller than me, reached up and brought the chicken down
by knocking it off the ledge. He seemed to want to keep it.

I said, 'No! That's mine!'

One Russian responded by getting hold of the chicken's head and he just
pulled it off, right in front of me. He didn't want to hand the chicken back to me
but I wasn't backing down.

'Give it back!' I said.

It was a bit of a gamble but he did hand it back in the end.

Those Russians must have just been to a local house, because one of them
showed me that his hands were full of lovely cake. It looked so delicious that I
dipped my hand into his and tried to take a piece. He hit me across the hand and
his look told me in no uncertain terms that I wasn't going to get any of that cake.

We cooked that chicken right there at the farm. We managed to pinch a table
cloth; we broke into the farm's wine cellar and had bottles of wine on the table.
We had a lovely meal, but we didn't invite the Russians. They were wild types;
you'd never have known what was going to happen.

My British companions told me I shouldn't have done what I did, that the
Russians could have shot me for standing my ground over the chicken, or for
trying to take a bit of their cake. We could all have been shot, they said. I suppose
they were right. It was all so chaotic, anything could have happened. But it didn't
stop us from enjoying that lovely meal. When you've risked your life for some
food, it tastes even better!

When I returned from that little escapade, the Americans came in and said,
'Who is the senior officer here?'

I looked around and there wasn't a British officer around. I'd been promoted
to warrant officer by then – you could be promoted even while you were a POW,

that was the one thing I liked about it. I was a sergeant when I was shot down and I was a warrant officer by the time I was free!

So I quickly realised I was the senior NCO and said, 'I am.'

I wondered why they wanted to know. Would I regret owning up to my status?

'There's a German officer who wants to surrender, in a house up on the hill,' he said.

So I had to go. I took a few men with me because the Americans said there was still trouble in the area. I went out, found the hill the Americans had described, and at the top of the hill was this very nice house. A very kind-looking middle-aged lady came to the door.

I said, 'I've come to take the surrender of the man in this house.'

She said, 'It's my son.'

I waited in the hall and all of a sudden a very big man came down the stairs in the full uniform of the German officer. He was absolutely immaculate but his leg was encased in plaster from his foot right up to the hip. He'd been wounded on the Russian front. He hobbled down the stairs, got to the bottom, then he clicked his heels to me and handed me his revolver. I took it and prepared to lead him out. He said goodbye to his mother, who was in tears. He was carrying beautiful leather valises, ready to go wherever I decided. But just as I took him out, an American jeep came up the drive and grabbed him. They took his revolver from me too, probably wanting to keep it as a souvenir for themselves. They were the most brutal blokes I've ever seen.

They took him, yelling, 'This way!'

They threw his leather valises down the drive towards their vehicle and he was manhandled onto the jeep. I hope he reached some prison-camp somewhere. But I actually felt sorry for him, because he seemed a really good chap. His mother was really upset at seeing him whipped away like that. I was glad my parents hadn't seen any of the humiliations I'd suffered. Now my war was over, because that was the last of the ugliness I was ever going to see first-hand.

I was going to be able to go home to them in one piece.

★ ★ ★

It was about three weeks to a month after the Americans had first liberated us at that camp, and I was finally able to go home. It was May by now; but I knew I'd see the people I loved soon. I enjoyed the sense of anticipation; I couldn't wait to get back.

First of all the Americans picked us up by lorry at the camp, and then they took us to an airfield just outside Bad Sulza. We boarded some American plane, I can't even remember the type, and we were flown to Le Havre, on the French coast.

From there we went by ship across the English Channel, towards Southampton. Seeing the English coast come closer by the minute, knowing I had finally made it; that was so special. The last leg of the trip back to London was done by train. But I was still in the RAF; and it still wasn't time to see those people who were dearest to me.

Mother and father knew I was coming home. They also knew I'd had to go to Cosford Medical Centre with the other returned POWs, for a full medical check-up – it was standard procedure – before I could get back to them.

At Cosford they told me that there was no chance of me going back out to fight. They said I was unfit to serve any more. I was to be discharged because of my general condition. I'd had jaundice in the prison camp and I'd had that nasty bout of dysentery on the march. I was no longer as fit as I thought I was, apparently.

I wasn't upset about it, to be honest. I just wanted to get home as soon as I could. I still hated the Germans but I also wanted my own normal life back. I wouldn't have been disappointed to fight again either, because I felt I'd been wasting my time for three years. I had mixed feelings. But the verdict was inescapable: my war was definitely over, unless of course some belated German bomb was going to blow me up in London.

I phoned home, broke the news to mother and father, and told them I was coming home that very day.

Technically I was on leave, but I'd made it. To know that I'd come through and didn't have to go out again, that just made it even more special. I'd just been told about my medical discharge, but I felt alright in myself. As far as I was concerned, there was nothing permanently wrong with me, nothing that a few weeks of good food and happiness couldn't put right. I was in good spirits, ready to enjoy the moment.

My parents were living still in East Dulwich. It was a lovely spring day and as I neared the house, I could see that they had put flags up for me. Union jacks and a 'Welcome Home' banner.

I thought, 'Oh my God!' It was all a bit much, but I was ready to accept it.

Mum and Dad were waiting for me and they saw me walking down the street towards them. They were struck by how thin I looked, but they did a good job of hiding that concern. Besides, hadn't we all worried enough? Nothing could rival the joy we all felt at being reunited. They came rushing down the road towards me and Mum got there first, smothering me in one of the biggest, warmest embraces she ever gave me. Once we got inside we were all in tears, including Dad. I gave him his present from Germany – that roll of cloth for the suit – and it made him smile.

But after all the initial greetings in the front room, I started to wonder what had happened to Sylvia. She hadn't got cold feet after all that time, had she? When the reality of my homecoming had hit her, had she realised she didn't want to be tied down after all? Had she run a mile?

Mum looked at me as if she had something to say, as if there was something I should know, something important that I hadn't yet been told. I didn't quite know what to make of it, but she was still smiling, so I began to think it couldn't be bad news.

'Maurice,' she said. 'Someone in the next room wants to see you.'

It couldn't be, could it? I went into the next room, and there she was – Sylvia, looking as beautiful as ever. I hadn't seen her for four years but she hadn't changed, not to me. She didn't say I'd changed either. I knew for sure right then that I was going to spend the rest of my life with her.

No words were necessary. She looked lovely. And as far as I could tell, she thought I looked lovely too! What did we say? There wasn't much 'saying' done! Didn't need to be! It was wonderful!

This was everything I'd hoped for. The surge of passion, the knowledge that all I'd hoped for in the dark days of captivity was coming true, right here in my arms. For years I'd dreamed of holding her, but it had only been a dream. There were moments when that dream seemed to have been slipping away. A few weeks earlier I'd almost been a dead man. Now it was impossible to feel more alive and joyful than I felt as we kissed. I wasn't imagining it any more; we really were kissing and holding each other.

Sylvia also remembers the day vividly:

I'd been in his mum's house, we were in the lounge. I was looking out of the bay window and I could see him coming down the road, very thin. I could sense that, even though he was in his uniform, which sort of filled out his shape. But no, he looked fine, he wasn't too bad really. As far as I was concerned, he was the same boy that had left back in 1941! I knew I still loved him and now at last I could show him!

The joy I felt, it was just incredible! The feeling of being free, of being loved by more than letter, to be no longer in the camp; it is impossible to describe if you haven't been locked up for years like that. A lot of us felt like this. Absolutely free! It was a marvellous feeling! And I had all that back-pay to spend, so nothing could stop Sylvia and me from painting the town red.

I had to do everything as quickly as possible. Pubs, West End theatres, everything! Live life! We had a wonderful time in London, Sylvia and I. *The Shop at Sly Corner* was one play we saw at St Martin's theatre. It was a new play, a murder thriller by Edward Percy, who was a Conservative MP. It wasn't exactly a whodunit because we knew whodunit. It was more of an 'is-he-going-to-get-away-with-it'! Very enjoyable to see a professional production again! Mickey Orr would have been proud of me. The prisoners had put shows on in the camp occasionally; but this time there were no German guards watching over us. I was free and I was surrounded by free people.

We stayed up in London for about a week. We still didn't make much of an impression on my back-pay, because I had so much of it! Shows every night, having fun, then home to sleep at Mum and Dad's in East Dulwich. Heaven!

I'd always said in my letters that I'd wanted Sylvia to be with my people when I came home, and she'd kept her promise. The other thing I'd said over and again was that I wanted to marry just as soon as we could, once I got home. She told me she still wanted that too. We'd had great days in dear old Braunton so we decided to get married there, at the local church near Sylvia's home. A few days later we went down to Devon to see a vicar to get it all sorted out. We were going to be married as quickly as possible, just as I'd imagined in my dreams, for all those cruel years in Germany.

As a builder, Sylvia's father had a sizeable workshop with about seven or eight men working in it. There was a bit of land down there around the workshop too. When we reached Braunton, Sylvia's dad announced that all normal work was suspended. The new job for the men was to transform the workshop into a beautiful hall fit for a wedding reception. He got all his men to clear the tools out of the workshop and they decorated this room with flags and made it very nice for the reception. Sylvia's mum was busy getting all the food ready, including cakes and peaches with traditional Devon cream.

My mum and dad came down with some other relatives, my aunt Sue and aunt Ivy. My cousins Pam and Iris came down too and they became bridesmaids. How did they manage to drive such a long distance? Sylvia's dad had managed to work some magic with some petrol coupons. Remember, the war hadn't even finished and everything was supposed to be rationed, but Sylvia's dad solved all that somehow.

There was nothing we could do to get my brother Ken back from active service though; so he just had to make do with sending us a telegram. It was nice to know he was thinking of us when he wasn't dodging German bullets! Sid Knight sent best wishes too, though the RAF still hadn't finished punishing him for going LMF, so he couldn't be there.

All sorts of people were doing things to make our wedding nice – and I wasn't doing a bloody thing!

My dad and Sylvia's mum made a good combination. As you know, my dad was in textiles, so he wasn't short of clothing materials. And Sylvia's mum was an excellent dressmaker, so between them they had everything needed to make Sylvia a beautiful wedding dress.

Irene, Sylvia's eldest sister, asked me, 'What are you going to wear, Maurice?'

'This,' I said. I showed her my army battle dress and the navy blue trousers that had been dyed for my escape from Germany.

'Oh you can't get married in that!' she said. 'Sylvia's got a beautiful wedding dress.'

'It'll be alright,' I told her, wondering what the fuss was about. 'I'll be wearing a collar and tie.'

'No Maurice,' Irene said, knowing full well that a collar and tie weren't going to make the combination of the battle dress and dyed old trousers look any more impressive. 'We'll have to find you something else. I'll see what my husband has got tucked away.'

Her husband was called Maurice as well – and he was in the RAF too. Maurice Adams was a Flight Lieutenant and at one time he'd even flown Beauforts. He was away in India at the time, but he'd left some uniform in Braunton. His Flight Lieutenant's uniform was beautiful, but there was one problem – he was about 6 feet 2 inches tall and I was quite short. Once again, Sylvia's mum and her friends went to work. They did an amazing job on that uniform. They tucked the sleeves up and made sure the belt went round in a way that you couldn't tell the whole thing had been made for a much taller man. I'm not sure what Maurice Adams made of that uniform when he came home again, but it was all ready to work a treat on my wedding day, even if technically I wasn't supposed to wear the uniform of an officer like that!

One day before the wedding, to get out of everybody's way, Sylvia said, 'Let's go out for a bicycle ride.' But I couldn't ride a bike. You may remember that my dad had banned me from having a bike when I was a boy. Now I was twenty-four and I'd still never ridden one! That didn't put her off, she said there was an extra bike down in the cellar, so I got it out and away we went. We were going down the road and my short legs were pedalling like nobody's business as I tried to keep up with Sylvia.

It had been a lot easier walking up the lanes with Sylvia three years earlier, hand-in-hand, singing our song, 'Amapola, my pretty little poppy …' I'd been in control of my movement then. I knew how to walk without causing any trouble. Cycling was different. All of a sudden a man came out into the road with a wheelbarrow. He was pushing it across the road with a pile of newspapers in the wheelbarrow. He must have been in a rush to deliver all those papers, because he wasn't going to wait until I'd gone past. But unbeknown to him, I didn't even know how to steer a push-bike, so I just went straight into him. It's a wonder I didn't go over the top of the handle bars, but I didn't. Instead I knocked this poor man over and his newspapers spewed all over the road. I should have helped him up but the only thing going through my mind was to catch up with Sylvia, because she was pedalling away like mad! I couldn't get started again though, so she stopped and came back.

Sylvia recalls:

I don't think I saw the little accident, because I was ahead of Maurice; but then I turned round to see where he'd got to. I cycled back to see Maurice trying to get back on his bike and pedal away, with his handle-bars twisted sideways. Can you imagine? How was he going to get the bike going like that? Together we straightened the handle-bars out again so we could carry on. This chap had picked himself up by then and gone off irritably, so we didn't need to worry too much about him any more. They make 'em tough in Devon!

Perhaps it was just as well that the wedding day arrived before I could cause any more chaos in Devon. Sylvia's two brothers were away serving, in India and France. My brother Ken was in Europe, so my best man was Sylvia's sister Betty's boyfriend. He was a French-Canadian called Jerry. That's all we could rustle up at the time, because the rest of the lads hadn't come back yet. I hope you'll be relieved to hear that Jerry did fine; nothing was going to stop this day from being perfect. It was a wonderful wedding and the guard of honour was formed by some of Sylvia's friends, girls who had been in the Land Army with her.

I can't describe the excitement I felt. A wedding … My wedding … Our wedding! Marriage! Of course it was exciting! Some cynical blokes will think I'd spent time as a POW being shackled, and now I was daft enough to be getting myself shackled all over again. Let me assure you I didn't feel like that at all. Picturing that wedding day was what had kept me going so long. To me, marriage was freedom, a culmination of all the joy our love had been giving us during the worst possible times.

You might think it was hard to cope with so much happiness, after I'd been days from death only a few weeks earlier. But I didn't find it hard at all. Hard is realising you can't walk any more and you are about to disappear from the march, like hundreds before you. Hard is watching men shot in the POW camp for daring to run from servitude. Hard is being shot down and watching your close friend slip beneath the waves forever. Hard is spending year upon year away from your loved ones, even though you have their letters in your hand. It is the frustration, the torture of being denied your liberty and your normal life as a young man.

Was adapting to the big day hard, when it came upon me so quickly? Of course not! Like I say, I'd been dreaming of this day for three or four years, I'd savoured every moment in my mind and soul when I couldn't have it. I doubt there has

ever been a happier man than me on my wedding day. Nervous? Of course not!
The one who was nervous was Sylvia's father.

Sylvia chuckled as she relived the memory:

My father was so nervous when he was walking me up the aisle to Maurice,
I could almost feel my dad trembling. Was I nervous? No, the occasion didn't
bother me at all like that; I was just happy and excited. It was great!

We came out of that beautiful little church as man and wife, with the rest of our
lives to look forward to. We'd live that adventure together. Happy? I don't think
that even begins to describe it.

Don't take my word for it; just take a look at the wedding photo! I've got this
huge grin on my face, as though I still can't believe what is happening to me; that
it really has all come true at last. I look well; I don't even look thin any more; I've
already left behind the horrors of life as a prisoner. I'm back in the normal world,
where you could pedal down a hill on an English lane, completely out of control
on an old bicycle, just to catch a glimpse of the woman you love as she disappears
round another corner. Look at Sylvia's smile too, so full of joy.

POSTSCRIPT:
HAPPY EVER AFTER

We began married life with a honeymoon in Boscombe in that summer of 1945. We were still enjoying married life in a Gloucestershire village in 2013. So marriage must have been alright for Sylvia and me, mustn't it? When Sylvia was asked what had kept us happy for so long, she once said, 'I think it was the way he held my hand!'

I was glad of the way she held mine too, because in a sense the war never really went away – not entirely. My brother Ken was wounded in the back by shrapnel before it finished. He survived his wounds and came home too. Mercifully he also enjoyed a long and happy life, one of the luckier ones.

It didn't take me long to hear about all my friends who hadn't made it. Tommy Keegan, who had called me a cradle-snatcher when I'd first gone out with Sylvia; he'd been shot down in Malta and didn't survive the impact. Jack Featherstone, my old mate from Chivenor; he'd been killed coming home on a boat.

I could go on for ages about friends who died, because most of the Beaufort crews didn't survive. Bill Carroll did, and at the time of writing he was still enjoying life and his own long marriage to his wife Brenda in Canada. We had a good old chat in the summer of 2013 and laughed as loudly as we had when we'd been young men in Devon.

Little more than a year after the war I had a letter from the German Admiralty to say that three crew members from the German ship which shot us down wanted to write to me. I didn't do a thing about that. It was too soon. It only took me about a year to stop hating the Germans after I was free – but that didn't mean I wanted to be pen pals with them.

Len Murray and his family came to stay with us soon after the war. He was an absolute gentleman, and we were able to recall the months when I was him and he was me. Sadly he still wasn't well and died not very long after the war. But we stayed in touch with his daughter and we're still in touch at the time of writing.

John Sinclair had survived the Long March too, and I called him up after the war. He came to visit Sylvia and me, which was nice of him. We'd shared the intense experience of being shot down together, so we had that much in common. But the truth was, we didn't have anything else in common – so we quickly lost touch again. He did help save me though, and I'll never forget that.

Sylvia and I had thrown ourselves into the London life we'd planned together for so long. I didn't have to become a farmer's boy, as Sylvia had once suggested to me. My Amapola was happy to be my wife in the big city – she loved it there. As she had told my parents during my period of captivity, she so loved all those shops! I was soon fit, well and back up to full strength. We could enjoy all that RAF money and we had a jolly good time!

Then my father – who knew a thing or two about coming home after a nasty war and fitting back into peacetime London – reckoned he had seen enough.

He said, 'Don't you think it's time you went back to work?'

Reluctantly I said, 'Suppose so.'

'Well you can't keep floating around like this, you're a married man. You're supposed to settle down.'

We were thoroughly enjoying being married, but we hadn't worried too much about the 'settling down' part!

I sat down with Dad in the end.

'Where are you going to work?' he asked. I didn't know exactly. Then I heard the same sentence I'd heard all those years before, after I'd dropped that accountant's calculator and cost myself so much money. 'Why don't you come and work for me?'

'How much are you going to pay me?' I asked.

'How much do you want?' he replied.

'I want five pounds a week,' I told him.

'Good God! Five pounds a week? That's ridiculous!'

'I don't think it is,' I said, holding my ground. 'The manager and accountant who were working with you before took five pounds a week.'

We came to an agreement and I went back to work for my dad. On the first Friday, I was waiting for my wage packet and opened it eagerly. There were only three pounds in there.

It was his way of bringing me back down to earth and making me knuckle down. He really worked me hard. He'd give me heavy materials to carry upstairs and then come up behind me with a stick as I climbed the stairs. 'Quick, quick, quick!' he'd say.

When I look back, it was all for my own good, to make sure I was going to be a hard-working, stable man who could build a happy future for Sylvia and me. And a happy future did await us, thankfully.

We had four children together – Madelaine, Nigel, Wendy and Stephanie. We've got nine grandchildren and a few great-grandchildren too!

I still loved my cricket and I'd missed it. I didn't play as often as I had during my teenage years before the war, of course. Once I started working for my father, there was hardly any spare time to play cricket at all. I still went back and played the odd game for Old Vauxonians on a Sunday. What a pleasure it was to be able to do that.

I never did have quite the same touch with the bat after the war, not like I had when I was a teenager before it all started. I was nothing special with the ball any more either; but it was nice just to be able to play again when the opportunity arose. Down but not out! That's what I'd been during the war. I certainly wasn't down any more, and as far as I was concerned, I was still 'not out'!

Later I became a member at my beloved Surrey County Cricket Club – and watched that famous RAF fighter pilot Bill Edrich, the England batsman. I was a regular spectator at the Oval for years, I had a season ticket, and I loved every moment.

In 1949 I played in a trophy-winning football team called Suffolk Villa FC. I hadn't changed deep down. I still loved my football, too.

A bit later some former POWs went back to Lamsdorf, which was by now part of Poland again. They found that the whole of Stalag VIIIB had been knocked down – good thing too, if you ask me. The graves of British military men had been moved to Krakow Military Cemetery. Bill Routledge sent me a press cutting about the visit, in which it was observed, 'the Poles took a little educating in our desire for a cup of tea and were at first a little nonplussed when we insisted on having milk.' There were said to be no complaints about the vodka, though!

I stayed five years working for my father after the war; then my uncle Fred had a vacancy to manage his shop in Deptford. So I went back to my roots, so to speak, and ran that shop. In the end I bought it and another in Welling, near Woolwich, with my brother Ken. He ran Welling, I ran Deptford and we did very well, selling up when the leasehold finally ran out in 1985. They always said Britain was a nation of shopkeepers, didn't they? Well it was true in my case!

After I retired, Sylvia and I went on a cruise. It was 1995 and soon after we booked it, I realised we would more or less be passing the place where I was shot down. I asked the ship's line if they would be prepared to slow down when the Oriana sailed past the spot, just to give me a few quiet moments.

P&O Cruises wrote back to say, 'We sail from Southampton on the 9th of June, bound for Norway. During the cruise we shall be passing at a latitude of 57 degrees, 57N at 23.30hrs on the evening of the 11th June.'

It turned out this was 109 miles west of where I was shot down, but they'd gone to the trouble to work it all out, and to tell me when I'd be closest to my lost friend. Wasn't that nice? On that given night, I climbed out of bed and went out on deck to look at the black water. I thought of those days, and thought about poor old Stan going down under the waves.

2 JULY 2013

More than seventy years have passed since I was shot down and here I am, preparing to enter the gardens of Buckingham Palace for a spot of tea. I've got Sylvia with me and she still looks beautiful.

We drive through an entrance just to the left of the front gate where the Queen usually comes out. The police look under our car, just in case of bombs. The outer car park is getting so full that we're allowed to drive on, through an arch and into a quadrangle. We go into the palace from there and up some steps. I'm helped up those steps by a soldier and a RAF man, one on either side, because I'm a bit frail these days at 93 years of age. I always say of my body that nothing works very well any more except my tongue. That is as strong as ever; in fact, it's in first class condition, which is why I can still tell my story. Anyway, when you get to the top of those steps at the palace, you go through a drawing room which acts like a bridge, and once you walk through that, you are across and you go down some more steps into the garden.

It all looks very nice and I enjoy every moment. It's nice to be recognised in this way at my age.

The invitation came out of the blue. It read:

> The Not Forgotten Association request the pleasure of the company of Mr and Mrs M. Mayne at a garden party in the grounds of Buckingham Palace by kind permission of Her Majesty the Queen in the presence of the patron, Her Royal Highness The Princess Royal on Tuesday the 2nd of July. Lounge suits or blazers and medals may be worn. Various tables will be presented to The Princess Royal and Vice-Admiral Sir Timothy Lawrence between 4pm and 4.30 pm. You have been selected to sit at table 27.

The royal family hasn't forgotten us; and we airmen haven't forgotten what happened during the Second World War. How could we?

I'm excited. I'm proud. I'm nervous. We're here at the palace for the boys who died and we're here for ourselves too. A moment of recognition; a moment to savour; and a moment to remember.

But the moment Princess Anne appears, she is surrounded – almost mobbed – by veterans' wives, and we never do get to meet. Never mind, I have a wonderful chat with Air Vice Marshal Sir Stephen Dalton, head of the RAF. Someone must have pointed me out to him. I'm one of the oldest there and a former POW, so I suppose I stand out a bit. He comes over and makes quite a fuss of me and I feel thrilled to bits with that.

There is an atmosphere of mutual respect and it rounds off a beautiful day in a satisfying way. Tea at Buckingham Palace, to show we really hadn't been forgotten.

It's a fitting way to end my story. Maybe this book will help other people to understand the kind of things we went through – and still do.

Sometimes I still have nightmares about being shot down.

'What's the matter?' Sylvia says.

'I was back in the water again,' I tell her.

INDEX